I Can Put in Windows and Doors

Pennsylvania Carpenter-Kenya Missionary-Family Legacy

by Darvin Byler, Shon Messick, and Nadine Rhoads

ISBN: 979-8-9873521-7-5

Dedication

We dedicate this book to the Author and Finisher of our faith, Jesus Christ. "Let us look to Jesus, the Author and Finisher of our faith, who for the joy that was set before Him endured the cross, despising the shame, and is seated at the right hand of the throne of God." Hebrews 12:2 MEV

One of Darvin's favorite Scriptures, Ephesians 3:16-19

"According to the riches of his glory, he may grant you to be strengthened with might through his Spirit in the inner man, and that Christ may dwell in your heart through faith, that you being rooted and grounded in love, may have power to comprehend with all the saints what is the breadth and length and height and depth and to know the love of Christ which surpasses knowledge, that you may be filled with all the fulness of God."

Table of Contents

Introduction

Jambo Hello! Darvin and Sandy Byler celebrated 42 years since they traveled to Kenya as short-term missionaries with Africa Inland Mission in August 2024. This book is a combination of Darvin's sermons that he kept filed, items that Sandy preserved, and stories that were written down from conversations Darvin and Sandy had with Shon and Nadine. We are preserving and presenting a piece of our family history and legacy. Our purpose is for generations to believe in the Lord Jesus Christ and fulfill our divine destinies. We are raising generations of righteousness for the glory of God. "Believe in the Lord Jesus Christ, and you and your household will be saved." Acts 16:31 MEV.

As I've read my dad's sermons, I hear his heart beating with love for God and love for people. I remember my dad preaching with an urgent sincerity for people to love Jesus and obey God's Word (Nadine). I'm glad my dad saved his sermons for now is a great time to hear the Word of God. May you also experience the love of Jesus beating in your hearts and choose to obey God as you read these timeless messages.

We are sharing some of what we remember from our perspective. We look forward to filling in the missing memories and story details as you reach out to us with your part of our story, "Pray for the Byler's in Kenya". We pray that you will choose to follow Jesus, accepting Him as your Master and Teacher, and walk the same path of life that Jesus walks. "And He (Jesus) said to them, "Follow Me [as My disciples, accepting Me as your Master and Teacher and walking the same path of life that I walk], and I will make you fishers of men." Matthew 4:19 AMP

> ***Shout in celebration of praise to the Lord! Everyone who loves the Lord and delights in Him will cherish His words and be blessed beyond expectation. Their descendants will be prosperous and influential.***
>
> ***Every generation of His godly lovers will experience His favor. Great blessing and wealth fills the house of the wise, for their integrity endures forever. Even if darkness overtakes them, sunrise-brilliance will come bursting through because they are gracious to others, so tender and true.***
>
> ***Life is good for the one who is generous and charitable, conducting affairs with honesty and truth. Their circumstances will never shake them and others will never forget their example. They will not live in fear of dread of what may come, for their hearts are firm, ever secure in their faith.***
>
> ***Steady and strong, they will not be afraid, but will calmly face their every foe until they all go down in defeat. Never stingy and always generous to those in need, their lives of influence and honor will never be forgotten, for they were full of good deeds. Psalm 112:1-9 TPT***

On behalf of the children, grandchildren, great-grandchildren, and generations to come of Darvin and Sandy Byler, let it be written, Asante sana thank you very much Dad & Mom/Papa & Sho Sho! We are grateful, enriched, encouraged, and appreciate you! Love, Nadine & Shon

SECTION ONE – Romans (1977), Ephesians (1978), Daniel (1979) Sermons Written & Preached by Darvin Byler. The Forming of a Missionary.

Study to show yourself approved by God,

a workman who need not be ashamed,

rightly dividing the word of truth.

2 Timothy 2:15 MEV

I heard that my grandparents moved from the hills of Hershey, PA to the Rift Valley escarpment of Kijabe, Kenya. I wanted to know more. I never heard my papa preach but I hear his voice ring out from the pages of his sermon notes. (Shon).

In August 1982 I traveled with my parents, my three siblings, twelve overweight suitcases, and twelve oversized carry-on items. The plane landed us in Nairobi, Kenya, an hour's drive south of Kijabe. I loved listening to my dad preach. His passion for the Word of God and love for Jesus is transferred into many transformed hearts. (Nadine).

My wife, Sandy, and I have piles of memories, four children, twenty-two grandchildren, four great-grandchildren, and many married into our family. It's time to gather my sermons and share stories of our desire to serve God, love people, and testify of God's faithfulness in our lives, so pull up a chair and enjoy. (Darvin).

How did a Pennsylvania carpenter end up as a missionary in Kenya? It began with my salvation. I accepted the Lord Jesus as my Savior on March 26, 1952. I recorded my new birth on the cover of my first Bible. I am told that my mom, Gretta Byler, called our pastor and asked him to come to our farm fields to talk with her boys about accepting Jesus as their Savior. I'm glad she did.

God was preparing me to serve Him in Kijabe. One year after my salvation God was preserving the lives of His children on the other side of the world in Kijabe. On March 28, 1953, the Lord sent an angelic army to protect and preserve RVA and the Kijabe mission station from a brutal attack. Everyone who has ever lived in Kijabe has heard about God's miraculous rescue. We continue to testify of God's miraculous protection. Mary Anderson Honer recorded the testimony in her book, *The Downing Legacy.*

> *"A band of Mau Mau were captured by the Home Guards, with the assistance of the RVA boys. These men, under questioning, admitted an attempt on the school. The Mau Mau men said that when they had come down to attack the school, they had abandoned the idea because the school was so heavily surrounded by British soldiers all dressed in luminescent white uniforms. Ironically, in March of 1953 there were no British soldiers at the school. Many believe that God sent angels to protect the children at RVA, surrounding them with His guardian angels in the form of British soldiers." (Honer, 104).*

I always saw myself as someone who supported missionaries, ministries, and my local church. I enjoyed working with my hands, building houses, meeting needs, and blessing people. I enjoyed being part of committees, teaching Sunday School lessons, praying for missionaries, and sending money to help ministries. I regularly helped ministries and my church with work projects, locally and as far as Guatemala City. Sandy and I, volunteered to teach English to Vietnamese refugees in 1974. We became a host family to a Vietnamese teenager named Long, in 1975. We consider Long as family and he blessed us with a recent visit. This is how I shared the Gospel of Jesus Christ.

I wrote the following sermons and taught them for Sunday School, Youth Group, and other services at my home church, Spring Creek Church of the Brethren, Hershey, PA.

File folder marked "Romans 1977". Sermons written and taught by Darvin Byler.

Romans

1

Introduction - Ridenour

Paul's letter to the Romans
acclaimed by scholars & theologins as the highest & best of All of Pauls letters.
thorough - systematic -
Romans is an eloquent, passionate declaration of the gospel - the greatest document on our salvation
This is the book that changed Martin Luther & started the reformation - listen to what he says about it.

Romans is ~~at once~~ simple & straight to the point concerning the steps to salvation - and yet deep & complex in other areas.
There seems to be always something new for the diligent scholar.

Romans will require all the mental make up we have - and then it must be bathed in Prayer & supplication before the Holy Spirit can teach us.

And the HS will certainly be our teacher for this quarter - I promise to you that I'll do my part - to submit to the HS - I would ask you to do the same - So we can learn together!

(2)

Paul - the great apostle

Born a Jewish blueblood - from the tribe of Benjamin - Born a Roman Citizen - He recieved the best education availiable - fluent in Hebrew & greek - A Pharisees Pharisee blameless under the law.

Daniel

But what can we say about a man who ~~[illegible]~~ was used to write over half of the New Testament!

Well --- I prefer we hear the words of Jesus concerning this man.

Lets turn to Acts 26:15

START

Ch.1:1-7 there is no doubt in Pauls mind about who he is - what his purpose in life is etc.

Read ↗

He is A Slave of Jesus Christ

"new" form of education - who am I?

We Should All Say with Paul - A Slave Set Apart To Serve

8-15 This is perhaps the only letter written by Paul to aplace & People he had never been to or knew - Yet he is always in Prayer for them - he wants to have fellowship with them - he is happy for their witness

3

WRS-14 Paul says he is a debtor to the greeks & barbarians - to the wise & foolish --
What does he mean?
Paul recognized who he was - a sinner saved by grace - Christ had done so much for him -- he had a debt to pay
How About Us? How Are We paying Our Debt?

VS 15 Paul Says I'm Ready To Go -- I'm eager - as soon as God gives the word - I'll be there.
Why??

16 For I Am Not Ashamed of The Gospel
Now I want to ask you to think back to some time when you were ashamed of the gospel - you didn't want anyone to know you were a Christian Mark 8:38

Do You Ever Think about What It's going To Be Like When You Meet Jesus Face To Face? I Do

That's the greatest motivation I have -- when I look into the ~~face~~ eyes of Jesus -
If You've Never asked Jesus To Forgive You For Those Times When You Were Ashamed of Him - I'm going To Ask You To Do IT -- Right Now!

(4)

Now the introduction is over - Paul has set forth his theme - the gospel is God's power unto salvation -- because it reveals the divine righteousness to be recieved through faith!

Why Is Righteousness Necessary?
Because We Have None Of OUR OWN!
There Is None Righteous - No Not ONE

Ever since I can remember, I have heard various persons propose this type of argument
If God Is A God Of Love -- How Can He Condemm Ignorant Savages In Africa To Hell, Who Have Never Heard The Gospel?
By So Saying they show their own ignorance!

① If they had really known God - they would know he is a God of love - He Saved Them!

② God Does Not Condemm Anyone To Hell
We Condemm Ourselves.

③ If they really wanted to know the answer -- rather than questioning God --- they could have looked right here in Romans and found the answer!

(5)

In the rest of this Chapt. & the next, Paul explains how the Heathen (Gentiles) have fallen short of their standards - - - and then the Jews also - who have the law - have also fallen short of their standards

Lo 12:48 to whom much is Given

Therefore - All The World Is Guilty Before God - As Paul Says In Ch, 3 - all have sinned & come short of the glory of God.

18-23 People don't like to talk about the "wrath" of God -- they prefer to talk about the love of God

But Paul tells us here that God hates sin!

Oh he doesn't fly into a fit of rage --

Rather -- Gods wrath is a fixed attitude of displeasure with sin

God hates sin --- but loves the sinner

Should Also Be Our ATTITude

19 Paul says that God has revealed himself to all men in at least 2 ways

① the light of conscience

(David Livingstone) knew they had sinned

(6)

(2) the witness of creation

Ps 19:1 the heavens are telling the glory of God

* Book Pg 6 -7

creation should point us towards a creative God -- But ---

21 although they knew God -- they refuse to acknowledge him.

Idolatry is the parent of immorality

22 and they turned to idolatry (we)??

24 Therefore - God Gave Them UP!

3 Times →

25. Because - - - -

26-27 For This Reason - - -

Read From Messenger

2

1st Chapter - Paul vividly describes lost condition of gentiles

vs 29 all manner of wickedness, evil, etc

Pg12 We Are Like The Jews

Remember - Paul was writing to both Jews & gentiles

Jews were morraly upright -- but self righteous

Paul Therefore In Chap 2 Begins To Show Them That They Too Are Lost

Living Bible Read Ch2 1-11

Paul doesn't mention the Jews by name yet (he will in verse 17) But he is primarily thinking of them

However -- Because we recognize that Gods' principles are universal -- And that all scripture is inspired & profitable

We need to read this as a personal letter -- To Us

The Jews thought they would get special treatment because of their "heritage"

Do We?

Pg14 Book

"Blameless" Phil 3:6

You Can Have A "Religious" experience & Feel Pretty Self Righteous

But When You Meet Jesus - You Will See Yourself As You Are - A Sinner

(2)

We must never compare ourselves to Others
Only To Christ

When We Meet Jesus = Humility

These Verses Point Out The Certainty of JUDGEMENT

God Is Love - But Truth out of Balance Is Heresy

(1) UNIVERSALLY - No one Shall Escape
2 Cor 5:10 We must all stand before the judgement seat of Christ

Principles of Judgement

(2) Judged According To Truth - ver 2

(3) According To every mans work ver 6

(4) Absolute Impartiality vers 11

(5) According To The Gospel of Christ verse 16
All Meant To Lead Us To Repentance

God Will Judge Us According To The Light We Have - Verse 12-15

Read - 17-24

Sermon on The Mount

Adultery = Look in Lust   Murder = Hate

(3)

Verse 24 The name of God is Blasphemed

Pg 17 More People Stay Away From Church - Because of OUR Lives - Than Any Other Reason!

Vrs 25-29 Paraphrase Phillips

Baptism - commandments

Ch 3 Paul now, as if sensing some objections raises several questions -- and then answers them

Ver 1 What advantage has the Jew? (Christian)
what value circumcision (baptism)

2 answer Jews have O.T. - Law - Promises
God Will Honor His Promises

Ver 5 If a mans unfaithfulness and sin bring about greater glory to God - How can he justify punishing man for it?

6 answer - God Forbid

9 - Are Jews any better off?
answer - No NOT AT All
None is righteous no not one

10-18 Paul quotes from O.T. - Will Many Times
Psalms - Eccles - Isaiah Remember his training

(4) So Now – after answering all of these questions – we're back where we were

VRS 19 ALL The World STands Guilty Before God

VRS 23 FirsT STep On Romans Road To SalvaTion

~~Back up to vers 21~~

The PROBLEM

HOLY God ———————— Sinful Man

Pg. 23

VERS 21 BuT Now!

VRS 24 JusTified = Declared NoT Guilty

JusT-As-If-He-Never-Sined

More than forgiveness – No GuilT

GRace = UnmeriTed, Undeserved FavoR of God

GifT – We must accept it

RedempTion = to deliver by paying a price

(5)

vrs 25 Propitiation - Expiation

Satisfying the righteousness of a Holy God

Used As An ~~Verb~~ Adj or A Noun

~~Verb~~ Adj. = That Which Propiates = Jesus

Noun = The Place of Propitiation

The "Mercy Seat"

To Properly Understand This We Must Go Back To The O.T.

This word is used in The OT to describe the lid of the ark [redacted] - the "mercy seat"

Once a year, ~~the high priest~~

a Covering For Sin

On the day of atonement, the high priest would sprinkle the blood of a bull & a goat on the mercy seat - To Atone For

Lev 16:14 The Sins Of The People!

To Satisfy The Demands Of The Law

Verse 25 God Put Forward - Christ

No Guilt!

K.J - Set Forth

Read Is 53:4

Greek = Publicly Displayed

Did More Than Forgive Sin He Completely Removed Them!

Heb 9:11-14 By His Blood!

22

25-26 Through Faith = Faith is the means by which the benefits of Christs death are appropriated

(6)

(JusTness)

vs. 25 This Was To Show Gods "RighTeousness"

Paul is saying here, that the propitiatory death of Christ - makes possible the justification of the sinner - without compromising the Holiness of God.

This Is The HearT of The Good News

Many people stumble because - its so simple & Nothing required of us - but FaiTh

We Would RaTher Do SomeThing To Earn Our Way

Men have tried down through the centuries to add to -- to make it works righteous

vs. 28

vs. 27 Paul says there is no way you can boast of this salvation

3

(8)

Ch 5 - Therefore - since we are justified by faith. -- End of Debate

What Are The Benifits For Us

1 Peace With God

Once We Were Seperated From God - Because of our sin - Now we have Acceptance

Many Christians don't have Peace with God because they can't accept his Justification

2 Access To His Grace

Access = right to enter

The justified man has free access to God!

We May Now Come Boldly To The Throne of Grace Heb. 4:16

3 Rejoice in our Hope of Sharing The Glory of God

4 Rejoice in our ~~Sufferings~~ - Tribulations = Pressure

God Can Teach Us Some Things In Adversity -- That We Cannot Learn In Prosperity

Count It All Joy Brethren - James 1

HOLY SPIRIT Pg 38

Rom 5:8 - 2nd step

Sufferings - better translated - trials or tribulations
Orig Greek = to apply pressure

We must remember that Paul is writing to Christians

This is one of the principals of the ways of God in dealing with us.
I Just Want To Point Out Several Scriptures To Further Explain
Rom 8:28 - 29 → Gods Perfect Will for Us
1Pet 4:12 - 1:6
2 Cor. 1: 3-9

Many of you Can Testify To Gods Hand Upon You -
I Praise Him Also -- If He Had Not Pressured Me -- I Wouldn't Be Standing Up Here!

For God So Loved The (you) World (me)
that he'll do whatever it takes to draw us to him.

A Perfect example of alot being lost in translation.

That's why we always say that the Bible was inspired in it's original text.

Character - (experience KJ.) = acceptable - approved - tried

Hope = to anticipate with pleasure to have confidence

Read from Amplified Bible.

(2)

But in pointing us to the Problem
He also points us to the remedy

Paul shows 2 Heads of the Human Race
Adam - Christ

Through 1 Man	Through 1 Man
Sin & Death	Righteousness & Life

Man Is A Fallen Creature

Pg 43

Ch. 6

Read 1-11 Go Back To Page (1)

Sanctification Then Is A Lifelong Process of growing In Holiness.

Rom 8:29 - Conformed To Christs Image

We'll see later in Ch 7 that this is no easy thing.

verse 3-4 The Principle Upon Which Our Holiness Is Built, Rests Upon Our Identification With Christ In His Death and Resurrection!

Gal 2:20 Should Memorize IT!

verse 6 - The Purpose Of Our Crucifixion With Jesus Is Stated.

that the body of sin might be destroyed

(3) The Greek Word Translated "Destroyed"
means – to render inoperative – or to annul
When you annul something – you break
its force or power – (As A Contract)

Sin May Still Be With Us,
But Now It's Power Over Us Is
Broken! Praise God!

Pg 48

verse 11 We must Recon ourselves dead to
sin -- This Does Not Mean That We
Will Not Have Temptations!

The Word Recon means = To Take Inventory
So -- when temptation comes – we take
inventory – that is we remember we were
crucified with Christ – therefore we have
died to sin – we will not let it
dominate us

verse 16 Pg 50

verse 23 – 3rd step on Romans Road
For The Wages of Sin Is Death, But
The Gift of God Is Eternal Life

4

Review Rom 6:3
Must identify with Christ in his death
4- So we might walk in newness of life

6- Our old self was crucified with him
No Longer be A Slave To Sin

Our Salvation was given to us -- a gift from God - there is nothing we can do to earn it. But - - -
Our Sanctification is not quite the same - there are some things we can & should do!

vse 11 - We must Recon ourselves dead to sin
we must stop & take "inventory"
We may not feel it -- but God said it - - - we must accept it.
When Christ Was Nailed To That Cross --
My Old Sinful Nature Was Crucified
Right There With Him. Gal 2:20

vs 13 - yield ourselves to God
16 - you are slaves to the one you yield to
Sin OR Obedience - why do you call me Lord, Lord & not obey
19 - yield your members to righteousness

(2)

verse 22 - sanctification is a part of eternal life.
Heb 12:14 - without Holiness no one shall see the Lord!
To Make Our Bodies A Suitable Place
For The Holy Spirit to dwell.
Absolutely Amazing! - that God - -
would live in me! I Cor 6:19-20

verse 23 Romans Road No 3

Ch. 7 - Paul Gives Another Illustration
Marriage - Woman married to law - Christ
verse 4 - Likewise you have died to the law
In Order That We May Bear Fruit For
God!
Jesus Was Completely Controlled
By The Holy Spirit - - & His Life Bore
Much Fruit = Love - Joy - Peace - Patience - Kindness

As We Are Conformed To Him - We
Too Will Bear Much Fruit.
Is there evidence in your life?

Now What Good Is The Law?
verse 7 To point out our sin.

(3)

Now we've seen how we are justified before God, -- and how we can become more like him -- And IT Sounds As Though Our Problems Are Over.

But Unfortunately That's Not The Case

Ridenour Pg 58 Read verse 14–25

In Ch 6, we learned the doctrinal truth that we have died to sin -- its power over us is broken -

But then we find ourselves failing miserably in day to day living -- and we wonder why

Sin Is Not Dead -- We Have Died To IT

Before we identified with Christ in his death we were defeated Christians -- & NO threat to Satan -- BUT NOW!

So He Steps Up His Temptations & Accusations

SATAN Would Take Us To The Law & Condemn Us

(4)

The Holy Spirit Takes Us To Calvary & Jesus -- & Shows Us His Wounds - His Shed Blood & Says To Us

I Know Your Every Sin --
I Anticipated Every Failure ---

I Have Paid The Price

Come to me in Repentence -- & I will Forgive You

It is Good To Come Under Conviction But Not Condemnation!

Ch 8: 1 - There Is Therefore No Condemnation
Romans Road

In Ch 7 -- We Saw The Struggle - We Were Condemned By The Law
But Now -- it matters not what the law says - it cannot condemn us anymore
If -- We Are In Christ

Important to memorize scripture - to rebuke Satan
Jesus used it in his temptation
It Is Written

(1) Rom Ch 8

5

Up to this point Paul has shown us how the whole world stands condemned - all have sinned
How the law cannot save us, but rather condemns us also -
How through faith we can be justified before God

Last week we saw that we are dead to sin - - that we need not be dominated by sin -
But we also saw that sin is not dead - - and that we have an even greater inner conflict - - as we try to follow after our new nature.

Ch 7 Points out our conflicts

But Ch 8 Starts Us OUT on The Victory Trail

verses 1-2-3 - for God has done what the law could not do

~~Read verses ... Amplified Bible~~

(I)

Before the law we did not know sin --
then God gave the law --- and man
could not keep it -- it condemned him

But Now! God not only tells
us what to do -- He Does IT For Us

He shows us what he wants through
the word -- and then he gives us the power
to do it through his spirit!

And What Must We do?

(week 4) ①. Walk according to the Spirit
(week 5) 2. Set our minds on the Spirit
Then Trust & Obey -- Through Faith!

1 Walk in the Spirit Gal. 5:16 - 25

Many times in the Bible we're instructed
how to walk --- But before we can
walk -- we must learn how to sit
Watchman Nee in his book Sit-walk-stand
Makes this point
Pg 11 Is 40:31 - They that wait
upon the Lord shall renew their strength

③ Now all that Paul has shown us up to this point has been a kind of "sitting" experience.

Showing us all that God has done for Us

But Now he's going to show us how to walk.

But first we must be firmly rooted & seated with Christ

Pg 22 EPh 4:1 amplified

To Walk then refers to a way of life - a daily lifestyle

NoT JusT SomeThing We Do on Sundays

This word Walk means much more though

To Walk in the Spirit requires a certain amount of faith

IT Does Not mean though that we take a blind leap

To Walk according to Webster = to advance by steps - lifting one foot while the other foot is securely on solid ground

And that's exactly how God will lead us!

(4) We always see some Super spiritual person way up there somewhere -- & we think to be like that we must let go of ~~all~~ everything and take a do or die leap of faith. NO! NO!

God will not Push us -- the Holy Spirit leads us -- & only as we have one foot firmly planted.

Walking is a series of steps

But Walk Also means something else

In The Greek = it means to follow as a companion -- a trusted friend --

Is it hard to follow a trusted friend ?

And Why do we trust him ?

He's Proved himself over & over

Now in verse 5 Paul tells us further to set our minds on the Spirit

Amplified

(5) What is the mind of the flesh?

verse 6 ---

Why death?

verse 7 --- cannot Please or satisfy God

we may for a time be "religious" -
but sooner or later we will seperate from God

We will have a "form" of godliness --
but deny the Power thereof

Now **how** do we Set our mind on the Spirit?

Gothard - Moral Freedom Pg 184

Indwelling - Acts 2:38 - Repent & be baptized & you shall receive the gift of the H.S.

(H.S. abbreviated for Holy Spirit)

(1) Answer to carnal Christians - 6

Indwelling - Acts 2:38

Persons who do not show evidence of salvation -

Did They ??

Repent = turn from sins

believe = trust - rely on - put your faith in

no 9 Must be a spiritual rebirth - new birth

if anyone is in Christ he is a new creature

Not Intellectual!!

But it is possible to be saved --- & Not yielded to the H.S.

I Cor. 3

But Why would anyone just want to barely make it to Heaven?

Christ came to give us a full & abundant life right now! To bear fruit

Eternities greatest priviledge will be casting our crowns at his feet!!

(2) Many christians remain *spiritual babies* their entire life

They don't even know that there's a *war* going on -- much less *fight* in it.

Jesus told us that Satan was the enemy of our souls

Peter tells us he's a roaring lion

Paul tells us in Eph 6 how we are to be prepared to fight this war.

Do you know there's a *war* going on?

Do you know who the *enemy* is?

Do you have your *weapons*?

That's what this diagram is about

Satan has already *neutralized* many Christians -- because he's *convinced* them that he doesn't exist!

That's a pretty neat trick -- *No enemy* -- *No War*!

But let's see what Paul says in *Eph 6*

① 7

verse 17 Paul brings us to "glorification"
we've seen Justification -- & "Sanctification"
(Walking in the Spirit) saved from the Power of Sin

But there's more to come
an "heir" is a person who has not yet
received his inheritance!
I Cor 2:9 - Eye Has Not Seen - Nor
Ears Have Heard - Nor Has IT Entered
Into The Heart of Man, The Things Which
God Has Prepared for Those Who Love Him

18-25 Not only do we look forward to
future deliverance -- But Paul says
All of Creation yearns to be
free!
This tells us that Sin when it
entered the world with Adam - affected
all of Gods creation
God Said Cursed Is The
ground for Thy Sake Gen 3:17

verse 23 But we who have the first fruits of the
Spirit --- Praise God! There's More
To Come!

(2)

Some day our fight will be over -
we'll no longer have to struggle with Sin
(Our lower nature)

FOR In This Hope We Were Saved

Our hope lies in the 2nd coming of Jesus --
when our mortal bodies shall be changed

We will receive new & glorified bodies
like Jesus --

Then -- & Only Then
Our Salvation Will Be Complete!!

verse 26 - Amplified

Eph 6:18 - Pray In The SPIRIT

Helps = Stands With Us Against All
Opposition

27 H.S. Pleads before God on our behalf

28 That's why all things work together for
good

36-37 - We may not be being killed -- but
no doubt many of the Roman Christians to
whom Paul wrote were --
They probably read this section right
before they went to the Arena = "all things work for good"
??

8

① Last week we finished Ch 8 - a stirring declaration of faith

But then --- Paul remembers his
Ch 9 fellow Jews -- And his heart breaks for them

We Saw in verse 4 a listing of all that God had given to the Nation Israel

Now The question Arises ---
Did Gods purpose fail? Are his Promises void? Paul Says NO! - 6

God Is The Same Today - Tomorrow & Forever! Heb 13:8
His Purpose Is Unchanged

1st - Paul Shows Us That God Has
11 Always operated under the principle of election

2. That The True decendants of Abraham are those who have been "recond" as righteous by faith

(2) 3. But Some Will say that God
14 is unfair
Paul Says By No Means!

15 God Is Soverign
16
17
Then another objection v 19
if that is the way God governs--
how can he hold us accountable??
20 God Is The Creator!

Now Paul Isn't Just Spouting His
Own Ideas Here-- He's quoting Scripture
We must remember that Paul knew the O.T.
front to back-- & He refers to Is. 45:9

This Refusal to accept our Created
Place In Gods Universe Is The Very
Heart Of Sin

It is Rebellion!
Satan Did IT - I will Be Like God!
Adam & Eve Did IT - They Wanted To Be As Wise
as God!
Pg 80 And Man Has Been In Rebellion Ever Since

(3) 23-24-25-26 Gods Purpose all along was that his call of election would include the gentiles

27 But He Shall Save A "Remnant"
He has not rejected Israel -- rather out of the remnant come the chosen seed

~~4~~ Election Leads To Christ
30-(32)
It was impossible for the Jews to attain righteousness by following the law -- So they were destined to failure

Ve Too Must
ome By Faith!

Because of their blind adherence to the law they stumbled over the "Rock"

leb 11:6
vithout Faith
mpossible To Please
God

Jesus Is The Chief Corner Stone
The Elect of God

32 This "rock" will have a twofold effect
it will cause some to stumble --
and others to be lifted up
The Cross Is The Turning Point For Men
it will either lift you up -- or condemn you

Read Vrs 1–4

(4) Ch 10 – Paul again expresses his concern for his fellow jews.

NOTE – that nothing he has said about election has changed his prayer -- that they might be Saved

2–3 He points out 4 Major Areas Where they have failed

Perhaps if we look closely we can identify with some of them?

(1) Religious Pride

they had a kind of "Zeal" for God -- but it was based on religious performance

How about us? Are we proud of being "Brethren"

(2) Spiritual blindness

they were "ignorant" of Gods righteousness they were so wrapped up in their "religion" -- that they did not recognize the son of God.

How about us?

(3) Self-righteousness

they thought they could make it on their own

How about us?

O how we hate to say -- I can't make it myself Lord

(5)

(4) Unyielding Stubborness
Because of their self will - they refused
to submit to Gods righteousness
How about us?
Have we died to self?

v. 4 Now Paul says that Christ is the end of
the law. -- How?
2 Ways

1. He is the fulfillment, the completion
the perfect consummation of the law

Amplified v. 4 — 2. He is the end of the law in that
he has replaced the old order of legal
religion, with the new order of the
indwelling spirit

Scofield - Types!

5-8 Paul makes reference to Deut 30:11-14
No one need go to Heaven to bring
Christ down -- He has already come!

Neither do we seek him among the dead!
For He Is Risen!
And He Is Near Us Through His Spirit
& The Word

(6) verse 9 – Romans Road

There is much more implied here than merely verbal consent to Christ's diety

To Believe = adhere to, trust in, rely on
To confess Him as Lord = Obedience
More than Savior

13 No predestination – "Whosoever" may come

Read 14 – 21

Ch 10 9

① vv 9-10 Amplified

We need to confirm our Salvation

11 No one will be disappointed

13 Calls = to invoke as Lord!

14-17 - Read

This is the heart of evangelism -
go & Tell

I Cor 1:21 - God chooses To Use
17 Preaching - as His Primary Method

Now there is a difference between
Preaching & a Glorified lecture!

Preaching = To proclaim the gospel
itself

Gospel = good news! = scripture

18-21 - Has Israel heard?
did they not understand?

(2) Ch. 11 Read verses 1-10

4 God always keeps a remnant

8 Paul quotes from Isa. 29:10

Notice - God only hardened their hearts AFTER they had rejected Christ

Hardening is the natural & necessary effect of Mercy that is rejected

11 Amplified - fall = irretrievably?

No! - but through their transgression Salvation has come to the Gentiles

12 Someday Israel Will Be Reinstated

Read 13-22

16 Amplified - dough = Abraham

18 We do not support the root

Draw tree

③ 21 Eternal Salvation?

23-24-25 - untill the full number of the gentiles comes in

Some day The Last Gentile Will Accept Jesus Christ As Saviour - & The Full Numberr Will Be In - - - -

Then - - God Is Going To Turn His Full Attention Once Again To Israel

Now - - I don't claim to be a Prophet or an O.T. scholar

But - - I can read!

and as I read the bible, I can clearly see that God has a special plan for the nation Israel.

From the very begining - God chose them through the centuries they have been persecuted, scattered, and slaughtered - - -

Yet they are still intact as a Nation

Why?

we can read in the bible about the Jebusites - the Hittites - Girgashites - Babylonians - - Where are they??

(4) From Gen to Rev God is dealing with the nation Israel

There is much Prophesy concerning the future reinstatement of Israel

Ezekiel 37:11 - These bones shall rise again

Paul quotes much from Isaiah

Zechariah 12:8 -

Some day the Jews will recognize Christ - They shall look upon him whom they have pierced -- & cry out in Anguish

32 - Mercy on All - Not Salvation For All
Consigned = Adamic Sin

Pg 89 - Ridenour

26 - ALL Israel = Not Necessarily Each person
Rather enough To Make The Believers
Representive of The Nation

ALL - Without Exception ? - No
ALL - Without Distinction - yes

10

(1) Ch 11: 33-36
Paul breaks out in Praise
quotes Isaiah & Job

Ch 12
Paul is finished dealing with the question of what will become of the Jews.

He has given us much Doctrine & some deep theology

Now he is going to show us how that doctrine works out in everyday practical living.

The Bible never teaches doctrine just for the sake of knowledge.

Rather That We May Translate IT Into Practice!

Read verse 1 & 2 Amplified   Romans Road

So IMPORTANT!   So Much!

We're going over it word by word!

Beseech - Appeal - EnTreat = To Invite
To Exhort

2 Therefore = this is the connecting word
It connects this section with all
that has gone before

Mercies (compassion) = All that Paul has shown
us up to now -- is a result of the
mercy of God - By Grace are we Saved

When we begin to comprehend
all that God has done for us --
we will be ready & able to do what
Paul is asking us.

Present = in the greek this word has
the connotation of a sacrificial
offering. Used In Eph 5:27 --
where the Church is presented unto Christ
It is a voluntary giving

Bodies = a comprehensive word meaning
body - Soul - Spirit All of us

A living sacrifice = in contrast to O.T.
sacrifices of dead animals -- We are
to make a living sacrifice

(3) even so, there are similarities -- the animal
represented the life of the offerer --
Our life now is a New life in Christ
we are dead to sin - Our Lives Are
Not Our Own -- But Christs Who Bought Us
With His Blood! And we should willfully
present them to God!

Because of All of this -- Our sacrifice is

Holy -- and AcceptTable To God
and is well pleasing
Do you want to please God ?
Do you want to know what his will is for
your life? Present Yourself To God !

And Paul Says This Isn'T SomeThing
Irrational or Far OuT or Weird - Rather

IT Is Your Reasonable SpiriTual Worship

Paul says this is the logical outcome of
our position as believers in Christ
It is only through Christ that we are made
acceptable to God.
No Man comes to the Father - but by me

(4) verse 2 - amplifies

DO NOT BE CONFORMED TO THIS WORLD
Now heres where you're going to have to make a decision

Is this World good or evil ?

WORLD = AGE = it consists of all those people who think and act and live apart from God.

There are those who think that this world is basically good -- that given enough time Man will eventually create an orderly utopia.

AND THERE ARE MANY THEOLOGIANS ESPOUSING THIS VIEW -- We heard it expressed in this very Church several weeks ago!

NOW LETS GET SOMETHING VERY CLEAR -- It really doesn't matter what Rhienhold Niebor thinks --

It really doesn't matter what I think - or anybody else on this matter

(5) The question is What does God Think - and Say about this & Am I Willing To Believe Him?

1st What did Jesus say?

Jo. 8:23 - 8:43-45 - 12:31 - 14:16-17
14:30 - 15:18-19 - 17:15-16
18:36

2nd John says - I Jo 2:15-17 - 3:8
4:4-6 - 5:19

3rd Paul - Gal 1:4 II Cor 4:4
Eph 2:2-3 (When Satan Tempted Jesus He Offered The World)
Jms. 4:4

Now You Decide

Phillips translates this - don't let the world squeeze you into it's own mold.

That's The Negative - the don't - - here comes the do

Be Transformed = changed

this is the same word that is used to describe the Transfiguration of Jesus on the mountain

(6) By the renewal of your mind
Mind = complete intellect

So That You May Prove = to test & attest

to have spiritual discernment --
the inevitable result of inward transformation

Now IT ALL Sounds Good -
But HOW? do we renew our minds?
HOW do we transform ourselves.
I want to Share another diagram

Memorize - Jesus Did IT - Paul Did

Personalize - Change the pronouns to I me & my.
Example - II Chronicles 20:15
Only 1 interpretation - But many applications
II Tim 3:16 - profitable for teaching & reproof
correction - training in righteousness

11

① Ch12: 2 -- II Cor 10:4-5
Be transformed by renewing your mind -- But How?

Read verses 3-8

vrs 3 Moffat - In virtue of my office, I tell every one of you

Paul now is going to tell us how a Christian ought to think of himself

And how in view of our many & varied spiritual gifts -- we are to relate to fellow Christians

After we have established a right relationship with God -- then we are free to establish a right relationship with our fellow-believers

There Is Only One Thing Worse Than Pride -- Spiritual Pride

We need to see ourselves as God sees us -- and our gifts given to us as God wills

11

① Ch 12 : 2 -- II Cor 10 : 4-5
Be transformed by renewing your mind -- But HOW?

Read verses 3 - 8

vers 3 Moffat - In virtue of my office, I tell every one of you

Paul now is going to tell us how a Christian ought to think of himself

And how in view of our many & varied spiritual gifts -- we are to relate to fellow Christians

After we have established a right relationship with God -- then we are free to establish a right relationship with our fellow-believers

There Is Only One Thing Worse Than Pride -- Spiritual Pride

We need to see ourselves as God sees us -- and our gifts given to us as God wills

(3) 4 Paul portrays for us here his favorite view of the Church -- as a body having different members

I Cor 12: 14-

5 One Body - Though Individuals -- we need each other

6 Having gifts = Charisma greek

We all have been given some spiritual gift - So We're all Charismatics

Sad & Shameful - The Division & Hostility That Exist With In The Church

Spiritual Pride!

No Reason = God Worked Through A Donkey - So What If He Chooses To Work Through You!

I believe Satan is behind it all --

MT. 13 Parable of the wheat & tares - CounTerfiT

A genuine EncounTer With The Holy Spirit

HumiliTy

The Holy SpiriT Unities - SaTan Divides

(3) Let Us Use Them

Do you know what your spiritual gift is? (spiritual gifts are)

You are a necessary part of this body!

If you are a foot & you are not functioning - Our Church Is Going To Limp - it is your responsibility to find your gift - Don't Say - Nobody Even Asked Me!

MT. 25
Parable of talents

In The Same Way -- if I am not a foot & I try to act like a foot -- we're in trouble

One of The Biggest Problems of Church

Individuals Doing Jobs That They Have No Gift For!

When we select individuals for various positions -- we should do it on the basis of -- do they possess the needed gift for that particular job.

Lets Look Now At These Particular Gifts Paul mentions

(4) Prophecy = unfolding the message of God
preaching

Service = helping with physical needs
preparing meals (lovefeast) setting up chairs -
ushering

Teaching = Ability To Explain Scripture &
Make It Clear To Others

Exhorting = to encourage & admonish
to counsel

Giving = Ability To Make Money
give with "simplicity" & Hilarity = greek

Leadership = gift of administration - ability
to moderate a meeting - is to possess
Zeal = enthusiasm

Mercy = Greek word literally means
"Sick - Visitor" ability to express
sympathy - - to do it with cheerfulness

This is only a partial listing of
spiritual gifts - - Others are given in
I Cor 12 & Eph 4

5

Wisdom - Knowledge - Faith - Healing
Miracles - Tongues - Interpretation of Tongues
Apostles - Evangelists - Pastors
Testing of Spirits
Which gift is most important?

Paul always begins his listings with Prophecy
However the most important gift is - - -
the one that is needed at the present

I believe today we have an over emphasis on healing & tongues
We need to be careful
Remember Satan is a deceiver -- he is able to imitate any of the spiritual gifts - -
He also can heal! (Gift of Testing Needed)

The Presence of A Spiritual Gift Does Not Mean Spirituality or Spiritual Maturity - ie Church At Corinth

Rather The Presence of Spiritual Fruit Does - Fruit = Jesus Character
Gifts = Jesus Works - deeds
Jesus Said By Their Fruit - Ye Shall Know Them

12

LOVE WITHOUT HYPOCRISY

(1) Amp verse 9 - Hate what is evil
turn in horror from wickedness
Beware - lest we get used to the dark
Vance Havener - read

10/ Paul uses same pattern as I COR -- after
spiritual gifts - love A More Excellent
Way

giving precedence - hard to do "humanly"

11/ KJ - POOR Business = eagerness - earnestness
Zealous

FervenT = To Be HOT To Boil
Be Aglow
to be lukewarm makes God vomit
GoThard - PURPOSE - Pg 5

12/ be constant in prayer

14/ Bless & do not curse = can only do that
with help from Holy Spirit

15/ bear one anothers burdens

16-21 Excellent chapter to begin
MemoRizing

② Ch 13 1-7 Read
Phil 3:20 our citizenship is in heaven
Ch 14 1-4 read
Overall picture Jew & gentile
weak = Jew strong = gentile
Jews had some hangovers -- gentiles were free

verse 5 Jews had special feast days

7-9 - whatever we do - we do it unto the Lord

10, We are not to be our brothers judge

Lets make sure we understand what Paul is saying here

① - he is talking about those who have accepted all of the major Christians Doctrines. .. not someone who is reinterpreting the christian gospel verse 1
Gal 1:6-9 Rom 16:17

He is not saying that we should accept someone who will deny the inspiration of the Bible - or the virgin birth - the deity of Christ - his resurrection - our judgement

Jude:3 contend for the faith

Universalism

(3) Examples of some "weak in the faith"

some would say King James only version

some would say eating in Church - wrong

wearing of jewelry

"Brethren tradition"

these are all marginal issues -

Paul would say don't judge one another on these matters -

Because they will tend to divert you from Jesus who is at the center

verse 8

13

(4)

11 every knee shall bow, every tongue confess - Hallelvia

13 don't cause another to stumble

14-21 There Is A Tendency When One Has Truly Been Set Free In Christ -- To Want To Let Loose & Worship Christ In Freedom -

But we must apply this principle to all areas of our conduct

20 Do not for the sake of anything - destroy the work of God

23 Whatever does not proceed from faith -- the just shall live ~~by~~ faith

Play tape

Prayer

(7)

Now Paul has set forth here a very radical idea - in the eyes of the Jews

So Now - He's going To Illustrate Just What He Means. Pg 32

Read Ch 4: 1-12

Is Being Justified Through Faith A New Idea?

How Were People Saved In The OT?

Exactly The Same As Today By Faith

vs 16 Why Faith?

vs 18 Abraham Believed God
20
22

vs 23 Is Genisis A Fairy Tale?
A Story of Creation?

Paul Says No - These Words Were Written For Our Sake Also

File folder marked "Ephesians 1978". Sermons written and taught by Darvin Byler.

#1 Ephesians

Background - like Romans - a systematic setting forth of the whole Christian faith & practice

Not going to give you a lot of history - just a few important facts -

written by Paul - from jail - on trial for his life - 62 AD

To - as verse 1 says - all the saints who are faithful - Some manuscripts add "at Ephesus"
Was intended as a circuit letter - possibly to the 7 churches mentioned in Rev.

Paul was writing to a very poor group of people - they were poor in spirit as well as materially poor - Many were slaves - Depressed - Afraid - Anxieties - Superstitions
They Had No Hope - Either In This Life OR The Next

It was to this kind of people that Paul first spelled out - the vast riches that were theirs !!

I- These riches - when they were accepted as facts - would free them - Transform their lives - give them joy - peace - love - hope!

And IT Did!

The Same Thing can happen to you! -- regardless of your situation

This letter is a storehouse of riches -- to which we ought to turn repeatedly -
When We get Discouraged -
When We Feel Defeated

Read This Letter Then As A Personal Letter - From Paul - To You - A Faithful Saint
Apply what he says as facts - whether you understand them or not - and just let God work in your life - I gurrantee you a Miricle - A Changed Life.

Pray

3/ Ch 1:1 Paul always states his credentials
An apostle - one sent - by the will of
God - It was not his choosing - rather
God chose him.
An Apostle of Jesus Christ - Paul
recieved his message directly from Jesus.
He didn't get it from Peter or James
or John - they never taught him -
His AuThoriTy came directly from
Jesus Christ
It's amazing - the audacity of some people
they'll say I don't agree with Paul about
this or that -
Do they realize what they're saying?
If You Say You Don't Agree With Paul -
What you're Saying Is, You Don't Agree With
Jesus Either!

2 Grace & Peace
3 He has blessed us with every spiritual
blessing - or "all the blessings of the Spirit"
There Is No Need For Us To Be SpiriTually
Poor - We have been given every spiritual blessing
4 Now Paul lists some of our blessings

1. He chose us
2. Holy
3. Blameless
4. He adopted us as sons

4 5. grace = unmerited favor of God
6. Redeemed us - (Slave Market)
7. Forgiveness = To Set Aside
8. Shows us his will
9. Sealed with the Holy Spirit

God Has Done All of This For You!
They are gifts from god - part of our spiritual blessings -
Only Possible "In Christ"
verse 7 - In Him 11 - 13 In Him

13 verse 13 shows us the whole process of SALVATION

1. Hear the word of truth = Good News

2. And Have Believed = To Trust In - Rely Upon
Adhere To

3. Saved - Sealed With The Holy Spirit
That's IT!

You can't be a Christian - without the Holy Spirit! Ro 8:9 anyone who does not have the Spirit is none of his
Acts 2:38

5/

14 Great verse of assurance - Sealed with H.S. which is the ~~g~~ earnest (K.J.) of our inheritance

Earnest = Guarantee = Pledge

When you buy a property - you usually are required to put a down payment of 5 or 10% - this is your guarantee that you will pay the rest at settlement.

Jesus Bought Us - with his Blood!

And has given us the Holy Spirit as a Pledge or Guarantee that Some Day He's going to finish the Transaction!

Hallelujah!

Remember the 3 stages of Salvation?

1. Justified
2. Sanctified — Book Pg 24
3. Glorified

Engagement Ring

3 Points Page 25

#2

Ch1:15 Review - all that God has done for us.

1. Chose us
2. declared us "not guilty"
3. adopted us
4. Redeemed us
5. Forgiven us
6. shown us his will
7. Sealed us with Holy Spirit

All through Christ

all unmerited

Now verses 15 - 18

Paul says - for this reason - He has just spelled out the great fundamental truths of the Faith - And now he's going to Pray for their understanding

1st he points out 2 things that convince him they are true Christians

1. Faith = always the starting point -
Heb 11:6 - without faith it is impossible to please God

But faith is not enough!

2.

1. James tells us that faith without works is <u>dead</u> -

So Paul goes on - he says

15 I've not only heard of your <u>faith</u> — but also of your <u>love</u> - <u>for</u> - <u>ALL</u> the <u>saints</u>

If your "<u>faith</u>" has not resulted in your being a more loving Person -

If your <u>faith</u> has not stirred you to <u>Action</u> - Then perhaps you're <u>faith</u> is not <u>rooted</u> & grounded in <u>Jesus</u> <u>Christ</u>

16 Paul prayed "without ceasing" - for these people - <u>FROM Jail</u>!

He was <u>so</u> <u>concerned</u> about the <u>spiritual</u> <u>welfare</u> of these people - that he forgot his own troubles - and <u>again</u> & <u>again</u> he lifted them up <u>before the Father</u>.

Is There Someone That You're Praying For This Morning?

3/

17. Let's look at verse 17 and see what Paul is Praying about

A Spirit of Wisdom

What is Paul saying here – is he asking again for God to give them the Holy Spirit? (No – verse 13)

He is Praying for a special ministry of the Holy Spirit

Turn to Isaih Ch 11 – Not 7 Holy Spirits – but 1 – who has a varied ministry

Here we can see a little bit of the operation of the H S in our lives –
Just because we have the H S – doesn't automatically mean we will manifest all the ministries of the Spirit – We Must Desire Them – Ask For Them – Don't Confuse This With Salvation – That's All Behind Us – Right?

Everything that God has is for us --
But Now There is something we can do -- Be Filled
Desire IT – Paul Says In I Cor. We Should Earnestly Desire Spiritual Gifts

4

Have you ever asked God to give you a spirit of Wisdom?
When you sit down to read your Bible? Is it Dull?
Does it make sense?
We have available to us the greatest teacher in the World!
But we must ask him to teach us!
James Says - Ye Have Not Because Ye Ask Not

18. Now look at verse 18 - Strange
The eyes of your heart

Why does Paul say that?
So Many things that God does are different than what we normally do.
(your ways are not my ways neither are your thoughts my thoughts
We learn with our Minds - our intellect

But Spiritual Truths Can Only Be Learned In The Heart
Head knowledge - without heart knowledge is useless
You could memorize the whole Bible - have an understanding of all the theological doctrines - and still be lost
Why is This So?

5

When the Bible talks about the heart -
it refers to the very core and center of
our being - - our innermost spirit
Difficult to understand - we know that
we are made up of 3 parts - Body - Soul -
I Thes 5:23 Spirit - Where does God dwell?

Rom 8:16 = God's spirit bearing witness with our spirit -
Many other scriptures tell us that the Holy Spirit -
comes and dwells in our hearts -
Therefore I Believe That The Heart &
Our Inner Spirit Are One & The Same

Now - in what part is our mind? - Body? -
Spirit? - No - Soul

Soul = Mind - Will - Emotions
Now why can't spiritual truth be learned
I Cor 2: 9-14 → in the mind? - Because God Communicates To
Us Through Our Spirits - His dwelling place
In Us.
We need to learn to be led by
our spirits - Opposite from what the world
tells us
Rom 8:14 - For all who are led by
the spirit of God - are sons of God.

6

Now why does Paul Pray all of these things? --- That You May Know What is The Hope To Which He Called You

What is our Hope? The ReTurn of Jesus

1. Hope
2. Riches
3. Power - we need power in order to appropriate our Riches

We don't have these riches just to be rich - but in order to use them to the honor & glory of God.

What kind of Power?

The Very Power That Raised Jesus From The Dead! IT's Available To Us - BuT We must Know how to Use IT.

Page 35

What a wonderful Prayer!

How unlike our prayers - Lord, Bless The Ephesians This Morning

Paul is Specific

Lesson # 3

verse 19 – 20 Jesus position in heaven

His name – above every name –
his power – above every rule & power

God Has Made Him The Head
of all things for the church

From This Position He Intercedes
for Us Rom 8:34 Heb 7:25 – He ever
liveth to make intercession for us

22 Paul introduces us to the concept of
the church as a body with Christ as
the head – will develop it further in
Ch 4.

Ch 2 In the 1st Ch. Paul has shown
us our spiritual possessions – now he
is going to show us our spiritual
Position

Pg 40 – Be Rich
Do You Believe That?
If so – what are you doing about it?
What are you going to tell God
when you meet him?

I/

I know all the reasons & rationalizations

We Believe Satans Lies - (We're All Worshiping The Same God)

But many times we are bound by fear

Fear of being rejected

I believe if we would concentrate on the needs of people - instead of our fear of rejection -- we would do something

Example - people in house - we would not want to intrude - But if we saw the Roof on fire -- we would overcome our fear and rush in and warn them -- knowing that our message was one that they needed to hear

Just So -- if we would see our friends & neighbors who are unsaved - as being dead -- as being eternally seperated from God!

We Would Do SomeThing About IT

2 Page 41 -> forces for disobedience

The Prince of The Power of The Air

Pg 41 - Point About Satan - Is Attractive

Angel of Light

Is Defeated

Liar - Deciever

3/ verse 3 – Page 42 The Flesh

verse 4 – But God – Praise God for the but gods in the Bible!

Rich in Mercy = We were guilty – we deserved Death – Mercy Has Pardoned Us

Love – An Attribute of God – Part of His very nature – Light – Just

5- while we were yet in our sins – He hath quickened us – Made us alive!
Each one of us is a Miracle of resurrection

6 Here we have the key – the most important fact of our Christian life.
Most Important Because – It's The Beginning -- And If You Miss The Beginning -- You're Probably Going To Miss The Rest

One of the greatest mysteries of the Faith – is the fact that when we Believe on Jesus – Trust him as Savior --
We are joined together with him --

1. In His Death
2. In His Ressurection Rom. Ch 6
3. In His Glorification

4 If you've never been joined together with Christ in his death - Let Me Help You
Paul has just shown us what we were - Sinners - Dead - Depraved

God Says - the wages of sin is Death
Yet - He loved us so much - he came and Took OUR Place.
Now - you can say that Christ died for the sins of the whole world - - and That's True - - But If you've Never Seen Him Die For YOUR Sins - - ?
Jesus Christ is the only person in the universe who is worthy to take your place - the lamb of God - without SPOT

Now - in the same way we died with him - - We are also resurrected with him - Eph 2:5 He - God made us Alive together with Christ. Rom 6:5

But - - That's not All - - He has also raised us up with him - - and made us to SiT with him - in the Heavenly places

verse 6

5 Now where is Christ?
Seated At the right hand of God the Father -- does that mean that he is litterally sitting up in heaven somewhere?
Yes but beyond that - it is a picture of someone who has completed their work - Jesus's Work Is Done
IT IS Finished!

Now here we are - what do we have to do ?? NOTHING!

IT's All Been Done -- So - We just SiT down beside him - and Enjoy Yourself!

vas 8 - By Grace - not of yourself

I said before that this was the Key To Victorious Christian living - Because its the Beginning -- IT's also the Key to our continuing walk with the Lord.

Probably the hardest thing that God will ask you to do is to WaiT
To SiT Down - Wait, I say on the Lord

6 Did you ever notice how incredibly SLOW god is?

I mean sometimes I feel as though I need to PUSH him.

It's So Clear to me what God Ought to do -- But do you know What?

He Completely Ignores Me -- (Thank Goodness) an just keeps on doing Nothing -- Untill I completely exhaust myself -- And then --

Ever So Slowly -- He Begins To Work and before I know it - he does More than I had ever dreamed possible -

and I don't even know how he did it! PRAISE GOD!

Lesson #4

Ch2:10 <u>Review</u>

Last week we saw in verse 1-3 - we were <u>dead</u> - because we followed the <u>Prince</u> of the power of the air
we were by <u>nature</u> children of wrath

Then verse 4 - But God -- rich in mercy & love - While we were <u>Dead</u> in our sins - he <u>resurrected</u> us.

And verse 6 gave us a new spiritual position - Right <u>alongside</u> Jesus Christ

verse 8 - Paul sums up all that God has done for us.

<u>Now</u> verse <u>10</u>
Workmanship = Greek = Poièma
from which the english - <u>poem</u> is derived
Literally = we are gods poem - or masterpiece
~~And what do you do with a Masterpiece~~?
~~Put It on Display~~!
What a beautiful illustration Paul gives us of the Christian life

Verse 10

2/ If we could grasp the full significance of this verse -- we could forever settle this issue of grace - verses good works.

What Paul is really saying here is this -- God did not raise you from the dead for nothing! - he didn't sit us in the heavenly places so we could take some kind of ego trip -

God Is Trying To Shape You Into A Lovely Poem -- So That The World Will Read You -- And Glorify Him!
MT 5:16 - Jesus Said - You Are The Light of The World - Let Your Light So Shine - That They May See Your Good Works & Glorify Your Father - Who Is In Heaven
That's How It's Supposed To Work
isn't it tragic -- that so many times -- The World Reads Us -- And Ridicules Our Father In Heaven
Why? = 2 Basic Reasons

1. Because We Have Not Died To Self
Can we say with Paul - I have been crucified with Christ, it is no longer I who live - but Christ who lives in me

1 As we pointed out last week - the Key
or starting point - for a joyous -
Victorious - Spirit Led - Christian life

IS - Being Crucified With Christ

If We Do Good Works To Glorify
Self -- The World Will See Through
Us

Read "Others"

2. Because We Refuse To Believe God
God Says He Has Raised us UP -
He Has Made Us To Sit In Heavenly Places -
Given Us Power - His Spirit
IT's All in The Past Tense

But we say - NOT Me -
Lord -- you must mean someone else

I'm Ugly - I'm Not A
Beautiful Poem!

Yes -- But God Does Not See Us
As We See Ourselves!

He Sees Our Potential

Example

4/1. God Said To Moses - You Will
Lead My People Out of Egypt..
But Moses Said -- I Can't even Talk
Without Stuttering!
God Saw His Potential

2. Jesus Said To Peter - You Are
A Rock -- Yet Peter Looked like AnyThing
But A Rock - As He Denied Jesus
But - Jesus SAW His Potential

We Must Purpose To Cooperate
With God - In Finishing Us
Please Be Patient - God Is Not Finished With Me
Yet

We Must Get Back On Gods Easel

Similar To Chalk Drawings --
Joni's Drawings -- Picture All Messed
Up --. A Few Strokes Here -- A Little
Color There -- Result - A MasterPiece

What Do You Do With A MasterPiece?

Put It on Display!

5 ✓

~~There is no place for self in the Christian life~~

~~If we do good works to glorify ourselves - the world will see through us~~

~~Key - Who are we glorifying?~~

But There is A Further Testing

Look at the last part of verse 10 -- Edy - Amplified

Paul says that God is prearranging preparing circumstances -- So That We Might Do Good Works For His Glory

Now - if we're running around arranging all the details so we can do some good work -- That should tell us we're on the wrong track.

Pro. 3-6 If You Will Acknowledge Him In All your ways -- He Will Direct your Path

Ps. 37:23 - The Steps of A Good Man Are Ordered By The Lord - A Principle of Scripture

For The Christian - There is No Such Thing As A Coincidence! If We Let Him -- God Will Direct our Path

6/ verse 11 Now Paul brings up one of his favorite subjects - Circumcision

The Bible has a lot to say about circumcision -- Paul devotes almost the entire letter to the Galations to it -- So IT MusT Have Some Very Special Meaning & Significance

Have You Ever Wondered Why God Chose This ParTicular Sign - To SeT ApaRT His Chosen People ?

Well one thing that has characterized Pagan, Godless people from Abrahams time to the present day -- is sexual degeneracy

God Made Us Sexual -- & He Knew ThaT If We Could NoT ConTRoL OuR Sex Drives -- We CouLd NoT ConTRoL Any OTheR AReA oF ouR Lives EiTheR.

And it didn't matter how "civilized" pagans got either -- The GReek PhilosopheRs of Pauls Day -- SocRaTes ETc. Have NeveR Been SuRpassed In TheiR Thinking - -
YeT They PRacTiced Homosexuality And OTheR DegRading Sexual PRacTices

7a

The One Thing That Has Marked Godly People Down Through History -- Has Been Moral Purity

A Persons Morality - Will Dictate Their Theology

Almost all of Modern day Cults came into being because of Immorality

That's Why It's Very Important To Check The Life style of Any one Who Would Preach Another Gospel

Good Example - Niche - God Is Dead Died of V.D. - Immoral Man

And SO - In this day of Gross Immorality -- We Would Do Well To look again at the Significance of - Circumcision

One More Thing About Circumcision - It Demonstrates The Trustworthiness of The Bible - And The Practicality of The Bible

Lesson # 5

Ch 2:14

He - Christ Is Our Peace

What is Peace ? - The Absence of Conflict ? Ex. - Two Armies Stop Fighting - Untill They Regroup
On - Husband & wife agree to live at peace - for the sake of the children -- Is That Peace?

Or How About 2 Church Members -- Who Agree To Disagree Civily -- Yet There Remains Deep Division & Distrust
Is That Peace ?

veese 14 → Peace Is A Person - Jesus Christ
Peace Is Oneness - Through Jesus Christ

That's Why I Have Great Difficulty With Peace Movements - Be It the Camp David Summit - On The Brethren March on Nuclear Arsenals

I Believe The Bible Clearly Tells Us - "We Will Not Have Peace -- Untill The Return of Christ
2. Peace Can Only Come As Individuals Experience The New Birth

2. What A Hypocritical Situation --
We Pray for Peace In The Middle East --

Yet Right Here At Spring Creek --
Where We All ~~Before~~ Have Been Born
Again - We Cain't get Along

With Each OTheR

Peace Is A Person - And Before
We Can Be AT Peace WiTh OThers --
We Must First Be AT Peace With
The Person Of Jesus Christ

verse 18 Both Have Access Through One Spirit

~~One of the main reasons we can't~~
~~get along in our churches~~ --
Jews Were God's Chosen People --
They Had The Law - Prophets - Temple --
They looked down on the Gentiles --
causing great hostility.

Today - We Do The Same Thing -
"We Brethren" Are Certainly More Biblical
Than Those Lutherans

3. And even in our own Church -- We Do The Same Thing --
God Chooses To Bless Us With Some Spiritual Gift - And Right Away We Become Proud -- As If We Were More Worthy -- When Really We Were More Needy

When we project ourselves in such a way -- as to make others feel 2nd rate --
That Causes Resentment & Hostility

The Ground Is Level At The Foot of The Cross
Everything God gives us is a gift of his Grace - unmerited favor

verse 19 Be Rich Pg 65

Jesus Is The CornerStone --
20 EveryThing Else Relates To IT - Him

21-22 Now Paul Shows Us How God Is Building His Church

FiTly Framed To Organize CompacTly
To Join TogeTher

4/ If We Would Just FiT TogeTher--
God Would NoT Have To Shape Us-

BuT - Because We're Each DifferenT
God Has To FiT Us - Shape Us
(IllusTraTe On Black Board) HOLY SPIRIT IS MORTAR

And One of the ways Gods
does this - is through other Believers

But many times we do not benifit
from this - because of a wrong response

We Become Offended - Develope
How? -- We are Crucified with Christ BiTTerness
GoThard Give IT All To Jesus
1.
2.
3. if God want's to teach me patience -
do you think he allows everything to
just go smoothly?

5/ Now – you might be ~~saying~~ thinking – –
thats OK For Some people – –

But, I'm the Independent Type – –
I Don't Need That

Yes But We Need _You_!

Our body is _Sick_ – There Are
Gaping Holes –
Many of Our Body
Have _Urgent_ Needs –
As Long As We're _Divided_ – –
The Holy Spirit Cannot _Minister_ Through
_Us_

To night = Love feast = _Opportunity_
To Submit To The _Body_

Unconfessed Sin – eat & drink damnation
unto yourselves

Lesson # 6

Ch 3 For This reason - What reason?

Because he preached that the gentiles are joint heirs - partakers of the same promises.
Ch 2: 19-20-21. Ch 3: 6

A Prisoner of Jesus Christ --
What? - He was actually a prisoner of Ceasar charged with treason against the emporer

What a lesson for us -- when we become concerned about the political happenings in the World.

Paul knew who was in control -- he knew he was a prisoner because Jesus willed it - And he was confident that when there was no longer any good purpose - he would be freed

Now - he gives some good reasons - On Behalf of You Gentiles - Paul recognizes that he is in prison for their sake - Yet he knows that some good will come -
This Letter!

We looking at history can see God's purpose - The Prison epistles make up a large portion of the New Testament

2) verse 2 - Stewardship of Gods Grace

Paul saw his responsibility - We have a responsibility Too!

One of the things that disturbs me about (Charismatics?) They only seem interested in a spiritual High - have no sense of Misson - Of Course We Don't either

verse 3 - The great Mystery - verse 6 made known to Paul through revelation - Paul Was Taught Directly By The Ressurected Lord - Gal 1:12

Paul preached for 14 years before he ever sat down & talked with the other apostles - And He Says - They Added Nothing To Me ! Gal 2:6

He Knew Every Thing They Knew - Even The Things That Jesus Had Done With Them When He Was Still Living !

Example I Cor. 11:23

verse 4–6
3/ Now Paul speaks again & again about this wonderful mystery – & you can really sense his awe – – That God Chose To Reveal This Great Mystery To Him!

verse 5 Paul points out that this mystery was hidden from the O.T. Prophets

skip to verse 9 – Hidden for ages

verse 10 – through the Church – You & Me

We're Going To Teach The Angels! Wow!

Pg 73

Now back to verse 7
Paul inserts this testimony of Praise
Look at what he says –
1. It Wasn't My Idea To Be A Preacher
2. It Was A Gift of God – Through The Power of The Spirit
Paul Undoubtly Had The Gift of Evangelism Ch 4:11

4/ How many more gifts he had I don't know – Apostle – Prophet – Pastor Teacher – Healing – Tongues I Cor 12

It is Possible That Paul Had All The Gifts of The Spirit

The Important Thing For Us Is That Each One of Us Has At Least One Gift 1 Cor 12:7

Have you found it – & are you using it? Do you Have A Ministry For The Lord?
Paul Had A Lot of Gifts – – & He Used Them – He Had A Big Ministry

verse 8 Genuine Humility – Always The Result of Gods Grace Gifts

verse 11 – All things are on schedual! – God Has An Eternal Purpose –

Through Christ – – Who gives Us Boldness – Confidence

5/ Now once again the deep concern for these people – which prompted this letter -- comes forth

verse 13 Paul is concerned that they are about to quit! Give Up

They're facing Trial & Hardship Daily – & Their Leader is in Prison – Soon to Die

& Paul Almost Shouts To them – Things Are NoT As Bad As They Seem!

Are you beginning to identify with these Ephesians?

verse 14 So – Paul begins his second Prayer

You remember in his first Prayer – Paul Prayed for Wisdom & understanding for them – But this prayer is a Prayer for Power –

Paul wanted them to understand & know All that God had done for them -- But he also knew that now they needed the Power To Implement Their Faith

6/ verse 15. Paul is not promoting the
universal fatherhood of God.

Another example of poor translation
Greek = PATRIA = Paternal descent
a group of families - under one
Father Pg 83 New International Version

verse 16 - Living Bible
What is the inner man? - His Spirit
This should be our Prayer - when
we're down

verse 17 The Main Work of The Holy Spirit
Is To Glorify Jesus - SO If
you Let Him Have His Way In Your
Life - He Will Bring You & Jesus
Together In the Most Intimate of
Fellowship

Rooted & Grounded In LOVE

Most of our problems spiritually --
come because we are not Rooted or
Grounded in Agape Love

6/ verse 15 Paul is not promoting the universal fatherhood of God.

Another example of poor translation
Greek = Patria = Paternal descent
a group of families - under one Father Pg 83 New International Version

verse 16 - Living Bible
What is the inner man ? - His Spirit
This should be our Prayer - when we're down

verse 17 The Main Work of The Holy Spirit Is To Glorify Jesus - SO If you Let Him Have His Way In Your Life - He Will Bring You & Jesus Together In the Most Intimate of Fellowship

Rooted & Grounded In LOVE

Most of our problems spiritually -- come because we are not Rooted or Grounded in Agape Love

7 Notice that Paul is taking us Step by Step back up the road to spiritual vitality - And It's Not UnTill The 3rd STep That We Feel AnyThing!

Many times we get discouraged because we don't "feel" the closeness of God

Paul Knows That First We Must Have A Fresh InFilling of The Holy Spirit

And Our FaiTh STrenghtened - Before We Feel AnyThing

verse 18 Once we're rooted & grounded in Love (Agape) we can begin to comprehend The Love of CHRIST which Paul says surpasses knowledge

Pg 87

19 - filled with all the fullness of God

We are complete in him Pg 89

Now we should be firmly seated in the Heavenlies -- Ch 4 - Walk

Lesson # 7 8

Ch 4:1 - I therefore beseech - beg - urge - you to WALK worthy of the divine calling.

1st 3 chapters = our position in Christ
Sitting - Resting on Him
Seated In The Heavenlies

Now - the practical outworking of that DOCTRINE

NoTe - we can only Walk - after we are firmly seated

To try to live the Christian life without being firmly seated with Christ is to try to live it in your OWN Power - IT Can't Be Done! = FRUSTRATION DeFeaT

2) Walk with all lowliness & Meekness

1. HumiliTy
2. Meekness
3. Long-SuffeRing
4. ForbeaRance

} FRuiT of The SpiriT
Same As Gal - Walk in The SpiriT - Only Way

J/

verse 3 Paul make a Plea for UniTy -
By Emphasizing SpiriTual FruiT

We CannoT CreaT UniTy -
Only the H. SPIRIT can do that!

We are to endeavor - to strive for

UniTy Is NoT UniformiTy Pg 95

We need not all be alike -
BuT - - we do need a common
Doctrinal Foundation Pg 96

verse 4 One Body - One SpiriT etc. Pg 97

BapTism of The SpiriT
In The " } 2nd Experience?
If we're going to have UniTy ~~we~~
we need to Agree on This DocTrine

I WanT To STarT With Our
Experiences - Because I Feel This
Becomes The Problem Area

3/ John 1:1 = The Word = Logos = Christ
Must Be Our Final Rule & Authority

When we have an "Experience" Do we then Interpret The Bible Out of That Experience? NO!
We must always interpret Our "Experience" Out of The Bible!

I Believe That The Bible Teaches That Ideally We Are Baptised Into The Body of Christ At Conversion By The Holy Spirit
But Unfortunately This Doesn't Always Happen – Many Reasons
CARL Ziegler - Very good
Wet 3 Times - Many of us were imature –
We had the H.S -- But He didn't have US Each Different!

But – This Doesn't Change The WORD!
If we try to change the word to suit our experiences - we put God in A BOX!
HE WON'T ALLOW IT

4 We can't use our experiences for the NORM - God IS Soverign - He Does What He Wills - He Meets Us Where We Are!

Examples - Missionary in Africa - people received H.S. before water baptism.

Housewife - went to refrigerator - received the H.S. - NORM?

O.K. - Maybe some of you are thinking SO What - What's The Big Deal?

In this area we are Probably more vulnerable to deception than in any other area of our Christian life.

SATAN IS A Decievers - The Father of Lies - He Works To DIVIDE US

Now - we should be open & desire All that God has for us - BUT if we are told that we MUST Have A Certain Experience - And We Need Too Seek After IT -

We Are Opening Ourselves To The Possibility Of Deception

5- Especially When We Say That This Baptism of The Spirit Must Be Accompanied By Speaking In Tongues.

Thats Unscriptural!

SATAN CAN Speak in Tongues

HOW Then Can We Know if We Have Had A Genuine Experience With The HOLY SPIRIT? (Humility) Said Before

What does the Bible Say?

Jo 13:35 - By This Shall All Men Know That you Are My Disciples - If you HAVE LOVE - (Agape Love) For ONe Another

And Mt 7:15-23 (Read)

By Their Fruit ye Shall Know Them

Why love? Why Fruit?

Because SATAN CAN Counterfiet The Gifts of The Spirit - But He Cannot Counterfiet The Fruit of The Spirit

Questions?

Read from Pamphlet pg 11

6/ I want to use Diagram because-
1. Helps us to Visualize
2. Different Terms have different meanings to different people

Sunday Evening
Not only missed Carl Ziegler - but missed a beautiful Testimony -
Sun Eve - Important - To Build The Body - Testimonies Important - We Need To Know What God Is Doing NOW!

We Need Committment! God Gives Us 168 hours every week - What Do We give Him? 1 hour?

The Bible Says IT's The Lords Day!
If we're serious about the Christian life - Surely We Could Commit Ourselves To More Than Sun Morning

Any Way --- Edies Testimony Really Summed Up This Whole Thing For Me: -- Diagram

Lesson #9

Ch 4:11

Spiritual Gifts I Cor-12 Don't be Ignorant

1. List is illustrative
2. Are Given For The Body (For Unity)
3. Are Not To Be Put on Display - Misused
4. Are Given As God Wills
5. Are Grace Gifts (Not Earned)
6. Do Not Make Us More "Spiritual" (Corinthians)
7. One Gift Is Not More Important Than Another - Whichever Is Needed
8. We CAN Neglect Our Gifts - Paul told Timothy to stir up the gift in him & not to neglect it - To Do So Is SIN

9. When We Restrain The Gifts - We Limit The Lordship of Christ

verse 12 - amplified

We Are working Backwards -

IT Will Never Work

Pastor - or Shepard - Does not reproduce - Sheep reproduce sheep

We Will Never Build The Body -- UnTill We Put This Into Practice -

Sun Eve --- Bible Studies - Visitation

7/ verse 13
To Attain The Unity of The Faith

We Are a divided Broken Body
we can't even sit down and talk about
our differences without HOSTILITY

CAN We ATTAIN UNITY?

Yes! If We ALL Yield
To The Spirit - Because He
Will Make Us All Like Jesus!

That's what it's All About

Why? - verse 14 - A Clear Witness

verse 15 - speaking the TRUTH in Love
Pg 104

verse 16 - Each Part Is Important
Must Be Concerned For Insignificant
Member

Lesson #10

Ch 4:11 - Review

verse 15 - Speaking the truth in Love - Hard!
But Necessary

Gal 6: 1 & 2 - Amplified

Complete What Is Lacking

verse 16 - Amplified - Each Part is Important

Growth comes when Each part is working properly--
With Power Adapted To Its Need
We must remember - that these abilities and Talents are NOT our Natural abilities

They Are SuperNatural Enablements Given By God

Read Pg 107

verse 17-18-19
They Can't Think Right Because They Do Not Have The Light Of The Holy Spirit - Minds Are DARkened

3/ Further – Sin Has A Way Of Blinding Us – Causing Us To Become Callous

Should We Be Surprised At The Direction Our Society Is Going?

According to this scripture it can't go any other way.

Once Again That's Why We Need A Healthy Body --

Individualy -- We Can't Survive In That Kind of A Society – We Can't Keep Our Families Together

Example – Lot – Did he think he could serve God in a godless town?

Read from Wycliffe

We need A Healthy Body To Help Us To Stay Seperated From The World

3/ verse 20-21-22

verse 23- Be Renewed In your Mind
How?
Gothard

verse - 24-25-26

Righteous Indignation

verse 30 - A Command - Do Not Grieve The
Holy Spirit
What Grieves Him?

verse 31
1. Bitterness - Wrath - Anger
amplified - 31 & 32

Lesson # 11

Only 3 sessions left - going to skip over to Ch 5 : 18

Paul has given 2 illustrations of the Church

1. Ch 2 : 20-22 A Holy Temple
Jesus The Cornerstone

2. Ch 4 : 11-16 Church Is Like A Human Body - Christ Is The Head

3. Now In Ch 5 He Gives Us The 3rd Illustration - The Church Is The Bride of Christ
And in this context He mentions the fact that the husband-wife relationship should be the same as the relationship between Christ & the Church.

I've talked before about the importance of sharing with one another what God is doing in our lives - Our Testimonies
To Share Not Only our Strenghts -- But Also Our Weakneses
That's how I want to begin this morning

3/ verse 18 - Many time we need to be broken before the Lord - He is

Then Able To Fill Us & Control Us

verse 21 - Me - Submit To One Another

This should be a Basic Attitude for the Christian

This scriptures main point is the relationship between Christ & the Church

The Husband-Wife Relationship Is Given As An Illustration

To Be Filled & Controled By The Spirit Requires Willful Submision

1. To Christ - Our Will
2. To The Body
3. To Husbands & Wives

As we develope a submissive spirit - we free the Holy Spirit to operate in Our Lives

Look For Our Rights -- None

3/ verse 25 - Christ gave himself up - -
When Our Wives See Us In
TOTAL Submission To Our Head -
Jesus Christ - - They Will Have No
Problem In Being Submissive To Us

Lesson #12

Ch 6:1 Read Pg 149

We've been looking at Submission in Practical Relationships

A Natural Result of Being Filled With The Spirit - verse 18

1. Joy Ful - 19
2. Thank Ful - 20
3. Submissive - 21

verse 21 - Be Subject To One Another a Basic Christian Attitude!

1. Submit To Christ
2. Submit To The Body
3. Husbands & Wives

Now In Ch 6 Paul speaks To Children & Fathers & Slaves!

Book Is Very Good on This Pg 150

verse 3 - a commandment with a promise Pg 152

2/ verse 4 Fathers – Should Discipline

Pg 153 – Duties of Husband & Father

I don't feel very qualified to
talk about raising Children --
I Have Much To Learn --
But I do know this – I Can't Do
It Alone -- I need My Wife

I Need The Holy Spirit

verse 5 – Amazing teaching – (Pg 156)

We need to be careful –
Brethren Are Too Involved In Changing
The Social Order – & NOT Preaching
The Gospel
Jesus Did NoT Try To Change Political
System – Neither Did Paul – Just
Preach Good News – Heal The Sick –
Win The Lost

3/ verse 10 – Finally -- Be STrong In The Lord!

Pg 163

Sooner or Later We All Discover That We're Engaged In SpiriTual WarFare

* Pg 164

Our Problem – (Sandy & Me)

We Were NoT Prepared!

We BoTh Were Growing SpiriTualy – Had A "Good" Marriage – But We Were NoT Ready – When SATan ATTacked

He Knows Where Your Vulnerable

If You Fail To Recognize Him – & FighT Back WiTh The Power Of God -- He Will DesTroy You!

Pg 164 – * 165

4 SiT - Walk - STand (Pg 41)

verse 11 - PuT on The Whole Armor of God

God Has Provided The Armor -
We Must Put IT On!

That You Might STand!
without this armor - we cannot stand against
SATAN (SiT-walk-STand Pg 43)

verse 12 - Pg 165 *
against principalities - against powers
against rulers of darkness -
against spiritual host of wickedness

various powers - different functions
SATAN ATTacks Us In Many
DifferenT Ways
1. TempTaTion To Sin
2. Bodily - (HealTh) Lu. 13
3. ATTempTs To Hinder
4. Oppression
5. Deppression
6. FrusTraTion

7. RepeaTedly Brings Up PasT Failures & Sin - To Accuse Us
8. Sows Seeds of DoubT

5/ We must learn to recognize his various methods -
Hard To Do Because He Works
Under Cover - Many Disguises

Pg 166

The Bible Tells Us Much About
The DecieTfulness - Lying - Methods of SATan
BuT--- He speaks DirecTLy only
3 Times -- In All of ScripTure
1. Garden of Eden Gen. 3 Seeds of DoubT
2. STory of Job Ch 1&2 Accuser
3. TempTaTion of Jesus Lu. 4

If you are the son of God

Lu 4 - verse 14 - Jesus ReTurned In The POWER
of The SpiriT
When we have resisted SATAN - & Stood
Firm - We Will Recieve POWER

Lesson 13

1, Ch 6:14
Gird Your Loins With Truth

Each piece of Armour is given us to protect us from corresponding attacks by SATAN

Girdle Is Mentioned First Because IT Holds The OTher Parts In Place
Also to gird up your loins - means -- to be prepared for action

Girded With Truth - Gods Word Is Truth - But We Must Allow IT To Become A Living Reality In Our Lives

SATANS ATTACK - To Sow The Seeds of DOUBT - About The Bible

Garden of Eden - Yea HaTh God Said ?
Doubts About The Bible -
Totaly Inspired - Inerrant -
If SATAN CAN CAUSE Us To Doubt The Authority Of The Bible -- The Battle's OVER

Verse 14

d/ BreasT PlaTe of RighTeousness
Breastplate guards the HearT - The Most ViTal Organ of our Bodies

HearT In SpiriTual Sense Is The CenTer of our Being - Where The SPiriT of God DwellS WiThin US.

If The HearT can Be Gotten To Then Again - The BaTTle IS OVER!

SATANS ATTACK - To GeT Us To DoubT Our SALVATion

For Us To PuT ON RighTeousness - Is To AccepT The SubsTiTuTionary DeaTh of JESUS ChRisT As FuLL PAyMenT For OUR SINS

We Have No RighTeousness of OUR OWN

When SATAN ACCUSes US -
we Can STAND Firm on The RighTeousness of ChRisT

verse 15

3/ Shod your Feet with The Gospel Of Peace

If we Are To STAND Firm - We Need To Have Shoes That will NOT SLip

These Shoes Are The Gospel - OR Good News - That Brings Peace - To OUR Souls & To Those We Come In Contact with

SATANS ATTACK - To Try To Rob Us OF OUR Peace

Oppression of SPIRIT - A Feeling That God Has Forsaken US

Repeated Failures

To Have OUR Feet Shod with The Gospel Is To Recognize The Completeness of OUR Position In Christ -

The "Good News" - We Were Guilty

SomeOne Else Took OUR Penalty
Don't Get COLD Feet --
PuT ON YOUR Shoes!

verse 16

4Y The Shield OF Faith

above all - lift up the covering shield of SAVING Faith (Ampli)

To quench the fiery darts of the wicked one

This Is A Special Piece OF ArMour - Able To Be Moved About - To Give Added Protection To Any Part

It was large 4' x 2' - able to cover the entire BoDY -

Edges Made To InTer Lock With OThers - SO SOLDIERS COULD MARCH InTo The ENEMY Like A SOLID WALL

We Do NoT Fight ALONE!

SATANS ATTACK - Fiery DARTS - SWIFT - Unexpected - DeaDLY

Causing us to doubt the very existance of God -

Giving Us Burning Desires To Sin

Verse 17

5/ The Helmet of SALVATION

The helmet protects the head & eyes - Our Minds & Direction - Vision

Our minds control our bodies - therefore whoever controls your mind - controls you.

SATANS ATTACK - He Zeroes In on OUR Thoughts - with suggestions to deceive us - to lead us astray

Our defense then is to fill our thoughts with our great SALVATION

Think of the wonder that God would love you So Much - to send his Son to die for you! - Or the Wonder of Regeneration

A New Creature

Example King SAUL - Lost His Mind To SATAN

Is. 26 - Thou WilT Keep Him In Perfect Peace Whose Mind Is Stayed On Thee

Jesus Is OUR SALVATION

Verse 17

6/ The Sword of The Spirit
The word of God - Sharp - Powerful
as A Two Edged Sword

Our only "Offensive" Weapon -
And We Don't Even weild IT

Ampli - The sword which the Spirit
Wields - IT Is The Holy Spirit In
Us who Uses The Sword - As We yield
To Him

You Cannot Use The Sword of The
Spirit -- Unless you Are Filled with -
& Controlled By The Spirit!

The Best Defense Is A Good Offense

Thy Word Have I Hid In My Heart -
the importance of storing up scriptures - So the
Spirit can bring them to our remembrance

Also - Word = Greek = Rema - A Divine
Utterance

God Will Give Us A Word of Wisdom
When We Need IT - MT 10:19

verse 18

7/ Praying in the SPIRIT -

OUR Secret Weapon

We're told to pray at all times -
elsewhere in the Bible we're told to pray
without ceasing - How Can We Do This?

Do You Remember Ro 8:26 ? - The H-Spirit
within Us Can Pray Constantly -

We Need Only Be In An Attitude of
Prayer

We Don't need to say Any Thing --
Just Let The Spirit Talk -

Again - Filled With & Controlled
By The Spirit - A Complete
Trusting

Closing - All This Armour Does Us
No Good - If We Don't Put It On!

God Has Provided It -- We Must Appropriate
It

Verse 23-24

File folder marked "Daniel 1979". Sermons written and taught by Darvin Byler.

Ch. 1

Daniel - well Known For Stories About
Lions Den + Fiery Furnace
But More!

Two great books of Prophsy in Bible
1. Rev. 2. Daniel
We will Look generally - not Specific

A great hunger Today For Prophsy - - -
Many Errors - great imbalance

The Book naturally Divides itself into
Two Parts - 1. Historical 2. Prophetic
It is written in 2 Different Languages -
Hebrew - Aramaic

Background on Daniel = Historian Josephus - Bible give
us Lots of Information
Tribe of Judah - Who Else?
Taken Captive in 606 B.C. - about 18-20 years old
Rose To A high Position - Led A Public Life
Associated with Kings + Politicians yet
Not one Flaw in His Character -
He Talked with Angels - Jesus Appeared To Him
Greatly Beloved of God.

2

Daniel Wrote This Book About 573 B.C.
(Read From Larkin Pg. 10) Josephus --

Begin - Dan. Ch. 1:1-2

Nebuchadnezzar Defeated Egypt -
Then Took Jerusalem - It was The Custom
To Take The Best of The Young Men & Women
As Captives
All This was ForeTold - Jer. 27:4-8

V 3 - Ashpenaz - Master of Eunuchs = Castration

V 4 - 1. without Blemish 2. good Looking
3. Intelligent 4. Able To serve in Palace

V 5 - A 3 year Course of Training Designed To
Convert Them To The Babylonian Lifestyle
1. Language 2. Religion 3. Names V 7

6-7

What A Hopeless Situation!
Taken From Home - No Chance To Return
Brain Washed!

V 8 But Daniel Purposed --
Inner Convictions

Ch. 2

Dreams & Visions - Used By God

Pharaoh - Joseph   Peter

Why Nebuchadnezzar ?
Just Like Pharaoh - God was going To
Use Him To Bring About His Purposes
JER. 27:4-8

4-11 Failure of Chaldean Wise men

12-13 Kings Decree

14-16 Daniels Response

17-18 Prayer Meeting !

19 - God Answers - A night Vision ?
20 Daniel Praises God

23 we - us Daniel Shared The Blessing

24 Daniel Did not Rush into The Kings
presence - but went Through His Authority = Arioch

26 - Are You Able?

27-28 - Not I - But God
Chooses To Reveal The Future

29-30 Not To Puff up Daniel - But To make
Known To The King The Thoughts of His
heart Swindoll Pg.22

31 The Dream

1st. An Over view - Swindoll Pg. 2,

Ch 3

The King has a short memory!
Actually over 20 years have passed
since his dream - He has Destroyed
Jeruselam - Sacked The Temple

Now He builds An Image of
Gold - Completely More Gold Than
FT. Knox!

A Lot of Symbolism -.
The height 60 Cubits = 90'
width 6 9'
Six is The number of Man
Man was Created on The 6th Day.
"666" Rev 13:18.

Just As The Image in The Dream was
A Prophecy of The Future - So This
Image Also ForeTells = A Type of AntiChrist

V2-6 The Kings PLan - To Create One
ReLigion And so Unify His Kingdom
The people were unaware - Thus The Furnace

V-8-10 There Are Certain Jews
where was Daniel ?

13-15 - The King Could not Believe That
Anyone - would not Obey -
Perhaps They Did not hear or
Understand.

V-15 - Who is The God who will Deliver you?

V-16 - A Nobel Response - Swindoll A.

Heb. 11:32

V-19 - Now The King acts Foolish -
7 Times Hotter ?

24 - Did we not Cast 3 Men in?
Who is The 4Th ? Is. 43:2

Swindoll B. - SomeTimes suffering is Necessary -
We must go "Through The Fire"
Only The Ropes were Burned Away

26 Servants of The Most High God

Swindoll C.

29 The Decree - No one shall speak Evil -
Purpose of Miricle - 1. To Demonstrate Authority
2. To Help Jews

Ch 4

V-1-3 This is one of The most Unique Chapters in The Bible
IT is A - 1. Proclamation - 2. Confession
3. Explaination - 4. Conversion

IT was Issued After He Recovered From His Insainity 562 B.C - 1 year Before His Death
The Tone - A marked Contrast To previous ATTiTude - Are The Words of A Changed Man (Peace Be UnTo you)
Daniel may Have Helped Compose
What happened To the King To Bring About such A Change? He Tells Us!

V-4-7 Another Dream I Nebuchadnezzar
A self Centered Man - All his Worlds were Conquered - yet He is Alarmed
Just Like Before - except This Time He Remembers the Dream - STill The "wise men" Fail Him

8-12. AT Last Daniel -

13-17 - The Dream
Who Are The Watchers? Heb. 12:1
Eph. 6:12
Mysterious World of Angels
An Angelic Court - v-17

Billy Graham - "Angels"
What Troubled Nebuchadnezzar was The
Personification of The Dream By The
Watchers - IT = Him 15-16

18 - Daniel is Stricken Dumb -
He had Becom A Loyal Servant
over The years --- But More Important
- Daniel was No Time Server - He
Invested Himself into The Life of Nebuch.
He Cared About The King!
19-B - May IT Be For Your Enimies!

The Interpretation

20-22 - You Are The Tree
24 - A Decree From God
25 - Untill You Know - That God is God!
27 - Daniel Takes This Opportunity To give Counsel
28 - All Came To Pass -- 1 year Later!
29 - Did God Forget? Was Daniel Mistaken?
O The Grace of God! 2 Pet.-3:3

30 - which I have Built
31 - Once The Grace Period is Over - Gods
32-33 Judgement Comes Quickly
34 - No Resentment - Just Praise
36 - Just Like Job? 37 - A Warning - God Resists The Proud. ↑ 1 Pet 5:5

Ch 5

Belshazzar - History - (World Book) Pg. 193
(Larkin) Pg. 81

The City of Babylon
(World Book) Pg 10 (Larkin) Pg. 79

Belshazzars Feast - The Turning Point
From The "Head of Gold" To The
"Arms & Breast of Silver"
The Feast is given in A Spirit of
Contempt & Defiance
Cyrus The Persian & Darius The Mede
had Defeated Nabonidus - And Had Besieged
The City - They had Enough Food For
Several Years!

V-2 Belshazzar Wanted To Do Something
Sensational - was Drunk

V-4 They Drank Wine & Praised The Gods - gold-silc
5 - "The Hand writing on The Wall"
(Famous Cliche)
6 - Quickly Sober!
7 - Bring on The Wise Men - Again!
Third Ruler - Because He Was Already 2nd

10 - The Queen - Not His Wife - Nabonidus Wife -
Nebuchadnezzars Daughter

11-12 - She Remembers Daniel - 45 years After
Neb.s Dream

13 - The King Says - You Are That Daniel -
one of The Jews -- Now He would
Pronounce His Doom

14-16 - Empty Promises

17 - Listen To Daniels Reply!
A Stinging Rebuke

22 - Belshazzar - Probably 15 yrs. old

23 - Who Told Daniel What They had Done?

24 - God sent The Hand
The Words -

25-28 Mene = Numbered Tekel = Weighed
(Peres) Upharsin = Divisions
Why Couldn't The Wise men Interpret This?
Simple Words Only Daniel Was in Tune
with God. Spiritual Ears

29 - Belshazzar Still Rewards Him

30-31 - Belshazzar killed - Darius Did Not Take
Babylon
Cyrus Did!
God ForeTold it 175 years Before
Isa. 45 (Larkin 92) Ezra 1:1-4

"The Taking of Babylon" Pg 90
Rebuilding of Babylon - Pg. 93

Ch. 6

The Lions Den

Review = Historical Setting - Ch5:30-31
Belshazzar is Killed - Babylon Falls To
Medes & Persians

The "Head of Gold" Ruled For 67 years
Now - The Arms & Breast of Silver Takes over

Daniel is Now 90 years Old - yet
Darius puts Him in Charge - V-1-3
Because -- An Excellent Spirit was in Him

Swindoll Pg. 50

The Problem - Jealousy - Envy - Fear

Steven

Daniel was honest - No Chance For Corruption
So -- They sought To Remove Him - 4-5

The PLoT - Pass A New Law - which Daniel
must Violate - 6-9
Verse 7 - A Lie! Daniel was NoT Consulted

They Appealed To Darius's Ego - He Fell
For The Trap

The Response - 10-12 Daniel Did NoT Waver

His Acusers Move Quickly
13 - That Daniel - That old Jew - A Captive - Slave

14 - But The King was NoT Angry - Rather Sad
He Loved Daniel - worked All Day

15 - RelentLess - Seeking Daniels Destruction
The King is Power Less

May
16 - Your God Will Deliver You - K.J.

18 - No Sleep
IS
19 - He Rose Early - Was Your God Able ?

21 - Victory - O King Live Forever !

22 - God Sent His Angel - Daniels Prayers Answered

23 - Just As in The Fiery Furnace - No Trace of Hurt

Because He Trusted His God !

* - God Does NoT Promise To Keep Us OuT of Trouble
JusT To Be WiTh Us - In The Trouble

24 - Daniel Did NoT RetaliaTe -
Vengence is Mine SayeTh The Lord

InnocenT Children ? - The Sins of FaThers
Ex. 20:5 - 34:7 Nu. 14:18 - Du. 5:9

25 - The Conversion of AnoTher King ?

God is Glorified !

28 - So This Daniel Prospered

Swindoll ?

Ch 7

1st 6 Chapters Focus on Daniels Life

Last 6 Focus on Prophetic Revelations

Not Intended To give Us A step By step Account of Future - Rather A Panoramic View - Designed To Comfort The Believer & The Jews

Historical Setting - The 1st year of Belshazzar

From The Death of Nebuchadnezzar To The Death of Belshazzar - 23 years - Daniel - Semi Retired Spent Much Time in Study & Prayer - 65-80 years old

Daniel - John
Both "OLd"
Both Captive or Prisioners
Both Greatly Beloved
Revelation given To Reward Faithfulness

Daniels Revelation - To Comfort & give Hope To Jews Nearing End of 70 years Captivity
Johns Rev. - To Comfort & give Hope To Christians Facing Severe Persecution

Ch 7 = Three Visions
1. Four Wild Beasts
2. Judgement Scene
3. Son of Man Receiving Kingdom
All Interwoven

These Visions Correspond with Nebuc. Vision of The Image of 4 Metals

V 2-3 Four Winds & Great Sea
Immediately We Have Trouble

One Book says one Thing - The Other Another!
Not The Central Point - We Must Be
Careful Not To get Hung Up on "Minors"
& miss The "Majors"

4 - 1st Beast - Lion w Eagles Wings v-17 = 4 Kings
Babylon - Nebuch.
Wings were Plucked

5. - 2nd Beast - Bear = Medes & Persians
Raised on 1 Side - Persia The Stronger
3 Ribs = Lydia - Babylon - Egypt

Bear is Inferior To Lion - Just as Silver
is Inferior To Gold

6 - 3rd Beast = Leopard = Alexander - Greeks
Four Heads = Four Kingdoms Divided
4 Wings = speed

7 & 8 - 4th Beast = Roman Empire
Iron Teeth - Ten Horns = (Ten Toes)

A "Little Horn" = Different From Image
No "Little Toe" Pg 124
Some New Revelation - For Gods People (Jews)
in the Latter Days
Before Daniel Could Ask - Another Vision

A Judgement Scene

V-9-12 The "Ancient of Days" Pg 127

V-11 The "Little Horn" Speaks

The 4th Beast is Slain = Roman Empire
But Not The "Little Horn" = Anti Christ

V-15-16 The Interpretation = Gabriel 9:21-8:16

17&18 = Simple Explanation But Daniel was Still
Perplexed By The "Little Horn"

19-22 Here Daniel Adds To The First
Description of The 4th Beast

The Anti Christ shall Rise out of The
New Roman Empire - Swindoll Pg. 66

12 Facts About Anti Christ

1. He Will Not Create A Kingdom - Rather Absorb it
2. He Will Be Just Another Ruler - Another Horn
3. He will Be Obscure - At First = Little
4. His Rise To Power Will Begin With The Takeover of 3 Kingdoms
5. He will Be Different From The Others
6. Very Intelligent
7. A Great Orator
8. Very Handsome - 9. Yet A Blasphemer
10. He Will Try To Change The Times
11. He Will Try To Destroy Israel
12. His Time Will Be Short

Ch 8 - Written in Hebrew

V-1 - In The Third Year of Belshazzar -
The Same Year of His Death - The Handwriting

V 2 - Susa - 350 miles From Babylon - Headquarters
of Cyrus - Center of Medo - Persian Empire

V-3 - The Vision - Read to verse 14

AT First - This Might Look Repititious -
Just A Change in Animals - - -

But - Some Differences - only 2 Animals
Daniel was Told - 4 World Powers

Remember - This is For Jews
Revelation - For Gentiles

A very Difficult Period of Time For Jews
Captivity

Now if Thats All - We Had = Trouble! - - -
But Daniel Again Asks For Help
V15 - Gabriel - Birth of John & Jesus

17-18 - Even Daniel - Righteous & Greatly Beloved of God - -
Fearful

19 - The End Times - Indignation = Great Tribulation

20 - Now God is Going To Be Specific -

Up To Now Daniel was Not Told The Names of
The Other World Powers

He was only Told That Nebochenezer
was The 1st

But Now - He is Told The Name
of The Second World Power - Medes & Persians

What Timing! Even At That Moment
The Medes & Persian Army Was Surrounding The
City of Babylon. This Knowledge Helped
Daniel To Interpret The "Handwriting on The
Wall"

Two Horns = Medes & Persians

21 - Greece = Alexander The Great = The 1st
King Verse 8 = when He was Strong

22 - Four Horns = Four Generals
Thrace - Macedonia - Syria - Egypt
North West East South

23 - Up To This Point Daniel Had No Problem -
The Four Beast Corresponds With The Image ---
The Ram & The He-Goat Also
The Four Heads on The Leopard = 4 Horns

But - Now we Have Again A Little Horn
Verse 9

Yet There is Nothing To Compare To
The 4th Beast - or The Ten Horns

1. Man honors the famous & soon forgets them - God honors the unknown & never forgets them.

2. Man gives his rewards now - . God saves his untill later

3. Mans methods are connected to time - But God's are connected with eternity

2

Back To What We Know - The Goat is Greece - The Horn is Alexander - The Four Horns Are The Four Kingdoms That Were Divided.

History Tells Us That These Four Kingdoms Were absorbed into The Roman Empire Gradually with The Last To Lose its Identity Being Egypt in 30 B.C.

So While There Are To Be Only 4 World Empires - Not Without A Break - This Gap is Covered By The 4 Kingdoms

23-24 At The Latter End of Their Rule A King Shall Arise - "Little Horn" Great Power

25- Prince of Princes? Up To This Point - it Could Be A Description of Some Historical King - But This Sounds Future

A Dilema! 2 Possibilities

1. Refers To A Historical King Antiochus Epiphanes - The 8th King of The Syrian Dynasty - Swindoll Pg 28

3

Verse 14 – 2,300 eve & Morn = 1,150 Days =
3 years & 55 Days

$$\begin{array}{r} 365 \\ \times\ 3 \\ \hline 1095 \\ +\ 55 \\ \hline 1,150 \text{ Days} \end{array}$$

2. A Dual Meaning – Antiochus Epiphanes – & The AntiChrist A Type of

3 Reasons

1. Shall oppose The Prince of Princes
2. Shall Be Broken By No Human Hand
3. Pertains To Many Days Hence V. 26

Now – if All This Leaves You Confused --- O.K. So was Daniel!
verse 27

Conclusion – Swindoll Pg 80

Confidence in Gods Word

Ch 9

1- In The 1st year of Dairius

2- Daniel is Confused - He Has Recieved 2 Visions - 4 Beasts - Ram + He Goat
Both Told of A Prolonged Period of Dispersion For His People

The Problem - The Prophets - Jeremiah Moses Had ForeTold A Captivity of 70 years
He Knew That 68 years Had Already Passed

He Also Knew That The Very Man Isaiah had Foretold That Would Let Them Return was Now on The Throne = Cyrus

How Could 3 World Empires Come and Go in 2 short years -
He Didn't yet see The Dual meaning in The Visions
So God is Going To Give Him Another one!

3 But First - Prayer

Sackcloth + Ashes - Humility

4 - Confession

5 - Honesty We Have Sinned

6-14 - Gods Judgement is Just

15-16 - Now Let Thy Anger Turn Away

2

16 - Thy People Have Become A "By-word"

17 - For your own Names Sake

Daniel Pleads For The Reputation of God

18 - The City Called By Thy Name

19 - Do you Sense The Agony of Daniels Spirit?

We ~~that~~ Should Have That Same Concern For The Reputation of The Lord Jesus Christ = Christian

20 - The Interrupted Prayer

21 - While I was Praying -- - God Can Communicate To Daniel Because He (Daniel) Has opened The Lines!

22-23-24 Seventy weeks of Years

Weeks = Literally - Seventy units of Seven
Swindoll Pg 91 - 92

This Applies To your People - your City

6 Objectives

24. 1. To Finish Transgression
Jesus paid the penalty For Sin on The Cross
But people still sin - when Christ Returns He will ~~put~~ Finish Transgression - with Israel

3

2. To Make An End To Sin or To Seal iT up (Israels Sin)

3. To Atone For IniquiTy
Isaiah said God Has Laid on Him The Iniquity of us All - True For Us - BuT NoT For Jews
when the Church is "CaughT ouT" then The Jews As A NaTion will Be converTed

4. To Bring in EverLasTing RighTeousness

The Millenial Kingdom - God Shall make A New CovenanT with IsraeL

5. To Seal up The Vision And Prophecy
Rom 11:25
when The Transgression of IsraeL Has Ceased - There will No Longer Be A need of Prophecy or Visions

6. To AnoinT the MosT HoLy
The HoLy of HoLies - TempLe

25- 70 "weeks" Are Divided inTo 3 DisTincT Periods

1. 7 "weeks" or 49 years - Swindoll Pg. 93
Neh 2:1-8

2. 62 weeks or 434 years - Swindoll Pg. 94

4

V;26. 3. Now - Difficult Interpretation - Aided By History

'An Undetermined Length of Time - After The Destruction of The Temple

verse 26 - "and even To The End" There. —

27 - One Remaining Week - 7 years

The Description Fits With Rev. Great Tribulation

Swindoll Pg 95

Mt. 24: 6-15 Lu. 21: 20-28

Rev. 5th Chapter To 19
written 26 years After The Destruction of Jerusalem

Key! - Daniel writing To Jews - The Times of The Gentiles - Not Important! = 2 verses
Rev. - written To Christians - 13 Chapters

Don't Forget! - The Christian Church was Not Revealed in The Old Testament
Daniel was Not Told! -

Thats Why He Jumps From Crucifixion -- To AntiChrist

Ch. 10

1. The 3rd year of Cyrus

Daniel - Almost 90 yrs old
Retired From Active Service

Some Jews Have Returned To Jerusalem -
But Many More Stay in Babylon

2-3 Once Again Daniel is Fasting & Praying
(21 Days) = 3 weeks

4-5 Tigris River - Flowed Through Babylon

5-6 - A Man? The Description - Similar
To Rev. 1:12
The Response - Similar
Rev. 1:17

7 Only Daniel Saw it

8-9 - Daniel Fainted

10 - A Hand - Possibly An Angel

11 - Same Words Used By Gabriel ? ?

12 - Believers Prayers Heard Imediately

Key - 1. Set your Mind To Understand
2. Humbled yourself

If We Seek - God Provides
Ethiopian Eunuch - Missionaries

2

13 - Spiritual Warfare
Swindoll Pg 99

SaTan Delayed the Angel For 21 Days!
SomeTimes our prayers Are Delayed By
Spiritual WarFare
Eph. 6:11-12 Jude 9 II Kings 6:8-14

Prince of Persia = A Fallen Angel ?

14 - your People in LaTTer Days

15 - 16 - Daniel Swooned Again
Another Angel ? ?

The Vision Makes Daniel Grieve

17 He Can't BreaThe!

18 - Angels can STrengThen Us! - Ex. Jesus
19 -
20 - A QuesTion - Then Another BaTTLe -
Spiritual Warfare is On Going

SaTan Has Organized Empire
Is NoT omnipresenT - Uses Fallen Angels

21 - Michael - Watches over Israel

Ch 11

Wars & Rumors of Wars

We May Desire Peace -- But The Bibles says Things will get Worse

Swindoll - Pg 104

Why? - Jms. 4:1 = Selfishness

Ch 11 is The Vision or Word of Truth Talked About in Ch 10:1

IT is A Detailed Description of The Wars & Conflicts of The "Kings of The North" - Syria - & "Kings of The South" = Egypt

This Prophecy is so Accurate - Not given in symbols or Figures as in Previous Visions - Critics say IT Could Not have Been Written Before The Events (533 BC)

2 Tim 3:15 - Holy Men of God - Moved By H. S.

Daniel was Mourning - 10:2

Because of What was To Befall His People - 10:14 For Many Days

The Kings of North & South would Use Palistine For A Battle Field For Centuries - 320 B.C. To A.D. ?

The Jews were Returning To Jerusalem - But Not For Long - God Had To show Daniel - That His People would Suffer For "Many Days"

2

V-1- Goes with 10:21

2 - Three More After Cyrus
Cambyses - Gaumata - Darius Hystaspes
and A 4Th = Xerxes = Ahasuerus = Esther

3 - Alexander - Ch8 = Ram + He Goat

4 - 4 To Succede Him
Macedonia - Thrace - Syria - Egypt - Swindoll Pg 105
Prophecy Narrows - To Syria - Egypt
Because - "Daniels People"

Syria = Seleucian Dynasty = Antichrist?
Egypt = PToLemies "

A Succession of 6 Different Kings
Swindoll Pg. 106

5-6 - Daughter - Berenice - Married Syrian King -
But After Fathers Death - The King
went Back To His 1st wife Laodice -
Who Poisoned Him! - Killed Berenice & Child

7 - Brother of Berenice - Angry at
Death of Sister - Killed Laodice
8 - Looted Their Temples

9-10 - Revenge - Marched Through Israel To
Egypt

3

11 - 13 - First The North - Them South

14 - Jews Caught in Middle - Learn To
Play one Against The Other

15 - Antiochus The Great - Captured
Sidon

16 - All of Israel

17 - Then Egypt - But A New Power - Rome!

So Diplomacy! His Daughter

But She Turned Against Him

18 - He Fought Against The Romans - Asia Minor
But Was Defeated

19 - His own People Killed Him

20 - Taxes Paid To Rome - Antiochus Son
was Poisoned

21 - A Vile Person
Antiochus Epiphanes

The Honor of The Kingdom - - He was
not The Rightful Heir - conniver

4

22-28 - He grows Strong And Tries To
Take Egypt - 2 Brothers

29-30 - He Tries Again - This Time
Egypt Appeals To Rome -

He is Enraged - Returns To
31 - Jeruselem - Desecrates The Temple -

32 - Maccabeen Revolt

33-35 - Jews Down Through Ages

Always Spoiled - Never Exterminated

36 - Sudden & Abrupt Appearance of
"The King" -- Because We Have Been
Told of Him Before

37-39 - General description of Antichrist

40 - The Time of The End --
Why will They still Be Fighting with
Horses & Chariots ??

41-45 Palistine - Israel
Gold - Silver

He Shall Come To His End
~~Rev.~~ Swindoll pg. 108

Ch 12

The Book of Daniel Begins with Captivity of Jews - And Ends with Armegedden 600 - B.C. - ??

1 - At That Time = Time of The End V 40 Ch 11

Michael = Stands Up For Jews
Jude 9 = Archangel
I Thess. 4:16 = The Voice of Michael

A Great Tribulation = Jesus Words MT 24 V 21
But For The Elects Sake =

Tribulation is Judgement For Jews - Refining Process

Every one Whose Name is Written in The Book Rev 20

2 - A Jewish Ressurection ?

Ezekiel - Dry Bones

3 - They Shall Shine - Because The Darkness Will Be Great

4 - Shut up The Words - Rev. 22:10

Opposite = Seal Not

MT 13: 10-15 = Willfully Ignorant

For Jews - Daniel - A Sealed Book

2

5 - 2 Angels

6 - Clothed in Linen = Christ ?

7 - How Long shall The Tribulation Last?
3 1/2 years

8 - Daniel Hears - But Does Not Understand

9 - Gods Revelation is Complete - Enough

II Tim. 2:15 Study To Show Thyself Approved

10 - Those who Are Wise - Shall Understand
Wisdom = Comes From God !
Understanding = Comes " God !

11 - 1,290 Days = Jewish Calender 360 Days
30 Days Extra = 3 1/2 years

12 - 45 More Days ? ? No Explaination

13 - Continue your Life - 90 + years old

Rest = in Grave - Stand - Raised Again

An Alloted Place For Daniel - Assurance -
Daniel Lived All His Life in Captivity - Never Returned To Jeruselem

Swindoll Pg. [redacted] 114

Around 1977 I met an AIM (Africa Inland Mission) missionary Fred Beam. We began to support them as missionaries. In a moment my whole perspective changed when Fred Beam told me that not all missionaries are preachers and teachers. He told me about a hospital in Kijabe, Kenya that did not have windows and doors. The doctors, nurses, and patients were very cold because of the high elevation. He showed me a photo of the surgeon putting in a door. I told him, "I can put in windows and doors!". I began to see how God brings different people and professions together for mutual benefit and the sharing of the Gospel of Jesus.

I didn't think about it too much because I was confident that Sandy would never go overseas with four children. A few years earlier we had a conversation with a ministry that we listened to on the radio and opportunities to serve with their ministry. They told us that they needed a family to go to Congo, Africa. One of the requirements was that my wife would need to homeschool our children. She told them that homeschooling would never work for us. End of discussion, or so I thought.

One day in 1980, Sandy shocked me when she told me that she thought we should become missionaries. The reality of what this would mean sent me for a spin. I no longer had an excuse. I had to make a choice. I wanted to find out more about AIM before communicating with them about potentially going as missionaries to the hospital in Kijabe, so that I could put in the window and doors. In January of 1981, I volunteered to work on a remodeling job at AIM headquarters in Pearl Harbor, NY. My observations and interactions with the people of AIM convinced me to start their process of missionary orientation and training.

One of my first assignments was to write a list of what I believed was important as a Christian. I wrote a list of several things. Then I was told to cross off everything that I would not need to share with a Kenya who was not saved. Soon I realized that there were only three things left on my list, Jesus is the Son of God, Jesus died on the cross, and the resurrection of Jesus.

One requirement was for me to complete Bible courses. I became a Moody Bible Institute Correspondence School student. I completed the Old Testament courses in July 1982 and went to Kenya that same year in August 1982. Nadine remembers Darvin studying early in the morning and showing her his test grades, every test came back marked with an "A". I continued my studies in Kenya and completed the New Testament courses in May 1985. God faithfully helped me complete my studies and prepare me to preach in Kenya.

AIM held a commissioning service for Darvin and Sandy before they left for Kenya. Although there were obstacles to overcome this service was held at our home church. This was a holy moment when God anointed us and set us apart to serve Him as missionaries in Kenya. We thank God for leading and protecting us like a very good shepherd.

You can find this sermon "The Commissioning of the Bylers" on YouTube & Spotify at "Darvin Byler Family Sermons.

"My Gray Wooden Toolbox"

When AIM told us to go share our mission and ask people to become our prayer partners,

I was not sure how I would do that

since I was only used to being a Sunday School teacher and youth leader.

Then the Lord showed me my gray wooden toolbox and gave me the idea to use what was familiar

to me as a starting point. I would use my tools and skills to help people in Kijabe.

So, I put a few of my favorite tools in my gray wooden toolbox and had "show and tell" in church.

SECTION TWO - Sermons Written & Preached in Kenya by Darvin Byler (1982-1989). Putting in Windows and Doors and So Much More.

That you may lead a life worthy of the Lord, fully pleasing him,

bearing fruit in every good work

and increasing in the knowledge of God.

Colossians 1:10 RSV

Sandy and I thought that we were ready to leave for Kijabe, Kenya in September 1981. But there was an important lesson that we needed to learn.

AIM wisely told us that we needed to have churches partner with us as missionaries because we would need their prayer support.

We began asking churches in our local area if they would allow us to share our mission assignments and request prayer partners.

We discovered that we had to travel further and take longer to find churches who were willing to give us this opportunity to share. God faithfully built a solid foundation of churches and families who committed to pray for us and our mission assignments. At one of the churches where we shared, an owner of a local business invited us to share at his workplace. It was here that God faithfully provided a family to rent our house while we lived in Kenya. A month before my family traveled to Kenya, God completed the last thing on our list to complete before we moved.

Darvin shares about the turtle on a fencepost in several of his sermons. A turtle needs help to get on a fencepost. He is grateful to the people who helped him, and his family serve on the mission field. In the following two sermons, Darvin Byler shares how he and his wife, Sandy, were led by the Lord from Hershey to Kijabe.

Acts 8:26-40 1

Greetings - Background

Not Ordained - Turtle on Fence post

Always Interested in Missions
not everyone can be A missionary -- 500-1
but everyone should have A missionaries heart!
not everyone can go To The Foriegn Field --
but everyone should Be Informed!

With A Family of 4 - Age 4 To 16 --
A building business - many other committments -
we Never Thought we would Be going either
But God had other Plans!

We were + still are Deacons in our Church -
we were Sr. Hi youth Leaders & S.S. Teachers and
were enjoying a great ministry with Them.
We Discovered That many Times - God calls
people right in The middle of a succesful ministry
And Asks Them To go or Do Something else
Acts 8:4 - Phillip was having a Revival!
verse - 26 - go To A Desert Place!
We Thought God was saying Go To Africa
A Desert Place!
We had A Thousand Reasons why we
Couldn't Go

2/

God had To Speak Clearly To Us --
And He Did iT Through His Word
Ecclesiastes 11 -
We were worrying About All The Details -
But God was Saying - Step Out
We were Looking at The Clouds -
But God was Saying - Sow!

That proved To be The Turning Point for Us - From Then on we Determined To go Through every Door That was opened To Us -- That Led us To A.I.M. - and Whithin one Year we were in Kenya

When we Arrived in Kenya - we found That just Like Phillip - God had Already prepared The Way Acts 8: 27-31

My Primary Assignment was To Supervise Building + Maintenance AT The Kijabe Med Center - A Large Mission Hospital - in The middle of A Building Program
But I Also Wanted To be involved in an Evangelistic ministry - and Soon I was Introduced To A National Pastor who needed Help Ps. 37:4 - Delight yourself in The Lord - He will give The Desires of your Heart

3/

The Church in Kenya is Young and growing Fast - Most Pastors have 4 or 5 Churches - Many Churches have No Pastor

We Discovered That many members had no Bibles - no hymnals
They were just Like The Ethiopian Eunech - eager To Learn - but needing some guidance

Seeing All These needs - we Plunged in To our Weekend Ministry

Bible Students - Preaching - Distributing Bibles 6,000

We were Kept Busy The entire 3 years - and still The question Came - Can you Come To our Church? - We need Bibles - Preaching etc,

IT is STill True - The work is Plentiful - But The workers are Few

One of The Saddest Things We hear as We go About Visiting Churches here - People will Come and Say To Us - you Know, some years ago I felt The Lord Calling me To The mission Field - But Things just Didn't work out - .
Are you Looking at The Clouds?

Darvin: "Given (presented) to Palmyra Rotary Club, 1986."

Greetings & Background

1. Why we Went - natural outgrowth of Christian Faith
First hand Experience

2. What we Learned - U.S. The Greatest!
Still Many Problems - But -- Based on
Christian Principles - Judeao-Christian Ethic
These Basic principles underly our Whole Society
you Also have benifited - Work Ethic = Buisiness Men

3. Pay Taxes With A Smile - No one Likes To Pay Taxes
I.R.S. Received This Letter -- Gentlemen;
Enclosed you will find a check For $150. I have
Cheated on my Income Tax Return Last Year,
and have Not Been able To Sleep ever Since. ---
If I still have Trouble Sleeping, -- I will
Send you The Rest!
We Take many Services For Granted

4. How Can We Help - Why Should We Help?
Our World is Shrinking -
We Can't Afford To Ignore Africa - Time Bomb!
Past Policy - In Adequate - Government To Government
Becomes Political Tool - Doesn't Work!
Fosters Resentment - Anger - Dependance
ILLUSTRATION - A Man who gave $100. Dollar Bill each week

End – I Believe – That much of The poverty, starvation, suffering – is A Result of Ignoring God's Principles For Living – Sending Food & Money is NOT The Answer

After 50 years → African Nations Are Saying -- Where's OUR Food –? Even Complain About Quality

There IS A better Way – Canada
Water Project – World Concern – 25%
Canada – 75%

Quiet – Effective
Aid → Given Through Established – Proven – Christian organizations
Most of Which Promote Self – Dependance --
Encourage Individual Responsibility – Work Ethic

There is A Paradox in Christianity --
That has To Do with Suffering
Today in America – We Live in A Painless Society – A Pill For Every Thing
Relief – NOW!
We Try To Do That when we Give Aid ---
Send A Million Dollars --- Quick Cure
But There is Much Value in Pain –
Some Things We Only Learn Through Suffering
Many of You Have Experienced This – Buisneses
The Fact is God uses Pain & Suffering as A Tool – To Achiev His Purposes – Easter = †

Jesus Said – Unless A Grain of Wheat Falls into The ground & Dies, it Remains Alone – But if it Dies, it Bears Much Fruit
Personal Experience – Parents – Children

It was time to put in windows and doors! In 1982 Kijabe was a large mission station. It has continued to expand. Nadine has included several links for those who may like to learn more about Kijabe, Kenya. Darvin's primary assignment was to work at the AIC (Africa Inland Church) Kijabe Hospital as head of maintenance and building. For more information about the hospital follow this link. kijabehospital.org/history.php Darvin's job list consisted of the following projects and ministry opportunities.

1. Fix the hospital's leaking roof
2. Finish and secure all windows and doors
3. Grind down all concrete floors and install vinyl tiles
4. Install a new clean water system (from a spring 7 Kilometers away)
5. Build 30+ housing units for the national hospital staff
6. Numerous remodel projects for the Kijabe missionary staff
7. Be on call to fix anything and everything that needs to be repaired at the hospital/station
8. Hire and lead a work team of 20-30 Kenya men
9. Trip to Sudan to help AIM Tech missionary (John Propst) build a new medical dispensary
10. Trip to Uganda to help AIM Tech remodel a missionary house and distribute Bibles
11. Assist Pastor Julius by bringing as many Moffat Bible students and Bibles that my vehicle could haul, to as many of his 8-10 churches on Sundays

The house that we were scheduled to live in was not completed when we arrived in Kijabe. I worked on finishing it for my family to move into as quickly as possible. The house was designated for a dentist, but we lived in it for three years until a dentist arrived. We lived in a small duplex apartment until I finished building our house (Aug.-Oct.). We lived out of our luggage for three months until the Lord faithfully released the containers we had packed and shipped from America in July. Nadine remembers celebrating Sandy's September birthday by sticking toothpicks in a slice of bread and lighting them like candles.

Our children attended RVA (Rift Valley Academy), an American-accredited AIM mission boarding school. When our children attended RVA it had several hundred students from kindergarten through twelfth grade. Our children loved attending this school. They were called station kids because they lived at home on the Kijabe mission station.

For those who are interested, the following links will give you more information about Rift Valley Academy. rva.org/campus/ and rva.org/history/

In 1982 our house was the last in line at the bottom of the mission station. When we walked out of our back door everything was uphill. The following article provides a brief history of Kijabe. johnkamau.substack.com/p/kijabe-only-kenyan-town-with-no-bars

Kijabe is home to Moffat Bible College. When we were in Kijabe several Bible students would pile into my vehicle on Sunday mornings and we would go two by two to several churches to preach and deliver Bibles. Several of these churches continue to flourish today. moffatbiblecollege.org/about/history

File folder marked "AIC churches", Kenya 1983-85, & 1987-89. Sermons written and preached by Darvin Byler in Kenya. (Note the names of the churches were often written at the top of the sermon)

Kazuri

Jo. 15:1-17 Gal. 5:16:26

Are you Happy?
Do you Have Joy In your Life?
Are you Living A Victorious Christian Life?
Today - Gods Plan For Joyful Living
1/ Jesus Is The Vine - The Whole Plant
God The Father is The Owner - CareTaker
H.S. is Sap
2/ Every Branch of Mine - They belong To Christ
Are Pruned - To Bear More Fruit
3-4 We Are Cleansed By The Word - Saved - So That we Can Bear Fruit
Abide = Rest
5 Apart From Christ - We Can Do Nothing
Are You Trying To Live The Christian Life Apart From The Vine?
6 You Will Whither & Die
7 ITs A Promise!
8 When We Bear Fruit - God Is Glorified
9-10-11 Obedience = Joy That our Joy May Be Full
12 The Commandment - that We Love one Another
Eph. 1:4 16 He Choose Us - To go & Bear Fruit - only The Branches Bear Fruit!
Gal. 5:22 What Kind of Fruit? Love - Joy - Peace
How? - Abide In Me How? - Through The WORD! H.S. Jo. 1:1-14
Are you Bearing Any Fruit?
If Not - Why Not? You Won't Be Really Happy - Untill you Are Bearing Fruit For Jesus
If You Bear No Fruit - You Will be Cut off - And Burned!

Ps. 73 - 1-20 Kagwe - Nduriri

I. Cor. 15: 12-28

Ps. 73

V2 I had almost stumbled

3 - Envy of Arrogant - Problem as old as Job

5 - No Apparent Trouble

6 - Proud - Violent

8 - Scoff

9 - Strutting Tongue

10 - People are afraid of them!

12 - These are the wicked

13 - In Vain have I kept my Heart Clean!

14 - I have Trouble

16 - How can I understand this?

From A purely Human Perspective You Can't

17 Untill - you Get God's Perspective

Then - We Can Understand!

18-19 - They are destroyed in a moment.

Ps. 1

1-3 = Blessed is the righteous

4-6 = Cursed is the wicked - Judgement

Heb 9:27 It is appointed unto men once to die - judgement

Rev. 20: 11-12 - 21: 7-8

HeLL Is Real! Eternity Is Forever!

I Cor. 15: 13 - If There Is No Ressurection

Than Eat, Drink & Be Merry - Tommorow We Die!

We Are In The Last Days II Tim 3: 1-4

We Must Pray For These Wicked People

Gal 5:13-26 Rom 8:1-17

Freedom

Jo. 8:36 - If Christ Has Set you Free -

1. No Condemnation
2. Free From The Law of Sin & Death
Rom. 6:23
3. God has Done it!
4. A. God is A God of Justice -
Jesus Paid The price for our Sin!
B. Who Live According To The Spirit - Holy
5. What Do you Think About?
6. Death - Life - we Have A Choice!
Pro. 23:7 - As A Man Thinks In his Heart - -
So is He! Phil. 4:8
7. Opposed To God.
8. Cannot Please God
9. you - who Are In The Spirit - you who Call
yourself Christian - - you Are in The Spirit?
Because - Anyone who Does Not Have The Spirit

10-11 He - God Dwells In Us!
12-13 If you Live To The flesh - you will Die - eTernally
14-15 we are Sons & Daughters of God!
16 - Gods Spirit - Tells our Spirit - That we
Belong To Him!
Do you have This Assurance?
God Wants you To Be Free!
1. From Condemnation 2. Sin 3. Death

Titus 2:11-15 MT. 28:16-20

This morning I want To Talk About A Bridge

On one Side - The Other Side -

Holy Righteous God  Sinful Mankind

V 11 God is going To build A Bridge != Salvation

1st Pillar is Grace = Unmerited Favor of God

Justice = gives us what we Deserve Rom 6:23 - wages of Sin

Mercy = Doesn't give Us What we Deserve

Grace = gives us what we Don't Deserve Eph. 2:8-9 - By grace

12 Grace Teaches Us To put Away worldly passions

13 Glory - 2nd Pillar 1. glorious Coming Acts 1:9 I Thes. 4:15

MT. 25:31-33 ← 2. Judgement

41

14 Two ~~Cables~~ Beams - Timbers

1. Redemption = Ransom - Jesus bought Us from Slaves To Sin

we were Captives I Cor. 6: 19-20

Purification

2. Sanctification = To Set Apart = To Purify

Only 2 kinds of People - 1. Those Who Know God

I Cor. 6:9-11 2. Those who Don't

God Is Setting Apart A People For Himself

These people Are Different - Called The Church of Jesus

Some people want redemption without sanctification - No!

15 Declare - Tell others! This Salvation Is For All men v11

MT. 28:18 - Orders Direct From Jesus - Go - Go!

1. Make Disciples
2. Baptize
3. Teach

} Jesus Is With Us!

This morning There Are Many people Who want To Cross over To God - But They Don't See The Bridge!

Will you show Them the way??

I Tim. 3:1-13 Titus 1:5-16

Elder - Deacon - Bishop = Old & Wise
Funtcion = Overseer - Shepard - Steward

Qualifications

1. Blameless
2. Husband of One Wife
3. Children Are Beleivers & Submissive
4. Not Arrogant
5. No Drinker
6. Not Violent
7. Not greedy For gain

1. Hospitable
2. Loves Goodness
3. Self - Control
4. Study the Word
5. Able To Give Instruction - Sound Doctrine
6. Able To Correct In gentleness II Tim 2:24

A Steward of Gods Church
A Sheppard

Kugway

Phil. 2:1-11 Greetings Rom 12 ~~[struck out]~~

I want To Talk about committment

V.1 bodies = whole person

which is your reasonable service

God wants All of you

Christianity Is Not A List of Do's & Don'ts

It Is A Relation Ship

Do you Know what God Thinks of a half Committed Christian?

Rev 3:15

V.2 The goals of World are the Same everywhere – Power

Prestige – Wealth – we are not to be like the world

That you may Prove what is the Will of God

I Don't even Know you -- But I Know What The Will of God

Commited Is for Your Life -- I Thes. 4:3 – 4:7

~~Sanctification~~ = Set Apart – Holy

Consecreated Rom 8:29 – Conformed To Jesus

How Do We Know the Mind of Christ?

Phil. 2:5 – Jesus had Power – Prestige – Wealth

but he emptied Himself – humbled

This Is The Will of God For Each of Us

V.4-6 God has given us each different gifts – to help build up the body

Not ourselves!

V.7-13

V.14 Bless Those Who Persecute You – different from the world

V.17 Do Not Repay Evil for Evil

V.19 Revenge Is Not For The Christian

V.20 Feed Your Enemy? -- give him Drink?

21 Over Come Evil with Good

You Can Only Do This If You Are Committed

MT. 24:36-51 MT. 25:1-13

Are You Ready?

We have just Celebrated Christmas -
The 1st Comming of Christ
Are You Ready For the 2nd Christmas?

When Jesus Left This Earth - The Angels
Said -
The next great event in history - 2nd Coming

Jesus Said - Be Ready - You Know not The Time

The Story of Ten maidens Teaches Us - Be Ready
v. 1-3 It was Night - The bridegroom was Coming

5 were Wise - 5 were Foolish

4 - 5 were Prepared
5 - They All Slept
6 - At Midnight - He ~~Came~~'s Comming!
7-9 - The oil Ran Out - Finished
10 - While They were preparing - He Came!
11-12 No 2nd Chance!
13 Watch & Be Ready Ch 24:36
No One Knows!

40-41 Two men - one Taken - Two Women
What Shall We Do!

23 - Some People will Panic - Christ is here!
24-26
44 - Be Ready - How? Have You Believed on Jesus?
Have You Received Him As Saviour & Lord

Just As There Was A 1st Christmas -
There will be A 2nd Christmas -

Women have played an important role in history
queens of Egypt - Ethiopia - England
Bible history - Ruth - Esther - Abigail - Mary
very fitting that we honor the girls cadettes

The Bible has a lot to say about women -
how they should live - Paul - Peter
But I'm chosen PROV 31 to think on the --

v.10 Yes it's true - girls can be intelligent & capable
& if their also virtuous - worth more than gold!

11 NOT necessary to be married - but most of you
will - when you do have a husband - he must trust you
13 Willing hands

15 Not lazy - rises at dawn & meditates
16 a careful planner - she doesn't take on more than she
can do - her husband trusts her to buy & sell
17 she prepares herself for her tasks
18 her lamp does not go out!
20 she is not greedy - she gives of her things & herself.
21 SNOW she sees that her family has warm clothes
22 she makes rugs & fine clothing
23 her husband has time to serve in the community
25 strength & dignity - security because she is prepared
26 she talks with godly wisdom - a kind tongue
27 she is not a gossip
28 her children call her blessed - her husband praises
30 charm & beauty is vain - it does not last - but a reverent
woman shall be praised --
31 her own life - work will praise her

Kagwe Nduriri Kahomahinda

MT. 24:36-51 MT. 25:1-13

Are You Ready?

We have just Celebrated Christmas -
The 1st comming of Christ
Are You Ready For The 2nd Christmas?

When Jesus Left This Earth - The Angels
Said -

The next great event in history - 2nd Coming

Jesus Said - Be Ready - You know not The Time

The Story of Ten maidens Teaches Us - Be Ready

v.1-3 IT was Night - The bridegroom was Coming

5 were Wise - 5 were Foolish

4- 5 were Prepared
5- They All Slept
6- AT Midnight - He ~~Came~~'s Comming!
7-9 - The oil Ran out - Finished
10 - While They were preparing - He Came!
11-12 No 2nd Chance!
13 Watch & Be Ready Ch 24:36
No One Knows!

40-41 Two men - one Taken - Two Women
What Shall We Do?

23 - Some People will Panic - Christ is here!
24-26
44 - Be Ready - How? Have You Believed on Jesus?
Have You Received Him As Saviour & Lord

Just As There Was A 1st Christmas -
There will be A 2nd Christmas

Kagwe Nduriri Kahumahindi

MT. 24: 36-51 MT. 25: 1-13

We have just Celebrated Christmas -
The 1ST comming of Christ
Are You Ready For The 2nd Christmas?

When Jesus Left This Earth - The Angels
Said -
The next great event in history - 2nd Coming

Jesus Said - Be Ready - You know not The Time

The Story of Ten maidens Teaches Us - Be Ready
V. 1-3 IT was Night - The bridegroom was Coming

5 were Wise - 5 were Foolish

4- 5 were Prepared
5- They All Slept
6- AT Midnight - He ~~Came~~ /S Comming!
7-9 - The oil Ran OuT - Finished
10 - While They were preparing - He Came!
11-12 No 2nd Chance!
13 Watch & Be Ready Ch 24:36
No One Knows!

40-41 Two men - one Taken - Two Women
What Shall We Do?

23 - Some People will Panic - Christ is here!
24-26
44 - Be Ready - How? Have You Believed on Jesus?
Have You Received Him As Saviour & Lord

Just As There Was A 1st Christmas -
There will be A 2nd Christmas -

Women have played an important role in history
queens of Egypt - Ethiopia - England
Bible history - Ruth - Esther - Abigail - Mary
very fitting that we honor the girls cadette

The Bible has a lot to say about women -
how they should live - Paul - Peter
But I'm chosen PROV 31 to think on the --

v.10 Yes it's true - girls can be intelligent & capable
& if their also virtuous - worth more than gold!

11 NOT necessary to be married - but most of you
will - when you do have a husband - he must trust you
13 willing hands

15 Not lazy - rises at dawn & meditates
16 a careful planner - she doesn't take on more than she
can do - her husband trusts her to buy & sell
17 she prepares herself for her tasks
18 her lamp does not go out!
20 she is not greedy - she gives of her things & herself.
21 SNOW she sees that her family has warm clothes
22 she makes rugs & fine clothing
23 her husband has time to serve in the community
25 strength & dignity - security because she is prepared
26 she talks with godly wisdom - a kind tongue
27 she is not a gossip
28 her children call her blessed - her husband praises
30 charm & beauty is vain - it does not last - but a reverent
woman shall be praised --
31 her own life - work will praise her

Kagwe Nduriri Kahumahinde

MT. 24: 36-51 MT. 25: 1-13

Are You Ready ?

We have just Celebrated Christmas -
The 1st comming of Christ
Are You Ready For The 2nd Christmas ?

When Jesus Left This Earth - The Angels
Said -
The next great event in history - 2nd Coming

Jesus Said - Be Ready - You know not The Time

The Story of Ten maidens Teaches Us - Be Ready
v. 1-3 IT was Night - The bridegroom was Coming

5 were Wise - 5 were Foolish

4- 5 were Prepared
5- They All Slept
6- AT Midnight - He ~~Came~~ 's Comming !
7-9 - The oil Ran Out - Finished
10 - While They were preparing - He Came !
11-12 No 2nd Chance !
13 Watch & Be Ready Ch 24: 36
No One Knows !

40-41 Two men - one Taken - Two Women
What Shall We Do ?

23 - Some People will Panic - Christ is here !
24-26
44 - Be Ready - How ? Have You Believed on Jesus?
Have You Received Him As Saviour & Lord

Just As There Was A 1st Christmas -
There will be A 2nd Christmas -

Ps. 23 NdURRi Jo. 10:1-18

Jesus used Sheep & Shepards in many of His Teaching - The Bible Compares Us To Sheep

Is. 53:6 - All we Like Sheep have gone Astray

Jesus Said In Jo. 10 - I Am The good Shepard

V1 DAvid Said in Ps. 23 - The Lord is My Shepard
I shall not Be in Want

Phil. 4:11 ⇒ Doesn'T mean Money & Material Things !

David Had Many Troubles - But God Met his Needs

Adam & Eve - Wanted For nothing -- UnTill SaTan came To The garden
Greed - Pride - Disobedience

Who is Your Shepard? - who Do you Follow?

V2 The Lord Leads Us To peaceful WaTers
He Restores our Souls

V3 The Lord Leads Us In Paths of Righteousness

V4 With The Lord - We need NoT Fear even DeaTh

V5 Even when we Are Surrounded By our Enimies - The Lord
meets our Needs - our Cup overFlows

V6 Goodness & Mercy in This Life -
We Shall Be With The Lord Forever!

Who Is Your Shepard?

Jesus Is The Good Shepard - He has given His Life For Us -- Who Are You going To Follow?

How Should We Pray For OneAnother?
Here Paul gives us a beautiful example

v.9 Filled with The Knowledge of His will
Spiritual Wisdom

v.10 Bearing Fruit - Increasing In Knowledge of God
v.11 Strengthened - Endurance - Patience - Joy
v.12 This produces Thankfulness = Qualified! | Us = Inheritance
v.13 If this doesn't make you happy Delivered! | Sometimes We
Then you haven't yet experienced it! Transferred | Need A Reminder
v.14 Muslims Redeemed! | of What God Has Done
Forgiven!
Is Jesus Just Another Prophet? ALL Past Tense!
The Bible says NO!

v.15 Image = Exact Likeness of God - First born of Creation
v.16 He had part In The Creation - ALL Things Were Created
Through Him & For Him!
v.17 1st!
v.18 Head of The Church - 1st born From The Dead
Pre-Eminent = No. 1 Phil. Ch 2:10
v.19 ALL The Fulness of God Dwelt
v.20 making Peace by His Blood
v.21 We Were Once Enemies of God - He has Now
v.22 Reconciled By His Death
To Present Us Holy & Blameless & Irreproachable
No one Can Touch You Without Gods Permission
Not Even Satan!
And We Don't need to wait until death for all of This -
its Availiable Right Now! I Jo. 5:13 - we May Know
v.23 Provided - That we Remain In The Faith.
Not Shifting

NDURILI
COL 1:9-23

Kagwa
Eph 3:14-21

1 Cor. 12:12-31 Rev. 5

"World Wide Body of Christ"

Greetings!

ITs Great To be A Christian!

One of Greatest - Universal Body

Nduvili - America - Russia

We Are one in Christ

God Is Building His Church!

1 Cor. 12: 12-13 one Body Eph. 4:4-5

Christ is The Head

Eph. 1:22-23 Col. 1:18

His Blood is The Foundation

His Ressurection is The Power

His Coming Again is The Climax Hope

Rev. Ch 5 Who is Worthy? To Bring This World To An End?

V. 5 - The Lion of The Tribe of Judah!

The Lamb of God - who Takes Away Sin

V. 9 - Worthy Art Thou - you were Slain -

By your Blood - Every Tribe & Nation

ITs great To Be A Christian -

A part of The Body of Christ

But Greater STiLL -- To join The Thousands & Millions Around The World - To Praise & Worship The Lord For Ever!

Heb 11:1-7 Ndurelli-kamahindu Karweti-kague Heb 12:1-4

Faith

We All Live By Faith - go To Bed - geT UP

v6 WiThouT FaiTh - IT is Impossible To Please God

The JusT Shall Live By FaiTh

v7 Noah - Abraham [8] - Moses [24] - Gideon [32] - David - Samuel

Some were Killed For Their "FaiTh" v36

What Is This "FaiTh"? What Are you willing To Die For

Country? Family? Christ?

Faith is NOT Blind obedience

Ch 11:1 FaiTh Is The Assurance of Things We Hope For

And The ConvicTion of Their ReaLiTy

Jesus Said you Can'T see The Wind - you Know iTs There

you Can'T See ElecTriciTy - No man Has Ever Seen God

Answered Prayer BuT we Know He's There = Power over Sin - New CreaTion

Rom 10:17 - FaiTh Comes By hearing - The Word of God

The H.S. uses The Word - To ConvicT - To Bring FaiTh Rom 10:10

Ch 12:1 Therefore - geT Rid of Sin - Sin seperaTes From God

LeT us Run with perseverence - The Race

Life Is Like A Race - you Don'T Run WiTh A CoaT

Object of Faith → v2 Looking To Jesus - The AuThor - Finisher

Joy - He endured The Cross - Jesus had FaiTh - he

Saw Beyond The grave

v3 Are you GeTTing Tired? Weary? Consider Jesus

v4 Have you Shed your Blood?

v5 Have you ForgoTTen? - We Are Sons & DaughTers

v6 Discipline

v12 Therefore - geT going! Draw Upon Your FaiTh

Look Beyond This Life - Keep your Eyes on Jesus

v14 STrive For Peace & Holiness - No one Shall see God

The Bible Says - now we see as In A mirror DimLy - BuT Then

Face To Face

WithouT FaiTh - IT is Impossible To Please God

Do You Have FaiTh This Morning? If not - Are

you Listening To The Word of God?

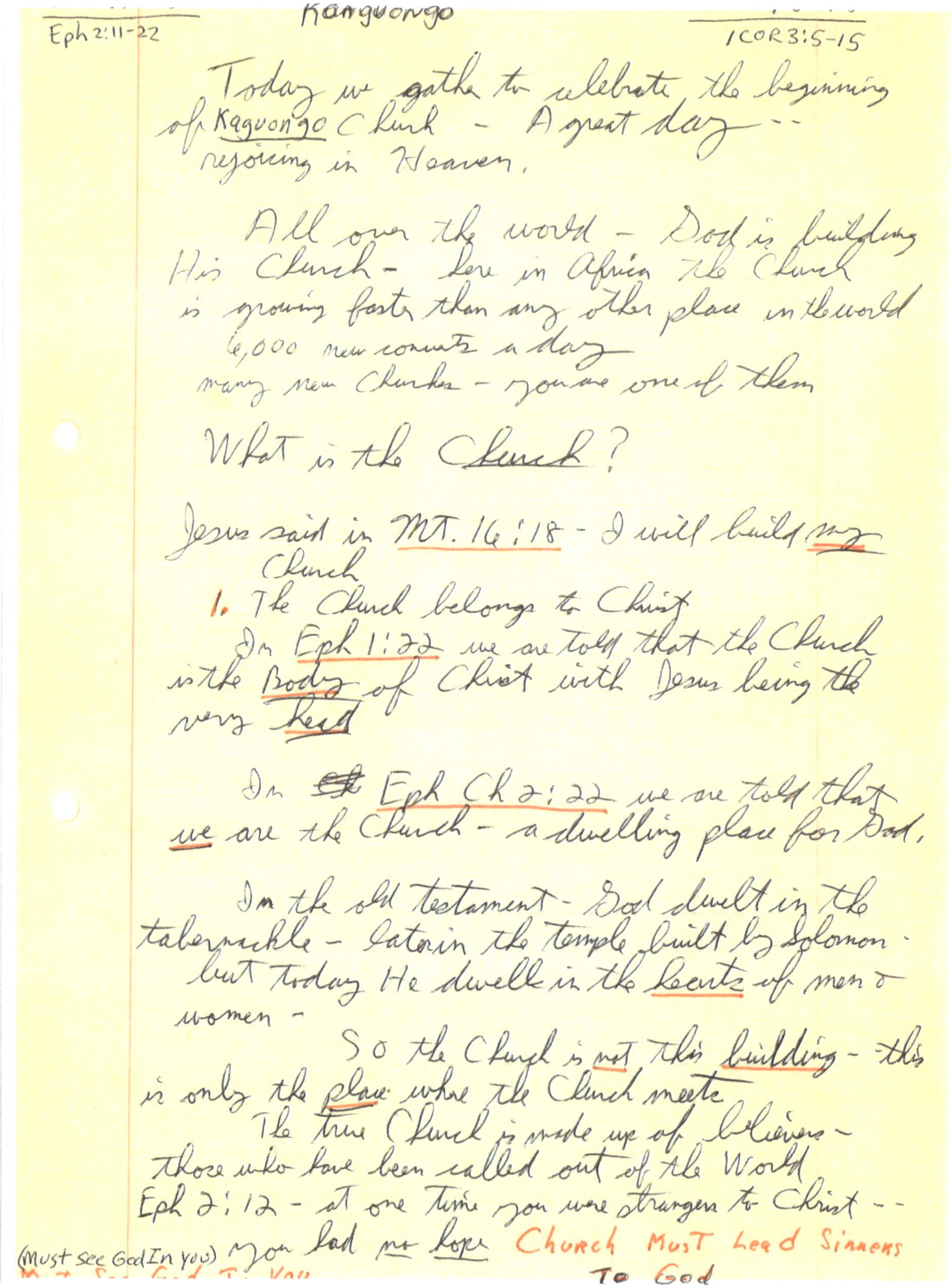
Kanguongo

Eph 2:11-22

1 COR 3:5-15

Today we gather to celebrate the beginning of Kaguongo Church - A great day -- rejoicing in Heaven.

All over the world - God is building His Church - here in Africa the Church is growing faster than any other place in the world
6,000 new converts a day
many new Churches - you are one of them

What is the Church?

Jesus said in MT. 16:18 - I will build my Church

1. The Church belongs to Christ
In Eph 1:22 we are told that the Church is the Body of Christ with Jesus being the very head

In Eph Ch 2:22 we are told that we are the Church - a dwelling place for God.

In the old testament - God dwelt in the tabernackle - later in the temple built by Solomon - but today He dwells in the hearts of men & women -

So the Church is not this building - this is only the place where the Church meets

The true Church is made up of believers - those who have been called out of the World

Eph 2:12 - at one time you were strangers to Christ -- you had no hope Church Must Lead Sinners To God

(Must see God In you)

Darvin: "Kanguongo was a new church in Kenya. I was privileged to speak at the building dedication."

13 But now you have been saved

19 no longer strangers - fellow citizens with Saints

21 you are a part of a world wide structure, joined together by Christ

But now comes responsibility!

If someone gives you a cow - - - great - but now you have to care for that cow

HOUSE - the same thing

CHURCH - the same - what direction will you go - what will be your priorities?

In Pauls 1st letter to the Corinthians, he talks about how he built that Church

Ch 3:10 - I laid a foundation - another is building on it

You have been given a good start - someone has laid a good foundation - - Take care how you build - Paul says remember the foundation is Jesus Christ

12 Whatever we build upon the foundation - - will be tested by fire - Hay Wood - Straw - To Please Men

Temporary

Eternity

Some Churches have large buildings and think they have a great ministry - - but they have move off of their foundation - - - they will be burned up by the fire of Gods judgement

Remember - 1. The Church belongs to Christ

2. The Church is the body of Christ

He is the Head - foundation - cornerstone, if you leave Him - you will have nothing.

Neh Ch. 2:1-10 Neh ch 4:7-20

Nehemiah Builds The Wall

Comment on Building Progress
Vision - When There Is No Vision Prov. 29:18

Years Ago Nehemiah had A Vision Ch. 2:5
The City of Jerusalem Was in Ruins
The people were being Ridiculed

He Prayed - Planned
I'm sure much prayer & Planning went Into This Building -- Someone Had A Vision

But -- Any Time There Is A Work of God - We Can See 3 Things happening
Whether IT's A Building - Ministry - Program Whatever

(1) Satan Will Oppose IT Ch 2:19 - Ch 4:1
I Pet 5:8 You Can be Sure - If God is in IT - Satan Will Be Against IT!
I'm Sure you've had Some Problems - Some Differences - But you Pressed on
Ch 4:6 - The people had A Mind To Work!

SomeTimes We Become Weary -- We Lose Sight of The Vision - Satan Succeeds In wearing Us Down -- Ch 4:10 Loss of Vision!

The Wall was Long - Verse 19 - The people were Seperated -- SomeTimes We become Seperated because of misunderstandings - Differences
What Did They Do? verse 20 They Rallyed Together! We need To Rally Together - To Defeat The Enemy - Stand Firm - Resist I Pet. 5:9

(2) Satan Cannot Stop The Work of God!
He Can't Stand IT -- But neither Can he Stop IT!
If The Work is Truly of The Lord ---
Satan Will not Stop IT
You Will have Trouble -- IT won't Be
Easy - You may Be Threatened - They may
Try to Frighten you - Nehemiah was Threatened [Ch6:2]
[Ch 6:9]
But God Will See You Through!
[Ch6:15-16]
Satan Cannot Stop The Work of God

(3) God Will be Glorified!
After The Wall was finished - Nehemiah gathered
The people Together -- And he had Ezra Read From The Bible
[Ch 8:3] From Morning To Midday! And All The people
Stood! verse 5
Then They Worshiped The Lord -- verse 6
They knew That IT was God who Accomplished
The work - And They gave Him Glory

When you Complete This Building -- God will
Be Glorified -- The Word Will go Forth Every
Sunday - The people Will Rally Together -
Souls Will Be Saved
Remember
Any Work of God

1. Satan Will Oppose You
2. Satan Cannot Stop IT
3. God Will Be Glorified
May God help you To Keep Your Vision.

(Gal 6:1-10) **Laws of The Harvest** Kagwe II Cor 9:6-15

One of The Facts of Life & Nature is The Law of Cause & effect - If one Thing Is Done - Other Things Occur

If we Ignore or break These Laws -- we must suffer the Consequenses

For Example - There is The Law of Gravity -- Objects That Are Heavier Than Air - Fall To The Ground -- If you Care To Ignore That Law -- And Step off This Roof --

These Laws are Fixed - Not Even God will Reverse Them -- The Law of The Harvest is one of These Laws [Gen. 8:22]

Whether You Are A Full Time Farmer -- have A small Shamba -- or just Plant Flowers You Will be Familiar with These Laws

1. We Reap The same Kind As We Plant
   beans - Maize - Potatoes
2. We Reap In A Different Season Than We Plant
3. We Reap More Than We Plant
4. We Can't Change Last Years Harvest - but we Can Do Something About this Years

The Laws of The Harvest Also Apply To our Spiritual Life - Whatever A Man Sows - That Shall he Also Reap

verse 6 Those Who Are Taught - have A Responsibility To share All good Things with he who Teaches -- You need To Support your Pastor But - Theres Also A Law of The Harvest here - II Cor 9:6

If you Give Little -- You Will Recieve Little

Darvin: "Kagwe was one of the churches in Kenya where I preached regularly."

V 7-8 God Is Not Mocked - One who Sneers AT
Gods Law - doesn't Change Those Laws --
God doesn't Suffer - Man Suffers
Law #1 - We Reap The Same As We Plant
Sow To the Flesh - Corruption [Gal 5:19]
Sow To the Spirit - Eternal Life [Gal 5:22]
How Can you Expect To Harvest A Field
of Holiness -- when you have Planted in Immorality

~~V 9~~ ~~In Due Season~~ -
Law #3 - We Reap More Than We Plant
Hosea 8:7 - They sow the wind - And Reap The
Whirlwind Examp. - Drinking - Cheating

V 9 In Due Season - Law #2 - We Reap In A Different
Season Than We Plant
ITs easy To get Tired of Doing Good --
If we Are Looking for Results Now
God Says - You Shall Reap - If you
Don't Lose heart
What Have We Learned ?
1. Give Generously

2. Sow In The Spirit Law #4 - You Can't Change
Last years Harvest -- but you Can Change this Year
Live In Holiness - Reap Eternal Life

3. Don't Lose Heart - We're Not home yet!
Remember - Our Home Is In Heaven - We're just Passing
Through here
What About you -- Is IT Time To Change
The Things You're Planting?

(I Tim. 3:1-13) (Acts 6:1-6)

This morning we are gathered together for a special purpose – To set apart & to Commission These Men & Woman To The Office of Deacon or Elder

Acts 6:2-5 From the 1st Church at Jerusalem, we see the need To Call certain men to Special positions

While IT Is True that Everyone In The Church Is To Be Involved In Ministry -- Some Are Set Apart for Special Ministry

Eph. 4:11

Your Duties Will Be Similar To Many who Have gone Before You – Assisting The Pastor in Worship – Communion – Baptism – Leading Committees

But! Don't Be Limited To These Traditional Duties

Steven – didn't just serve Tables -- He was a great preacher, He stood up to the Jews & None could withstand him

Philip – Traveled all over & was a great evangelist & Through the conversion of the Ethiopian Eunich was responsible for the Gospel 1st coming To Africa

Be Open To Gods Leading – He has Called You For A Special Reason

I'm very Happy That you wives are being included in this ceremony – Paul has a special word to you

I Tim 3:11 A man Is Only As Strong As His Wife -- He Can only Serve As You Support & Encourage Him

Be Ready For Satan To Attack Your Family!

Men - Your 1sT PRioRiTy Must Be Your RelaTionship WiTh God

BuT 2nd - Is Your Wife & Family

Your Church work Must Come After Your wife & Family -- God gave Them To you 1sT !

You Can Only Be EffecTive In your MinisTry If you Have A STrong Family.

I Pet. 5: 1-4 You have been Called To A Noble Task - To be involved in the Lords work is the Highest priviledge -- If you follow These words of Peter it will bring you much joy --

And When the Chief ShehERd Returns - You Will Receive the Crown of GLoRY!

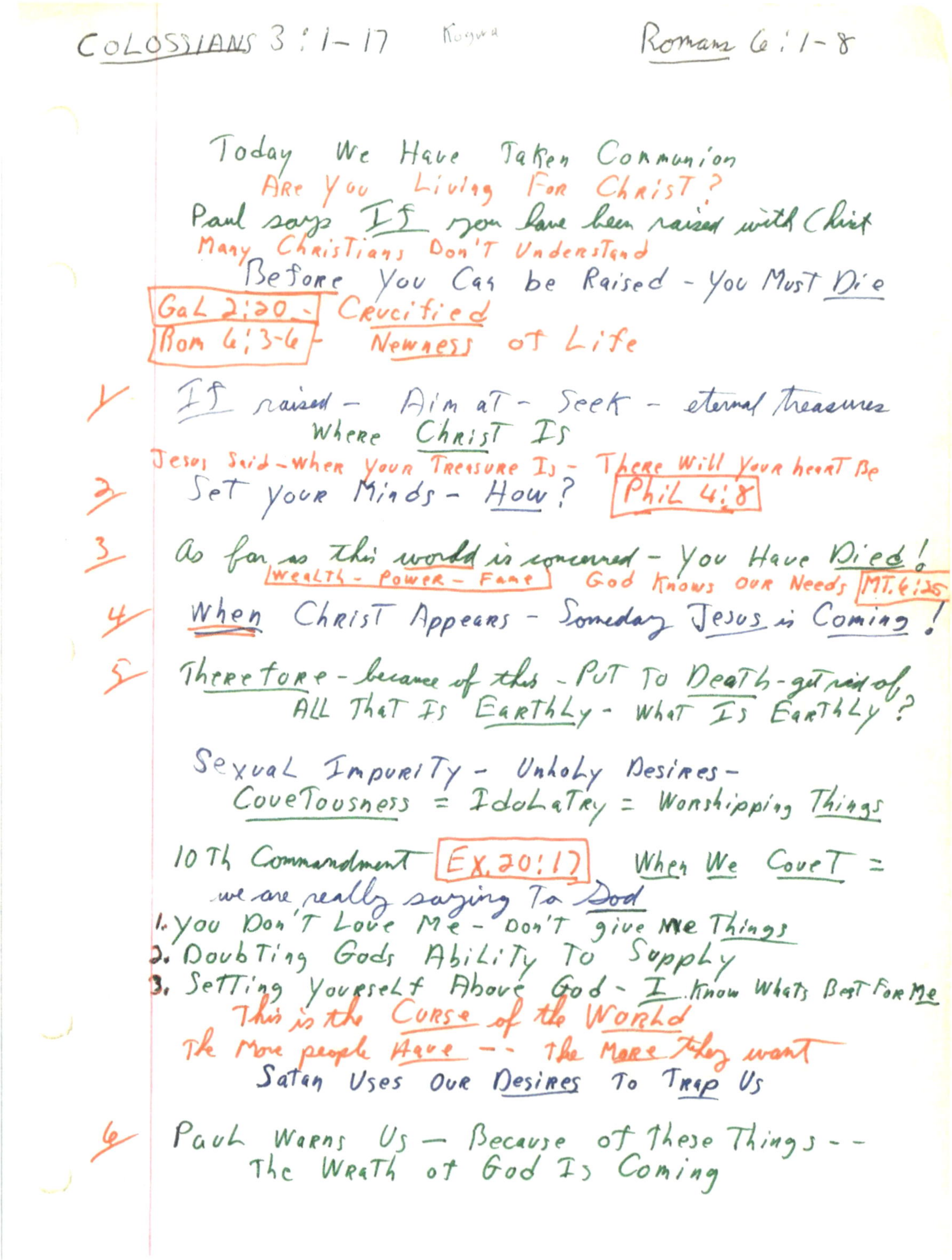

COLOSSIANS 3:1-17 Kagwa Romans 6:1-8

Today We Have Taken Communion
Are You Living For Christ?
Paul says If you have been raised with Christ
Many Christians Don't Understand
Before You Can be Raised - You Must Die
Gal 2:20 - Crucified
Rom 6:3-6 - Newness of Life

1 If raised - Aim at - Seek - eternal treasures
Where Christ Is
Jesus Said - where your Treasure Is - There Will Your heart Be
2 Set your Minds - How? Phil 4:8

3 As far as this world is concerned - You Have Died!
Wealth - Power - Fame God Knows our Needs MT. 6:25
4 When Christ Appears - Someday Jesus is Coming!
5 Therefore - because of this - Put To Death - get rid of
All That Is Earthly - What Is Earthly?

Sexual Impurity - Unholy Desires -
Covetousness = Idolatry = Worshipping Things

10 Th Commandment Ex. 20:17 When We Covet =
we are really saying To God
1. You Don't Love Me - Don't give Me Things
2. Doubting Gods Ability To Supply
3. Setting Yourself Above God - I Know Whats Best For Me
This is the Curse of the World
The More people Have - - the More they want
Satan Uses Our Desires To Trap Us

6 Paul Warns Us - Because of these Things - -
The Wrath of God Is Coming

Darvin: "Preached at Kagwe."

7-8 MORE! - Anger - Rage - Malice - Slender
Foul Talk

9 Do Not Lie to one another

10 Since We have been Raised with Christ - Lets Put on
our New Nature - The Image of Christ

11 In this new creation there are No distinctions
Christ is ALL - In ALL

12 Since We Are Gods Chosen Ones - Let Us Be -
Kindhearted - Compassionate - Meek - Patient
these Are ALL Fruits of The Spirit

13 Forbearing = Gentle - Forgiving - just As God has
forgiving You

14 Love

15 Thankful - for what God has given you
A thankful Spirit - hard to find

16 The WORD dwelling In You - Jesus Is The WORD

17 Whatever You Do - Do It In The Name of the Lord

If you Have been Raised With Christ - Seek
those things which are Above

If you Have Not been Raised With Christ -

MT. 13-1-9 MT. 1:24-27

MATIMBE/

S.S. - very important - PROV. 22:6

Children Spend Many hrs. School

1 hr. in S.S. | Teachers Are Important

Easier To Reach Children -

Jesus Said - Suffer The Children To Come

The Harvest Is Plentiful -

but The Laborers Are Few

If We Don't Win Them To Christ

Satan Will Snatch Them Away

MT. 13 Parable of Sower

We have Responsibility To Sow -

v. 19 Make Sure They Understand!

v. 20 S.S. Must build Roots!

v. 22 Must Teach To Delight In The Lord

v. 23 Hears - Understands = Bears Fruit

These Children Are The Church of Tomorrow - Fruit

Darvin: "Matimbe was a church in Kenya where I preached regularly."

We Must Be Faithful To
Sow The <u>Seed</u> -- But

He Who hears Also has <u>Responsibility</u>

Many Different Kinds of <u>hearts</u>

Hopefully you Children Will Be Like
The <u>Wise</u> man <u>MT. 7:24</u>

Jesus Told A Story - 1 Wise - 1 Foolish

If you <u>hear</u> The Words of Jesus And
Don't Follow Them - you Are Like The
<u>Foolish</u> Man - Building On <u>Sand</u>

<u>Rains</u> Come - <u>Floods</u> - <u>Wind</u>

Life Can Be <u>Hard</u> - Rains & Floods <u>Will</u>
Come

<u>Only</u> As you Build your Life
Upon The <u>Rock</u> of <u>Jesus</u> <u>Christ</u>

Many Years - Night of Terror
Details Still Vivid
Sandy & Children Experienced More
Difficult To Talk - Must

2 Cor 1 - To Comfort Others

Growing Awareness - Many Experience

Fear & Terror - Not Thieves

1. Loss of Loved one
2. Cancer - Sickness
3. Divorce - Abusive People
4. Bridge

How To Cope

Rom 8:28

1. All Things Work Together
Need To Trust God - Completely

2. Choose To Look For & Focus on Good - Gods Ways Are Not Our
Neg Feeds Fear - Destroys

3. Gods Grace is Sufficient -
At Time of Need!

4. Fear is Not From God 2 Tim 1:7
God Did Not Give Us A Spirit of Fear - But of Power & Love & Self-Control

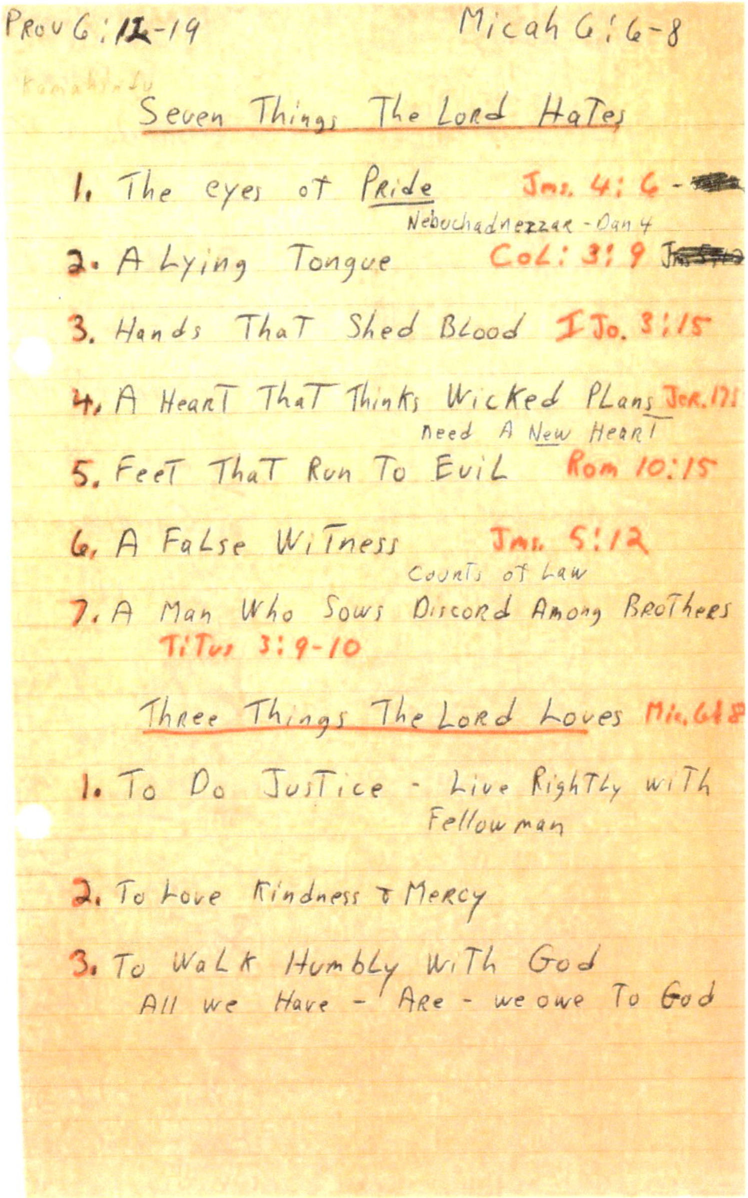

Prov 6:12-19 Micah 6:6-8

Seven Things The Lord Hates

1. The eyes of Pride Jms. 4:6 -
Nebuchadnezzar - Dan 4
2. A Lying Tongue Col: 3:9
3. Hands That Shed Blood I Jo. 3:15
4. A Heart That Thinks Wicked Plans Jer. 17:
need A New Heart
5. Feet That Run To Evil Rom 10:15
6. A False Witness Jms. 5:12
Counts of Law
7. A Man Who Sows Discord Among Brothers
Titus 3:9-10

Three Things The Lord Loves Mic. 6:8

1. To Do Justice - Live Rightly with Fellowman
2. To Love Kindness & Mercy
3. To Walk Humbly With God
All we Have - Are - we owe To God

Ps. 32

1 - whose sin is covered - blood of Christ

2 - imputed - if thou Lord should mark iniquities, O Lord who shall stand?

Ps 130:3-4

no deceit in our spirit

3 - the heavy hand of the Lord

4 - Selah = pause & think about that

5. Key - Many people acknowledge their sin - and gain forgiveness - but still feel guilty - Why? Phychiatrists Say It's Not Their Fault

Wilkerson - examples

Guilt & Iniquity - is it possible to have deceit in our spirits - Not being completely honest with God?

(6) the person who has experienced complete forgiveness - is ready to be used of God can stand the "trials"

Bible Examples = David - Moses - Jacob
Peter - Paul

8. I the Lord will instruct you

9 Do we learn from our failures?
or do we lack understanding?
How long will God have to keep the bit in our mouths - before we learn to follow him?

10 - A Promise

11 - SHOUT FOR JOY!
in Luke we read about the woman who washed Jesus feet with her tears & dried them with her hair - Pharisees objected
Jesus said Her sins which are many are forgiven, for she loved much - But to whom little is forgiven, the same loveth little.

Sometimes we may feel we haven't sinned very much - Ha! JUST ASK The LORD To Show You

Back To Verse 1
Blessed is He
Happy - Fortunate

Job - A Godly Father

One of The greatest needs of our Day - Godly Fathers!

Glad To See you here -- Tells me you Are Concerned!

Men who will Demonstrate To Their Children - The Love - Concern - Affection of A Heavenly Father

Statistics Show That young People who have difficulty Seeing God As A Father -- had A Poor Earthly Father -- etc.

God Planned For Families And for Fathers To Be Earthly models -- To point Their Children To Him! WOW!

2

Many Examples In Bible –

I Choose Job because Lessor Known – OverLooked – Always Think of Suffering & Patience

Read veres 1 & 2

Look AT that -- God Could have Said AnyThing About Job -- But He Chose To Talk About his Family!

~~[struck out]~~ Children Come before "things" -- Before Work! -- Yes Even Before The Church

verse 3 – A Picture of A very Wealthy Man – The Greatest man of His Time

15/ verse 4 & 5

Job Sent for Them ---
He Was Concerned About
Their Spiritual Condition

Fathers? Do you know
The Spiritual Condition of
your Children?

When Was The Last Time
You Rose Early In The Morning
To Pray For them?

Job Was A Busy Man --
But He Still had Time For
His Children!

Job Took The Responsibility
For Their Spiritual Training

How About IT Fathers?
Mothers Are Not equiped To Be
The Spiritual Leaders In The Home!

4. Oh But You Say I'm
NoT A Spiritual Leader --
I Couldn't Do That!
Why I Can't even Pray!

Well - You Can Be A Spiritual
Leader WiThouT Praying!

Well What Do we mean
Then when We Talk About
Spiritual Leadership In The
Home?

God Is A very PracTicle God
The Bible Is A very PracTicle Book
DeuT 6:6

7 PracTicle STeps
To SpiriTual Leadership

The Measurement of Time

I'm going To Ask you A question This Morning - How OLD Are you?

Gen. 47 Joseph Brought His Father before Pharoah, and He Asked Him - How old Are you?
Jacob Was 130

Right Way & Wrong Way To Measure AnyThing - I'm A Carpenter -

So IT is With Time

Some Measure Life By The Amount of ~~[illegible]~~ Money They Made.

Now Yes We need Money -- iT Can Do Many Things for Us -

BuT IT is A Poor Yardstick for Measuring Life

Some People would measure Life
By Reputation - They count Their
years By The Number of Honors
They Recieved - and Success Is
Measured By How far They Have
Climbed on The Ladder of Fame
& PresTige.

OThers Would Measure Life
Soley By Its Length
Now Regardless What Any one
Says You Are NoT As Young As
You Feel -- LeT's NoT Decieve
Ourselves - We Are As Old As We
Are -- And No Matter How Long
We Live -- if We Have spent our
Days In Self GratiFication - The
Sum ToTal Will Be Zero

3

Have You Ever MeT Someone Who Measures Life By ALL The Bad Things That Happen To Them?

What A Morbid Way To Measure Time. We Will Surely Remember The Pasing of Loved Ones ETc - But We Should NoT Measure Life As A Whole By Them.

Just As There Are Wrong Ways To Measure Time - There Are Right Ways Too

For Example We Measure Time By BirTh - Ps. 90:12 We Are Told To Number our Days, That We May Apply our HearTs Unto Wisdom

4

But I Trust That Many of
You This Morning have Not Only
Been Born, But Have Been (Born Again)
Not of Corruptible Seed, but of
InCorruptible, by The Word of God-
And So We Can Measure Life By
Our Birth, And our Rebirth.

We Can Also measure Time By
Knowledge. As We grow Older,
We Should Also grow Wiser. Our
Judgments should Be More Mature
As We Advance In Years.

We Can Also Measure Time By
Character - As We Look At The
Trunk of A Cut Tree - We Can
Chart IT's History By ITs Rings -
So We Can See The Inner Circles
of GrowTh

That show A Man[s] coming More And
More Toward A Full grown Character
To Mature Manhood To The Measure
of The Stature of The Fulness of
Christ. Are you A Better Person
Now Than When you First Began?
A Better Christian?

I Think IT is Proper To Measure
our Lives By The Growth In Grace
That God Has Enabled Us To Attain

We Measure Time Also By
Service - Certainly We Can NoT
count The Day AT All In Which We
Have Done No Good

So -- How Old Are You?
Are you Old Enough To Be Brought
Face To Face With God?- Or Have
You Learned The Ways of The
Master --

Have You Fought The Good Fight?
Have You Done Your Best For God?

And If You Are Not A Christian -- Are You Old Enough To Have Run Up A Fearful Account Against Your Soul on That Day of Judgement?

Are You Old Enough To Be Cynical and Bitter Towards God - Still Blaming Him For Your Failures?

Are You Old Enough To Make It Very Unlikely That You Will Ever Turn To God, and Accept His Offer of Salvation?

7

WhaTever Your Age Is This Morning -- You Are Old Enough To know Jesus ChrisT As Your Personal Saviour; -- you Are Old Enough To Be Ready For DeaTh If He Calls -- And Old Enough To Live For God And His Glory if permitted To Live.

May God Help you To Measure Your Life By His Word -- And To Call Upon Him For All of Your Needs. For Our God Is Able To Supply All of Your Needs According To His Riches In ChrisT Jesus

Study To Show Thyself Approved
UnTo Man

1 Cor. 2:2 - Paul - One of The
best Educated Men of His Time
A Pharisee - A skilled Orator -
Decides To Come In Weakness. Why

5 - That your Faith Might Rest In
The Power of God!

If Anyone Had A Right To be
Intellectual - It Was Paul - YeT
He Would NoT!

The Concern I WanT To Share
With you is This - We Brethren
Have Been Careful Over The Years
To Emphasize Rom 12:2 - Do NoT
Be Conformed To This World!

And We Have Applied IT To
Many Areas of Life -- Most Notably
Dress

2. But In The Area of Education,
We Have Mimicked & Copied
Almost Completely, Secular Institution
of Higher Learning
And Not Just We Brethren -
But All Denominations - Including
Fundamentalists -- Bend Over Backwards
To Gain State & Federal Accreditations.
The Curriculum Sounds The Same -
The Degrees Are Similar - Recent
Graduations Looked the Same (cap & gown)

And So My Title -- Approved
Unto Man

II Tim 2:15 Who Are We Trying To Impress
God or Man ?

I Have Been Thinking & Contemplati
That Very Question A Lot Lately -
As I Have Struggled With The
Idea of Perhaps Some Further
Training For Myself . . .

3. I Have Been Very Disapointed, As
I Have Had Opportunity To Observe
Various Colledges – and Their
Graduates -- A Recent Article
In The Messenger Concerning Pastors –
Stirred My Spirit – This Article
Was Generaly Bemoaning The Demanding
Life of A Pastor – With Comparisons
being Made With other "Professional"
Fields In The Area of Salaries etc.
Is That What The Pastorate Is
Just Another Profession ?
What Ever Happened To The Man
of God -- Who Was Called By
God -- To Give of Himself --
Sacrificially – To Tend The
Flock of God!

4. Today We Have An Abundance of Professional Ministers -- But Very Few Shepards - True Pastors

Why? I Believe A Big Part of The Problem Is The Way We Educate And Train Prospective Pastors

We Train Them In The Ways of The World - Not Gods Ways -- We Fill Their Heads With Knowledge But Very Little Wisdom

The Bible Says -- The Fear of The Lord - is The Begining of All Wisdom! Jn 1:5 - If Any Man Lacks Wisdom - Let Him

YeT Our Seminary Professors Systematically Destroy The Childlike Faith of These Young Men With Their So Called "Higher Criticism"

5. But Beyond All of That --
And of Much Greater Significance --
In Our Mad Scramble To Gain
The Approval of Man -- In Our
Desire To Achive Intellectual
Knowledge -- We Have All But
Ignored The Greatest Teacher
The World Has Ever Known --
The Holy Spirit!
Jo 14:26 Says The Holy Spirit
Will Teach Us All Things
And 14:13 - Says - He Will Guide
Us Into All Truth.

verses 6 - 11

Paul Says No One Knows The
Thoughts of Any Man Better Than His
own Spirit -- Like wise No One
Comprehends The Thoughts of God
Except The Spirit of God!

6. Chalmer Faw -- At Palmyra
All The "Right" Letters

A Professor At Bethany For Many Years - Great Intellectual Knowledge -

In His Own Testimony -- He Knew The Bible In Hebrew & Greek - Forward & Back -- Yet it Was All <u>Meaningless</u> -- Untill The <u>Holy</u> <u>Spirit</u> Became His <u>Teacher</u>!

IT IS A Very <u>Natural</u> Thing To Try To Reason Things Out for Ourselves - To Lean Unto Our <u>Own</u> Understanding.

But We Must Remember -- That <u>Gods</u> Ways Are Not <u>our</u> Ways - Many Times They're <u>Opposite</u>

7. Isa. 55:8 - For My Thoughts Are Not Your Thoughts - Neither Are Your Ways My Ways Says The Lord!

Verse 12

We Have Within Us - The Very Spirit of God!!!

Who Is Better qualified To Teach Us? - To Interpret Biblical Truths?

We Must Learn To Submit Our Minds - Our Intellect - To The Leading of The Holy Spirit!

We Must Stop Guiding Our Lives With Our Heads -- And Start Leading With Our Spirits

8. Gods Spirit - Dwelling In Our Spirit - Will Lead Us Into All Truth!

This Is Hard - Not As Easy Thing - This Is Opposite From What The World Teaches - Many Times It Is Opposite From What Our Church Related Schools Teach - -

Yet Isn't This Exactly What Paul Is Saying In Verse 13 ? The Holy Spirit Was Pauls Teacher - - And He Recognized The Inadequatsy of Human Wisdom.

Have We Come To That Point In Our Own Lives? Are We Ready To Be Taught By The Spirit?

9. Or Are We To Be Like
The People Paul Talks About
In Verse 14

God Has So Much -- He
Wants To Give Us -- But
He Won't Push Us

If We Insist on Understanding
Things With our Minds - of Trying
To Reason things Out - We Will
Never Recieve The Things Of
God -- They Are Spiritually
Discerned!

Study, To Show Thy Self Approved
Unto God!! A Workman Who Needs Not
To Be Ashamed - Rightly Dividing The
Word of Truth.

The Wedding Feast

Explain Parables - An Earthly Story
with A Heavenly Meaning

Why did Jesus Teach in parables?
MT 13:10 Amplified

verse 1 - King - Son - Marriage Feast

3-6 - 1st Invitation - Second Call
Explain Eastern Weddings -
Especially Kings
Invited Guests = Israel

7 - Burned Their City - Prophetic
destruction of Jerusalem

8 Invited Guests Not Worthy

9-10 Go out And Invite ALL
Both Good & Bad
Each Guest provided with
A wedding garment

(2)

11 King Spots An Imposter
Why No Garment ?

12 No Good Excuse - speechless

13 Through Him OUT!

What Is The Importance of The Wedding Garment?
Obviously IT Was An Absolute Requirement For Entrance

There Are Certain Themes you Can Trace Throughout The Bible & This Is One - Need A good Cross Reference Study Bible

Lets Begin with Isiah 61:10
64:6 MT. 6:33 Rom 3:21-22
Rom 13:14 Rev 7:9
14
Rev. 19:7-9
Marriage Supper of The Lamb

(3) I've gone Into All This Scripture To give Us Some Understanding of What Jesus Is Trying To Illustrate.

He Says IT Rather BlunTLy In Jo 14:6 - I Am The Way, The Truth & The Life, No one Comes To The Father But by Me.

In Light of All This -- I want To Share With you Some STaTements Printed In Our Annual Conference BookLeTs That I Find Very Alarming.

Pg 74 - 75

How About The Jews?

With That Kind of A Missionary OuT Look Can We Really Expect An Agressive Missions Program?

④ IT Also Helps Me To Understand
The Reply given To A query
From The ATlanTic NorTheast DisTricT
AT Annual Conference

(Read query on Pg 123)

I still Firmly Believe In A
LiTeral Hell - I Also Believe
That Everyone Who Does NoT Have
His Wedding GarmenT ON (The
RighTeousness of ChrisT, Through
His Shed Blood) Shall Be Thrown
InTo OuTer Darkness.

We Can EiTher Believe
The Lies of SaTan -- OR The
Truth of The Lord Jesus ChrisT.

'The Home Is The most Important Institution ever established.

No Church Is Stronger Than The Family Life of IT's Members.

We Hear So Many Statistics I Believe We're Numbed By Them 1 Million New Divorces each year etc

But Consider This One -

Our Divorce Rate In This Country Is Approaching 43% -- <u>No</u> Society In History Has Survived With A Divorce Rate of 50% or Over

Our Society Is Moving Rapidly Toward The Total Disintegration of The Family

And yet In Light of All This We In The Church Seem To Feel That We Can Each Individually Raise Our own Families!

7 We seem To Feel IT's Nobody
elses Business How We Raise Our Children
That We Don't Need or Want Each
Others Help.

I Need Help!

That's Why We join A Church
We're Supposed To Be A Family
Paul Say's We're Like A Body --
When One Has A Problem -- We All
Have A Problem

Last Week We Had Baby
Dedication -- Didn't We Stand And
Say We would Support Those Parents
What About Baptism?
What Is The Church Doing?
Sunday School? No Way!
IT Can't Be Done 1 Hour A
Week.

1 We Have Been Decieved
We Have Been Lied To
By SATAN

He Is Attacking Our Homes -
To Neutralize Us -
When Our Homes Are Unstable
We Cannot Have A Strong Wittness In
The World.

We Need To Recommit Ourselves
To One Another - To Recognize Our
Enemy And His Methods -- And To
Resist Him Together!

I Feel It's Wrong For The Church
Try To Discipline It's Members --
When We Have NoT Made An Honest
Effort To Encourage Christian Homes
We Need More Teaching & Preaching
I Was Encouraged By Jacks Sermons

7 We Need More Bible Study
Groups.
More Prayer Support Groups
I'm Concerned About
Our Public Schools - Why
Don'T We Talk About Them?
Should We Consider Christian
Schools?

I Want So Much For Our
Church To Develope Into That
Caring - Sharing Body That Paul
Talks About - - And We Have
Tasted A Bit of It - - But
There's MORE!
And I'm Convinced We're
going To Need iT ALL - To Keep
our Families Together!

Rev 3:17

Jo 4:19-24

1. Many Kinds of Worship
v22 False - Ignorant - Blind

2. God Desires our Worship
v23 He Seeks Us

He Alone is Worthy

How To Worship?

1. In Spirit = Gr. Pneuma
v24 God is Spirit - Not A Spirit
We Are Made in Image of God

Our Spirit + Gods Spirit = Worship
Directed By Holy Spirit

2 Truth - The State or Character of Being True in Relation To Being - Knowledge or Speech
Being Open, "True" or Transparent Before God

Two things that I remember about our first Christmas in Kenya. First, I found a cedar tree to cut down for our Christmas tree. We set it up inside and decorated it. But the tree made Sandy sneeze, so I put it outside on the front porch. We didn't use the front door because it was away from the road. We used the back door because it went out to the road that led to the hospital and RVA. We enjoyed looking at the tree through the window. The second thing we decided to do was celebrate by taking a trip to the beach in Mombasa, Kenya. The Indian Ocean was beautiful, the weather delightful, and the car drive was a long adventure. Mombasa is just over 300 miles from Kijabe. Without the numerous stops to fix flat tires from the thorn trees and drink hot Fanta it was a minimum nine-hour drive one way. Yes, God faithfully provided all we needed on our first Kenyan road trip. We would take many more road trips. They all included flat tires, animals, and fun!

Derek graduated from RVA in 1983 and returned to Pennsylvania. He brought my mom, Gretta Byler, to come and celebrate our second Kenyan Christmas with us. This family Christmas photo (next page) was taken in our living room. Nadine remembers the day that a bat came into the house through the chimney and how Sandy chased it down with continuous swings from a broom!

My job in bringing clean water to the hospital and hospital houses began by working alongside missionaries who devised the plan to pipe water from a spring seven miles away. I had three crews of 8-10 men digging ditches 3-4 feet deep. We carefully worked around a 10-foot python living in the spring, I made the pipe connections to the spring, filter, and motor system, and laid the piping to Kijabe. The whole system worked by hydro-power and pumped 20+ gallons of water per minute. Once we had it pumping the spring water, I maintained the system. This involved cleaning the filter and repairing holes that goat herders made in the pipe to water their herd. I watched for the python that lived in the spring and the Colobus monkeys that disliked my entering their territory. I felt that the Colobus monkeys were a greater threat to my safety.

No more dirty creek water. Later, we borrowed a well-pounder to pound three clean water wells. Two wells for the hospital and one well for Moffat Bible College. This took several months in 1989 to complete. Every morning I opened the Bible and led my workers in a study of the Scriptures and in prayer.

"Cement Mixer"

We purchased a large cement mixer that worked well when it worked. The diesel engine often needed to be repaired. It mixed cement the cement we needed to complete the large projects we were working on. It had iron wheels and took 8-10 men to move it. Later, one of the missionaries bought a truck with a cement mixer. We had to sift the sand before we mixed, even though the workers wanted to skip this step. They also wanted to use less cement in the mix, but I explained to them that it would weaken the concrete and make the foundation unstable.

Darvin: "Preached at Spring Creek Church of the Brethren, 1985-86."

MT. 16:13-20

"God is Building His Church" Rev. 5:1-10

Where? - Hershey? - Church of The Brethren?
Worldwide! "The Family of God"
Jesus Said - I "Will" build My Church
God is Calling OUT A People For Himself

This Morning, We Want To Help You See
This Worldwide Body of Believers --
To Have A Vision -- As John Did in Rev. 5
Every Tribe - Tongue - Nation
Surrounding The Throne - Saying "Worthy is the Lamb"

Before We Went To Africa, - Our Vision
was Limited -- But These Past 3 years - We Have
Seen Parts of Gods Church We Never Knew Existed
God is Building His Church!
Not The Way We Would -- Iss. 55:8

By The Way -- Did The Drum bother You?
I Just Wanted To Prepare You For Heaven --
Ahh -- You Thought Just Piano & Organs -----
We Need To Broaden Our Views ---
We, In America Are Just one Small Part of
The Body of Christ -- We Need To Catch
John's Vision - of Many Different Peoples --
Many Different Cultures -- ALL Worshiping Christ

2

God is Building His Church
NoT The Way We Would -- His Way!
When We Look AT Africa -- We See Poverty - STarvaTion - Famine -- We Are Overwhelmed
Where Do We Begin? Same Place As PeTer!
Who is Jesus? - The ChrisT - Son of Living God!
Jn 3:16 - For God So Loved The World

We Need To Keep ThaT in FronT of Us -- OTherwise - We Lose Sight of The Goal ---
We see The Suffering - The Poverty - And We Can Easily geT CaughT Up in The HumaniTarian EfforTs To Send Food -- Monies --- And We ForgeT ThaT - This is A SpiriTual BaTTLe!!
Americans Are GreaT AT Sending Food & Money
ThaTs NoT The Answer!
This is A SpiriTual BaTTLe! Much of The Poverty in Africa Can Be Traced To SpiriTual Bondage -- A Bondage ThaT Keeps Them in A Vicious cycle of WhichcrafT - SaTan Worship - Ignorance
In our Slides TonighT, - We'll Show You Some Young ChrisTian Men - Who Are Taking The ResponsibiliTy For Their Families - Who Are Living with **1** wife - Who Are Having Smaller Families - Because They know They Are Responsibel To Feed & Care For Them
(In TradiTional African CulTure - There is No Individual ResponsibiliTy For AnyThing)

3/

Christianity Has Within It - A Strong Work Ethic -- 2 Th. 3:10 - If A Man Will Not Work -- Niether Let Him Eat 1 Tim. 5:8 -- Anyone Who Does Not Provide For His own Family -

When People Come To Christ -- They Learn Responsibility -- They Start Caring For Their Families

Could It Be Possible -- That God is Using This Current Famine - To Open The Doors To Those Countries And Peoples Who Have Little or No Christian Witness?

Certainly -- There would Be No Missionaries Allowed Inside Ethiopia - or Sudan For Instance - Except For The Terrible Conditions There

God is Building His Church
Not our Way -- But His Way

The Bible is Filled with Examples of God Using Adversity -- Trouble -- Famine - Suffering

But Today -- American Christians Are Repelled -- By The Thought of Suffering -- In fact - There Are Elaborate Theoligies Built Around The Theme -- That Christians Should Never Suffer - We Should Not Be Sick - That God Wants To Bless Us With Material Posessions - Etc. Etc. That Sounds Good - When Seated on Your Lazy Boy Recliner - in Front of T-V - Eating Potatoe Chips - Pretzels & Ice Cream!

"You Deserve A Break Today" You Deserve The Best!

4

BuT -- IT Doesn't Sound So Good - When
You're SiTTing on The Ground -- In A Mud HuT --
And Your Chewing on Some Maize ---
And You're Having Fellowship -- WiTh Some of
God's DearesT Children

PeTer Says -- Don'T Be Surprised when You Find
yourself in Trouble -- ITs NoT A STrange
Thing - To Be Suffering -- Instead Rejoice!
Because God is GeTTing Ready To AcT!

Paul Reminds Us ThaT God Works BesT --
In Our Weakness ---
We WanT To Work For God in Our STrengThs! -
We Look AT Someone And Say - They're A
Good Preacher -- Or He's An ExcellenT Teacher --
They Would Really Make a Good Missionary --
BuT God is Looking For Obedience --
HumiliTy -- Willingness To Suffer --

STop!

When We FirsT wenT To Africa - We were
Eager To Share All of our TalenTs - our V-a-s-T --
STore of Knowlege -- We had All The Answers -
We Couldn'T WaiT To "Lay iT on" Those People

5

We had Some Success -- But There Was
A Seperation From The People - A Lack of Acceptance
A Coolness - if You Will
But Then God Did Something --
He Allowed A Gang of Thieves To Break
Into our House -- I was Beaten Severely
Around The Head -- My Wife Was Terrorized
And Almost Raped -- Our Children were Plunged
Into A Night of Fear They Will Never Forget --
Our House Was Plundered & Destroyed ---
And We Suffered --
And Like Everyone Who Has Ever Suffered -
We Said Why -- God!??

Didn't We Come To Africa To Serve You?
I Have All These Abilities I Want To Use
For YOU! -- I Can't Use Them Lying On
This Bed! --- Gods - Ways - Are - Not - our - Ways

No -- God Did Not Desert Us That Night --
We Felt His Presence As Never Before ---
And He Sent His Angels Round About Us ---
Certainly - One of Them Removed The Axe head
From That Steel Pipe -- Just Before It Crushed
Into My Forehead

6

And Another one Carried Me - Now Unconcience - To A Hidden Corner of The Room Where I Would Escape Further Notice -- And Be Safe From Flying Rocks & Glass. Still Others Surrounded My Wife Sandy -- Now Alone & Helpless -- Facing 4 To 6 - Armed & Demon Posessed Men -- God Gave Her An Incredible Calmness -- Supernatural Control & The Ability To Speak -- Quietly -- Confidently -- In The Name of Jesus!

STop!

The Events of The Following Hour Are Still Not Very Clear To Us --- What is Clear -- Is That When Human Strength & Ability Failed -- God Took Over --- Suddenly - This Strong - Confident - Skilled Missionary Was Laying Flat on His Back - And Now -- Instead of My going out To The People and Saying -- Look what I can Do For You -- I was The one Who Needed Help - Instead of Ministering To Them -- They Began To Minister To Us! --- Suffering -- iT PuT us on Thier Level As Nothing Else Could -- IT Opened The Door To Thier Hearts As Nothing Else Could -- And they Came - - And They Came! -- Some From miles Away - Bringing whatever They Could -- Some brought Vegetables - Some words of Encouragement -- But Mostly Just To Share in Our Suffering

7

I Felt Like Job of Old -- We would Sit in A Circle -- Some would offer words of Sympathy - Some Would Pray - But Most Just Sat in Silence - And Joined in Our Suffering

They Would Come And Touch My Head - Bend over And Look At My Black Swollen Eyes -- And just Slowly Shake Their Heads --

Now - We Became One Through Suffering -- Racial & Cultural Differences Faded Away ---

Now - When I Preached -- People Listened! They Knew I Believed what I was Saying. --

Now -- When I Presented Christ As One Who Also Suffered -- As one Who Knows Their Burdens As The Only one Who Can Lift Thier Burdens --- They Knew I was Speaking From Personal Experience And They Believed!

Yes -- God is Building His Church!

And He Has Chosen To Use Us!

He Wants To Use You -- But you Say -- I Can't Preach -- or I Can't Go To Africa

Did God Ask You To Go To Africa?

Or Did He Ask you To Go To That Neighbor -- Who you Know is Suffering -- And Just Be There

But you Say - I wouldn't Know What To Say --- SomeTimes - you Don't Need To Say AnyThing --- Just Join in Their Suffering

8

Many Times We Do NoThing Because We Don'T Know Where To Begin -- We Are Overwhelmed By The Tremendous needs All Around Us

The STory is ToLd of George Washington Carver -- He was A Black ScientisT Who Lived in The South During The 1800 Hundreds -- George WanTed To Do Big Things -- He wanTed To UnLock All The SecreTs of The Universe - And Share Them WiTh His Poor Neighbors -- So He Asked God To Reveal Them UnTo Him -- BuT God Said No -- ThaTs Too Big For You -- So Then He Asked God To Show him The SecreTs of PlanT growTh -- Again The Answer Was No --- Think Small George So George Asked God jusT To Show him The Value of The peanuT -- Up To ThaT Time Considered A worThLess Weed, -- Now God was Ready To AcT -- And He Revealed To George over 300 Uses For The PeanuT - From There he wenT To The sweeT PoTaToe - The Pecan - CoTTon - And he RevoluTionized The EnTire AgriculTure of The SouTh.

We ALso Need To Learn To "Bloom Where We're PlanTed"

God Has A Plan & Purpose For Each of our Lives As He ConTinues To "BuiLd His Church"

Where Do We Begin? RighT Here -- RighT Now Learn Obedience - DiscipLine - Learn To AccepT Suffering As A TooL of God -- And Rembe[r]er -- God Works BesT -- in our Weakness!

Jesus Learned Obedience Through Suffering! Heb. 5:8

Our missionary friends, Fred and Jan Beam, wrote this letter to our prayer partners about the thugs breaking into our house while they were spending the night.

Do you remember the story of the fiery furnace and the experience of the three Israelites, Shadrach, Meshach, and Abednego? Do you remember the lesson from that event: the Lord is with His children in the midst of even the worst ordeals! That is the joint testimony of the Byler's and the Beam's, and here is the story of our fiery-furnace experience we shared on July 9, 1983.

We were spending the week-end together at Kijabe and had talked 'til 12:30 Friday night (July 8th). We had been asleep less than an hour when 7-9 men, armed with hatchets, pangas (machetes), and rungus (clubs) broke down the front door. They overpowered Darvin and left him bleeding and unconscious on the floor. They also smashed the door to Sandy's bedroom, demanding money and threatening death.

Fred, Janet, and Karen had been sleeping upstairs with the three Byler girls. (Derek Byler and Fred T. Beam were away for the night.) Fred had started downstairs to assist Darvin, but had been driven back by the four men who shouted, "Give us money or we will kill you!" While the thugs had been looting Sandy's bedroom of money, valuables, and clothes, the Beam's were trying to garner some weapons and some plans. They decided their only hope was to scream for help and delay the thieves at the stairs 'til that help came. Their only weapons were prayer and the Name of Jesus, which they used to try to reason with the men to re-consider what they were doing.

However, the thugs didn't like the Beam's tactics, and began bombarding them with all types of missiles -- rocks, bottles, jars, fruit, firewood -- to try to remove them from the stairs and the upstairs window. (Three look-outs had remained outside to prevent anyone from escaping.) Twice the four men inside tried to rush up the stairs, and twice Fred met them half-way with a well-aimed footlocker -- in mid-air! A third assault brought the men to the top step, but the Lord protected Fred, and once again the men tumbled back to ground level.

Things happened quickly, yet the minutes dragged like hours as we prayed for help to come. We know the Lord never sleeps, but how could anyone else sleep through all our noise? Fred had salvaged a thirty-inch rungu from the objects being thrown at him and was using the club to pound the floor -- for more noise -- as well as to intimidate the men. The racket seemed loud enough to wake the dead in the nearby cemetery, but still no sign of help! (We later learned that the gang had already beaten the two night watchmen and broken their arms.) Then the phone began to ring; someone had heard and was trying to call! The gangsters angrily ripped the phone from the wall and threw it up at Fred. But help was on its way -- the twenty-minute screaming marathon had awakened some nurses whose approaching car frightened the men away. Our trauma was over except for the memories and the wounds, both of which needed to be healed.

Many came to express sympathy and concern as well as to help clean up and repair smashed doors and windows. And each one, like those around the fiery furnace, saw evidence of the Lord having been with us through it all. We had been outnumbered, but His presence made all the difference, so that we could say with Elisha, "...they that be with us are more than they that be with them."

Much could be said in the ensuing days about the experience of that night, and many days would pass before the memories of that terror would begin to fade. None of the girls saw the actual attackers; their fearful memories would remain faceless ones. But five year-old Darice recalled the essence of her memories in this brief statement: "Mr. Beam preached a sermon to the bad men on the stairs."

The Beam's and the Byler's were short-term hostages; their attackers, however, were actually the real hostages -- long-term hostages of Satan. They can only be released when they are killed by the police or converted by the power of the Gospel. Pray for their release!

The experience has changed us and given us new priorities and a new appreciation of His Word and His promises:

> The angel of the Lord encampeth round about them that fear Him and delivereth them...He that keepeth thee will not slumber... He preserveth the souls of His saints; He delivereth them out of the hand of the wicked...Whoso putteth his trust in the Lord shall be safe!

Were you a praying part of our victory? On July 8 and July 9 the Byler's and the Beam's were on the AIM prayer sheet; were you praying that the Lord would keep us and provide for all our needs? We <u>need</u> your prayers!

The Bylers
Sandy, Darvin, Nadine, Jolene, Darrel

Kijabe, Kenya, East Africa July, 1983

Sender's name and address Darvin & Sandya Byler
P.O. Box 34, Kijabe
Kenya, E. Africa

AN AIR LETTER SHOULD NOT CONTAIN ANY ENCLOSURE; IF IT DOES IT WILL BE SURCHARGED OR SENT BY ORDINARY MAIL.

Issued by Kenya Posts and Telecommunications Corporation

SECOND FOLD HERE KUNJO LA PILI HAPA

PAR AVION
AEROGRAMME

RHINOCEROS

Everyone in Kijabe would stop for a mid-morning chai break. This tasty hot drink, made with Kenyan black tea, warmed our bodies. Nadine remembers the large chai kettle set over an outside fire that the RVA kitchen staff prepared for everyone at RVA during the mid-morning school break. Darvin remembers that no matter where he was in Kenya, no matter what he was doing, everyone stopped for a chai break mid-morning and mid-afternoon.

Chai

6 cups water, bring to a boil

Add 6 cups milk, simmer

Add 7 teaspoons loose black Kenyan tea

And ¼ cup sugar.

Stir & Dissolve. Strain out tea.

Serve hot.

SECTION THREE: Sermons by Subject and New Testament Sermons Written & Preached by Darvin Byler. Kijabe Missionary Stories.

Therefore God highly exalted Him
and gave Him the name which is above every name,
that at the name of Jesus every knee should bow,
of those in heaven and on earth and under the earth,
and every tongue should confess that Jesus Christ is Lord,
to the glory of God the Father.

Philippians 2:9-11 MEV

"You can forget my name,

but don't forget the Name of Jesus."

Darvin

File folder marked "Sermons". Sermons written and preached by Darvin Byler at supporting and welcoming churches in Pennsylvania. Many examples from Kenya are woven into the messages.

Pharisees were Legalists - -
This man Knew The Law

Jesus Tried To Show Him another Way
We All know the story -
Let me Tell you Another Story - -
Well Known Seminary - Students Studying This Story
Prof. had acted out A present Day man in Need -
Out of 50 Students - 2 Stopped Why?

1. Legalistic Attitudes
What Must We Do?
What are the minimum requirements?
Everyones Looking For The quick Ticket To Heaven
Legalism has great appeal = Muslims
230% growth
Minimum Requirements - Maximim Benifits
What About Us Today?
Oh We Still have our Lists!
We Are Still Asking The question - - What Must we Do
1. You must go To Church Every Sun.
2. You must Attend Love feast
3. You must Be Baptised - Brethren Style
4. You must Pray Before Every meal
5. You must Never wear Slacks

1

Greatest Problem with Legalism -
No Joy! Jesus Said - I came
To give you Life - Abundantly - Joyful

Look Again At The Story -
Who had The Greatest Joy?

The Priest & Levite - Just doing their duty -
There is No Joy in Doing your Duty!

Joy Comes When You Go The Extra Mile
The Samaratin went Away Joyful!

Many people say we "Sacrificed"
We Recieved The Greatest Blessings

2 Self - Worth
The lawyer answered his own question
because previously they had asked Jesus - "what is
the greatest commandment?"
Jesus Gave The Same Answer - Give All
of yourself To God - And Serve your Neighbor
We All want To Serve our neighbor -
So -- What's The Problem?
"I - Can'T" - Self - Worth
Jesus Said iT - Love your neighbor - As you Love
Yourself!

Darvin: "'The Good Samaritan', Luke 10:29-37."

Do you Love yourself?
We Cannot Love others - Untill we have A Proper Self-Love
Christian Counselors Report The #1 Problem Poor Self-Image - Dobson

Many Christians have No Joy Because They're Dragging All Their Past Failures with them -- Love My Neighbor?? you Gotta Be Kidding! - I can't even Love Me!

1. A Proper Relation To God
2. A Proper Opinion of Ourselves
} = Love of Neighbor

Review - How To Be The Good Samaritin

1. Get Rid of Legalistic Attitudes
2. Improve Self-Image

Luke 14-1-6 Legalism = Satans Trap

Pharisees were "Watching" Him - Ha! No Need -
Jesus Healed The Man Right Before Their Eyes!

Today People Are Also "Watching" Legalists in Church!

The man had Dropsy - Perhaps A Sexually
Transmitted Disease - A Discharge of Fluids
Perhaps brought in By Pharisees - To Test Jesus
As He often Did - Jesus Turns it Around
with A Question v3 They were Silent

Their Silence is Revealing - The Law given
For The Good of The People has been Placed
in Opposition To The good of people

V6 - Jesus Asks Another Question -
Ass or Ox - not Son

The Law Instructed Kindness To Animals -
Even on The Sabbath - People Are More
important Than Animals!
They were Doctiinally Correct - But missed The Point
we Can Be Doctrinally Correct - Yet Know Nothing of
Christs Love or Compassion
Application = Balance
Law - Doctrine ← ⊥ → Compassion

Divorce - Poor - Unemployed - Teen Age Pregnancy

(Acts 10)

Good News For All People

Peters DiLeima - A Vision From God

Very Important - Luke gives it Twice

The Vision - verse 5 A Sheet From Heaven
A voice From God - v7
v.8. - But Peter Says NO!

Have you ever Said No To God?

There were All Kinds of Animals & Birds
Some Clean & Some Un Clean

ch 10:28 → God was using This Vision To Prepare
Peter For Something else - Animals = Nations

V-11. Three Men Sent By Cornellius Ch. 10

The Ways of God - 1. Preparing Peter
2. Preparing Cornellius

Pg. 52 → Same with Phillip & Ethiopian

Preparing For Kenya - Preparing Pastor Julious

v15 - As Peter Began To Speak - When God has
Prepared Things - All He needs is
An Obedient Vessel - it wasn't What
Peter Said

Example From Kenya

Darvin: "Preached at Spring Creek Church of the Brethren, 1985-86."

Now Maybe You Think Peter Learned
A valueable Lesson - Temporarily

Gal. 2:11 - Old habits Die Hard
Peer Pressure is very Strong

Before we're Too hard on Peter - What About Us

Pg - 55 - 54
Why Don't we have Any minorities
in our membership?
Alabama

Poor - Homosexuals - Singles - women who Don't
"Stay in Their Place" - Ex Cons - Prostitutes -
Alcoholics - Mentally Retarded - Disabled

Peter was Called on The Carpet

AnyTime You Try To minister To minorities --
Peer Pressure is Strong

v-16-17 But Peter Answered Them - Should I withstand God?

18 - They were Silenced - The only way To
Silence The Critics - is Changed Lives

Social Programs won't work - in Themselves
Good News - For All People - Not Food For All People

11 Water (Jn 7:37-38-39)

A New Appreciation 7/10 of Earth
Can't Live Without - Too Much - Too Little
We Are Blessed

Interesting - Jesus Used Water as Analogy of H-S
Look At Story - Vs 37

37- The Feast = Tabernakles - Booths
Thanksgiving For Harvest
Thatched Roofs - See Stars - Reminder of Past
Priest carried Water From Pool of Siloam

Jesus Stands - If Anyone Thirsty?
Jesus Used Common Things To Teach Spiritual Truth
Kikuya Garden
Were You Ever Thirsty? Sudan - Worms
Come To Me - Jesus The Source
And Drink

Believes in Me - The Messiah - God!

Not Just Mental Assent --
Satan Also Believes!

"Kikuyu Garden"

Kikuyu gardens were planted with no apparent order. Different seeds were planted together in clumps but not in rows. Our yard worker, Francis, would slip some maize seed in Sandy's flowers.

"Sudan Worms"

The people would be so thirsty that they would drink water from puddles. They would get guinea worms that would start growing in their stomachs and move down to their ankles. At their ankles they would emerge through their skin. They would begin wrapping these worms around stick until the long worms came out of their bodies. They would have sores and infections from this. It was urgent for clean water systems to be placed in as many villages as possible.

During the rainy season, rivers would spring up but the rest of the year they were dry river beds.

38- Rivers - Not All The Same - Kenya
Some Rivers Dry Up - (Darice Ocean?)
Some Christians Like That
"Rainy Season Christians"

As Long As Showers of Blessings Fall - -
When Going Gets Hot & Dry - - -
Jesus Promised Life From Within - Not
Dependent on Circumstances.

Some Christians Act Like They Have A Well -
Instead of A River - No Flow!
Well is Fine - Kenya - Sudan
Must Get Water Out!
Electric Pump - Hand Pump - Work
"Pump Christians"
Always Wears A Frown - Busy - Work
Appeals To Many
All Major Religions of World - Works Righteous
Not Christianity PTL! Eph 2:8-9

No one Will Ever Boast in Heaven
A Gift of God!

3 Many Times Water Is Availiable-They Lack Knowledge

Many Places in World - No Rivers - Wells
Must Carry Water - Cans - Buckets - Miles

Some Christians = "Bucket Christians"

Thier View of God is Small | Heb. 5:12 Milk-Meat
God Wants To Give A River - Bucket
God Has More! Eye Has Not Seen - 1 Cor 2:9

Bucket Christians Have A Problem -
Need Someone To Fill Bucket -
Sometimes Easy - U.S. - Radio - TV - Magazines
But Danger! - Is Water Good? - Polluted
Cults - "New Age"

Hospital - Kijabe - Went To Source
Don't Be Bucket Christian

38 - Rivers - Plural God Does Not Give
By Measure - Always OverFlowing!
Jesus Said - I came To Bring Life - Abundantly

Living Water = Greek - Alive & Causing To Live!
Plenty To Give Away
Love - Joy - Peace - Patience - Kindness - Gentle - Self Control

Evangelism = A Cup of Water in Jesus Name!

7

9- H-S NoT Given Because Jesus not Glorified

In Our Lives - Jesus Glorified?

Obedience - Do not Quench The Spirit
Don't Build Dams in River - Bitterness
Unforgiveness

Requirements For Rivers

1. Thirsty - God is NoT Playing Games -
Seek & you Will Find - Knock
Rev. 22: 17

2. Come - Where? Spirit & Bride
Pride? Jesus said - I Am Way - Truth

3. Drink - 10 Glasses A Day - Purify System
10 Min. A Day - in Gods Presence

Gods Promise - Rivers of Living Waters

Rev. 22: 1-5 → Close

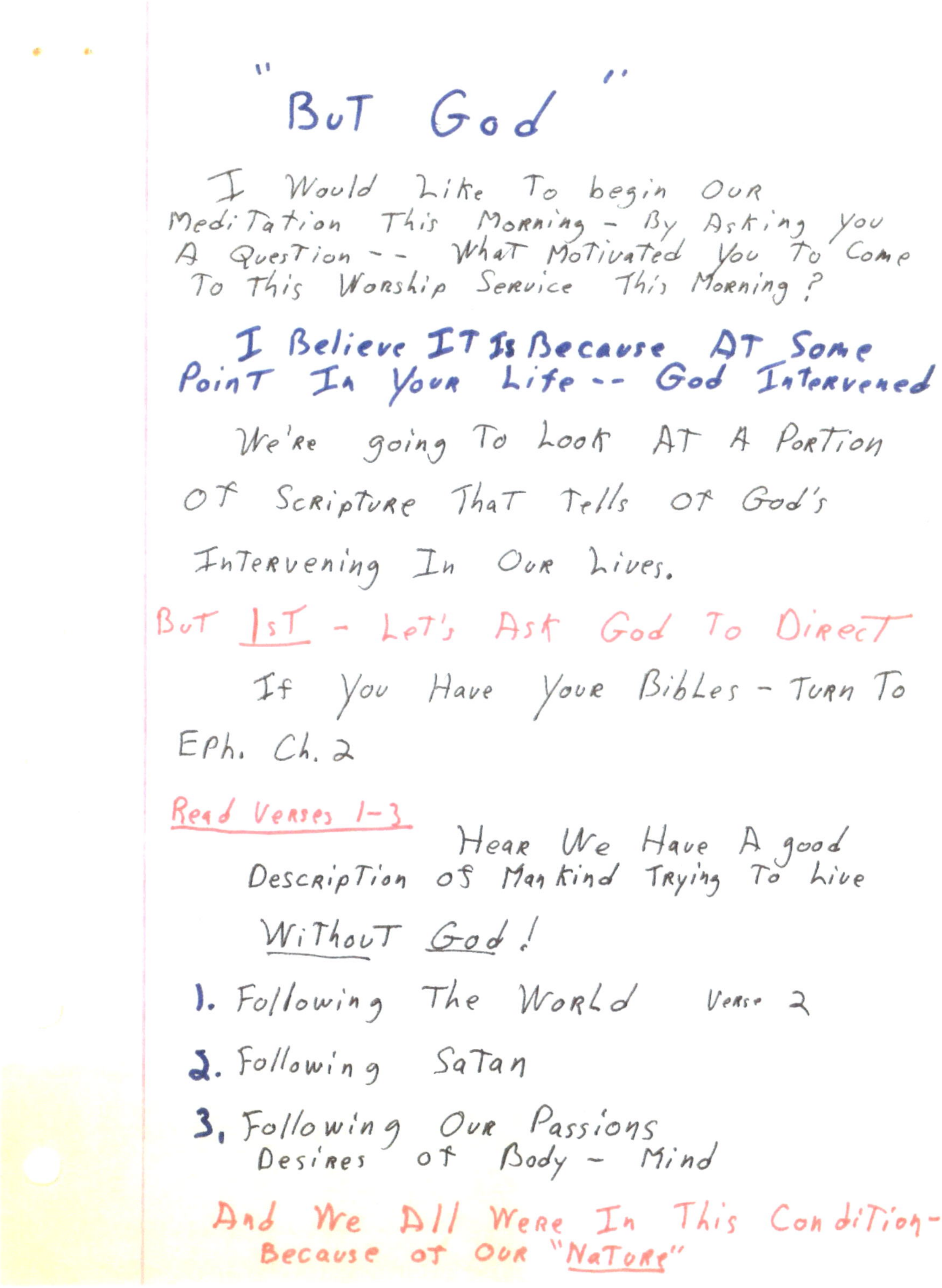
"But God"

I Would Like To begin Our Meditation This Morning - By Asking you A Question -- What Motivated You To Come To This Worship Service This Morning?

I Believe IT Is Because AT Some Point In Your Life -- God Intervened

We're going To Look AT A Portion of Scripture That Tells of God's Intervening In Our Lives.

But 1st - Let's Ask God To Direct

If You Have your Bibles - Turn To Eph. Ch. 2

Read Verses 1-3

Hear We Have A good Description of Mankind Trying To Live Without God!

1. Following The World Verse 2
2. Following Satan
3. Following Our Passions
   Desires of Body - Mind

And We All Were In This Condition - Because of Our "Nature"

Darvin: "Preached at Spring Creek, 1986."

2/

verse 4 But God!

Rich In Mercy – Unmerited Favor

Love

verse 5 Even When We Were Dead = (Spiritually)
(The Wages of Sin Is Death) Rom. 6:23

We Were All Guilty – Because of Our
Trespases = Sin

But God Hath Quickened Us – K.J.

Quickened = Made Alive – Ressurected

With Christ!

How? – Through Faith In Christ

verse 8 A gift of God

Through The Ressurection Power of
Christ – God Has Joined Us Together
With Him

Hence verse 6 Our Spiritual Position –

Seated Together With Christ! Wow

Where? – At God's Right Hand!

Look At Ch. 1:20

3/

This Is Literal - Jesus Is Seated
Some Where In The Heavenlies --
At God's Right Hand --
Interceeding For Us. ~~[illegible]~~ (Rom 8:34)
Also - It Is A Picture of
Someone Who Has Completed their
Work -- Jesus Said "It is Finished"

Verse 10 Workmanship = Greek = Poiēma
From Which The English Word Poem Is Derived
Literally = "We Are Gods Poem"
Isn't that Beautiful?
God Has Raised You From The Dead
To Shape You Into A Lovely
Poem -- So That The World Will
Read You -- And Glorify Him!
Now Maybe You Don't Particularly Feel
Very Lovely This Morning - Maybe You
Can't See Yourself As A Lovely Poem --

4

That's O.K. -- Because God Does Not See Us As We See Ourselves

1. We See Ourselves As Defeated

God Says We Are More Than Conquers - Victorious

2. We See Ourselves As Poor

God Says We're Rich - He's Given Us All The Riches of Christ

3. We See Ourselves Stuck On Planet Earth Untill We Die

God Says We're Already Sitting In Heavenly Places!

You See God Has The Ability To See The End Product!

He Sees Our Potential

We Must Stop Arguing With God -- And Start Cooperating

God Is Not Finished Yet!

He Will Make You Into A Lovely Poem -- If You Will Let Him

5

This Morning - How We Praise God
For Taking That First Step -- For
Loving Us - When We Were Unloveable
And Making It Possible To Be
Reconciled To God.

This Morning You're Probably Here
Because Somewhere - Some Time - God
Intervened In Your Life -- You Had
A "But God" Experience

Or --- It's Possible That God Has
Led You Here This Morning So That
You Might Have That Opportunity.

If You've Never Seen Your Need of A
Saviour Before -- If You've Never Experienced
The Grace of A Loving God -- If You've
Never Met Jesus Christ - And Trusted
Him As Your Saviour - I Would Be Happy
To Introduce You To Him At The Close
Of This Service

Hymn 453

Self-Denial

No one Wants To Hear About Self-Denial -
In our World of Instant gratification -
Every Thing Is Geared To Meeting Our Wants
NOW!
Even Among Christians - we're Told That
God Wants Us To Have All our Wants
And Desires -- After All He promised Us
A Full & Abundant Life Didn't He?

1st - I Believe Theres A Difference Between
Our Wants & our Needs --- 2nd When God
Speaks About The Abundant Life I'm Not
So Sure He's Talking About Material Abundance

Let's Look At The Words of Jesus - Lu 9:23

Untill We Deal With Self - And Learn
To Deny Our Selfish Natures - We Will Not Be
Fruitful For The Lord

Martin Luther Said - I Am More Afraid of My
own Heart Than of The Pope & All His
Cardinals!

2/ Gal 2:20

The Un Crucified Self Stains & Mars our Service To The Lord.

There Is A great Difference Between Realizing On That Cross He Was Crucified For Me --- And on That Cross I Am Crucified With Him.

The First Brings Deliverance From Sins Condemnation -- The second Brings Deliverance From Sins Power! Rom 6:6

Many Christians Don't Know This & Have Never Experienced IT!

As Followers of Christ our Goal -- Rom 8:29 – To Be Conformed To Him

How Strange - A Cross Bearing Christ, Leading A Band of Self-Indulging Followers! -- Who Shrink from The least Bit of Suffering!

Christ - our Example Suffered Greatly & Whenever The example of Christ Is presented To Us In Scripture For Our Imitation - IT Is His Example of Suffering!

3/ Phil 2:5 - I Pet 2:20 - 4:1 - 4:12

But you May Say Why Do We Have To Suffer ?

The Answer Is Found In Heb. 5:8-9

If Jesus Needed To Suffer To Learn Obedience - What About Us ?

God Needs Obedient Servants - And I'm Convinced He Allows Suffering To Come Into Our Lives To Teach Us Obedience!

In Jo 12:24 We Have Another Principle given For Productive, Fruitful Lives.

A Principle For Bearing Fruit - We Must First Die To Self

Jim Elliot - He is No Fool who gives What He Cannot Keep - To gain what He Cannot Lose.

Today Many Are Crying out To God For Spiritual Power & gifts -- But For God To Give Spiritual Power To Those Who Have Not Died To Self -- Would only Feed Their Vanity

4/ Today IT is The "In" Thing To Be "Born Again" - We Have Many Proponents Of "Cheap" Grace - ThaT Is JusT Believe In Jesus -- you Don't Have To Change your Life sTyle give Up Any Thing - SeperaTe From The World - & Certainly you Never Have To Suffer!

Rom 8:16-17 - Phil 3:7-10

We Make The Cross ATTracTive - people wear Large Crucifixes Around Their Necks eTc -

BuT In RealiTy - The Cross Was Horrible - Ugly & Shameful

Isaiah - 53 - He Was BeaTen InTo A Bloodied Pulp He Was Naked - They Couldn't Even Look AT Him!

Yes We Should Glory In The Cross -- BuT LeTs Never ForgeT IT Was Never ATTracTive!

Our SalvaTion Came AT A Terrible Price - IT is NoT Cheap

And We Are Called Upon To Take Up Our Cross Also - Daily -- To Deny Ourselves, & Follow Him.

Closing Hymn - Jesus Keep Me Near The Cross 452

"Suffering"

Pauls Sufferings - 2 COR. 1:8 - 11:24

Does God "Allow" Suffering?

Why? - 1 PeT. 1:6 Jm. 1:2

Since Job - We Have NoT UndersTood Gods
Ways

FruiT of SpiriT - Love - Joy - Peace - Patience -
Self - ConTrol

Suffering A Major Tool - Why?

You will Learn More In A momenT of
Adversity - Than in A LifeTime of Tranquillity

God Whispers in Our Pleasures - Shouts
in Our Pain!

Iraq - Cry out To God

We Have BoughT The Worlds View - If You Are
"Good" - God will Bless

Ps 73

2

17. Untill I went Into Gods Sanctuary
To Understand The Mind Of God
God is Not Sadistic - Love
Disciplines For Our Good
Heb 12: 3-12

Now Comes The Real Problem -
We All Know These Things - "Head Knowledge"
But Then Along Comes Something Personal
And our Heart Says Why God ? !

Read Letter -

Back To 2 Cor. - Paul Gives 3 Practical
Applications For Sufferings

Peace - Gods & Ours

Worlds

Definition - A State of Mental or Physical Tranquility - 2. The Absence of Strife or Conflict

Bible - Jo 14:27

Not The Worlds Peace

The Best The World Can Offer is The Absence of Conflict -

Jesus offers Peace in The Midst of Conflict

HOW?

By Giving Us His Peace - Its Gods!

God is Never Surprised - Afraid - Worried

Phil 4:4 - Rejoice - Praise - God Inhabits The Praises of His People.

You Don't Have To Feel Good To Praise God. Just Praise Him For Who He IS!

6 - Don't Dwell on Your Anxieties - Take IT To The Lord - With Thanksgiving

2

7 Peace of God - NOT OURS
Shall Keep - or Guard

Greek = Phroureo - A Military Term
meaning to Guard or garrison -

Gods Peace stands Guard over our
hearts & minds - The inner man

Yes - even our Emotions

Isn't That Good Theology?

IT's one Thing To Theorize -
Another To Live IT - - Especially When
your World Comes Apart

Confession - I'm A Pessemist!
Ask Sandy
I Belive in Murphy's Law!

Bad Things Do Happen To Good People

Just Because We're Christian - Does
NoT Spare Us

3

In Fact - That Very Well May Be
Why Christians Have So Much Trouble

This is Not A New Phenomonom

1 Pet 4:12 - Beloved - Do Not Be Surprised

All Who Live Godly Shall
2 Tim 3:12 Suffer WRIGHT (Pg. 170) Job
David
Why? Why? Isaiah

The Bible Tells Us - Again & Again
That Gods Purpose in Each of our Lives
is To Conform Us Into The Likeness of
Jesus - 2 Cor 3:18 From Glory To Glory

Is 53:3 Jesus Was Aquainted With Suffering
2, Vance Havner - Pg. 49
1, Lanny Arensen

God Whispers in ~~The Good Times~~ OUR PLeasure
But Shouts in our Pain!

3, Dr. Norman Wright = Front Cover

Pg. 166 --- Pg -171

4 Hymn – # 334
When Peace Like A River

Peace – Don't Settle For A Cheap Imitation

The Best The World Can Offer is To Remove You From The Conflict

Experience Real Peace – From The Prince of Peace

Listen To His Promises –

Come unto Me All Who Are Weary & Heavy Laden & I will Give you Rest – Take My yoke Upon you & Learn From Me – For I Am Gentle & Lowly in Heart & you will Find Rest For Your Souls

Eph. 2:13 But Now in Christ Jesus you Who were once Far off Have Been Brought Near in The Blood of Christ – For He IS Our Peace – who Has Made us Both One

Peace I Leave With You --
My Peace I Give To you -- Not As The World Gives – Let Not your Hearts Be Troubled Neither Let Them Be Afraid --
Be of Good Cheer – For I Have Overcome The World

MeaT Loaf - Burp - Thanks To Cooks

Encouraged By This MeeTing

Men of Spring Creek - give Up SaT Morn.!

Need Men Who Will Take A STand For ChrisT

Marines - Looking For A Few Good Men - -

God Also is Looking 2 Chron 16:9

God Has Always Called Men To STand For Him

Elijah - How Long Will you HalT BeTween Two Opinions?

If The Lord is God Follow Him!

PoliTicians - Wavering

Maybe you Say I'm No Elijah!

A Man Who Fails - is NoT A Failure!

All Have Sinned - None RighTeous

God is NoT InTeresTed in PasT - FuTure!

Promises BeauTy - For Ashes

God Allows Us To Fail - To Teach Us

When We Are Weak - God is STrong

Failure Does NoT Keep Us From STanding For God

Darvin: "Given (taught) to the Men's Fellowship at Spring Creek Church of the Brethren."

Greatest Hindrance To Standing
For Christ – A Clear Conscience

We Allow Past Failures –
To Silence Our Witness

Paul = Example – Persecuted Christians
Yet Was Able To Say –
I Stand Before God And Men –
With A Clear Conscience –– How?
chief of Sinners
Confess Sin – Hard For Men
Ego
I.R.S. Story = Try To Bargain With God

David Gives Us A Good Example
Ps. 51 My Sin – Own It

Confession – Washing – New Heart
Restoration – Beauty For Ashes

V13 – Then I will Teach Sinners
Clear Conscience

A Man Who Fails is Not A Failure!
God is Looking For Men – With Courage
To Confess Sin – Clear Conscience – Stand For Christ

(Communication)

Most Difficult Area For Me
Married 31 Years - Still Learning

Not Talking About Public Speaking --
Sharing our Feelings

Most Men Have Difficulty Expressing Feelings

Most Women Communicate Feelings Naturally
Examp. - 2 Women go Out For Lunch - O.K.
2 Men ? ... why ?

New Study - Women Speak Twice As Many Words

Why Do Men Have So Much Difficulty ?

1. They Have Few Models - Strong Silent Type

2. Not Feeling Oriented
Example - Couple No Children - Dog - Wife went on Trip - Called Home - Hows our Dog ?
Husband - Dog got on Roof - Fell - Died Wife - Why Can't you Be Considerate of Feelings ? - Gradually - 1st Call - Dog on Roof
2nd Call - Dog Fell - 3rd Call - Dog Died
Wife - By The way Hows My Mother ?
Husband - She's on The Roof

What Can We Do?

1. Recognize The Problem - Don't Withdraw!
   Prov. 18:21 - The Tongue has The Power of Life & Death And Those who Love it will eat its Fruit.
   Jms 3:5-8

2. Commit Ourselves To Learn How To Communicate
   Not just Words - Feelings - Heart

3. Learn To Listen
   Prov. 18:13 - He who Answers before Listening - That is his Folly And Shame

4. Do Not Respond in Haste
   Prov. 29:20 - Do you See A man who Speaks in Haste? There is More Hope For A Fool - Than For Him

5. Learn To Encourage One Another With Words
   Prov. 15:23 - A man Finds Joy in giving An Apt Reply - How Good is A Timely Word!

"The image of God", we are the same inside even though we may look different on the outside.

Why Praise

1. God Desires our Praise
   Jo 4:23 - The Father seeketh such to worship Him | Lords Prayer - "Hallowed" Be Thy name
2. God Deserves our Praise
   1 Pet 2:9 A natural Response To A Loving God - Jesus said if the People Didn't Praise - The Rocks would cry out
3. God Commands our Praise -
   Ps. 150 - Heb. 13:15 1st of Ten Command.
4. God Inhabits The Praises of His People
   Ps. 22:3 Where 2 or 3 Are Gathered in His
5. Praise Releases The Power of God
   2 Chron. 16:9 Joshua - Jehosaphat - David - Paul & Silas
6. Praise gives us A Thankful Spirit
   Praise is A Function of our Spirit - Our Spirit + Gods Spirit
   We Are Created in The Image of God (Kenya)

How To Praise

1. Singing - Eph. 4:18-19 All The Psalms
2. Playing Musical Instruments Ps. 150
3. Dancing ? - David
4. Lifting Holy hands Ps. 28:2 - 63:4 - 119:48 134 - 141
   (Ex. Boy) Lamen. 2:19 I Tim. 2:8 Heb. 12:12
5. Prayer - in The Spirit
   Eph. 6:18 - Rom 8:26 Conversational Prayer
   Close

(The Emmaus Road)

The Emmaeus Road

Doctors Are Now Calling iT "One of The Best Forms of Exercise"
"A great Way To Relieve STress & Clear The Mind"

Thousands of Americans Are Rediscovering The Theraputic Benifits of Walking!

For The Two Men in our Scripture Lesson This Morning - A means of Transportation

They were Going To Emmaus -

IT was The 1ST Day of The Week -
3 Days After Crucifixation -

They were Sad - Depressed - Defeated

Jesus, Their Leader - Teacher Had Been Put To Death - IT was Over -

They were Going Home - - -

V 13 Follow in Your Bibles

V14 - Many Things STill Puzzeled Them
Walking Slows The Pace of Life

15 - The Risen Lord Joins Them!

Jesus Wants To Come Along Side of Us
& Walk with us - in our Darkest Hour

16 - Why Could They Not Recognize Him
Glorified Body?

I Cor. 15:35

17 - Sometimes We Can't See The Forest For
The Trees! "More Than Conquerers"
Should Have Been Rejoicing!

18-19 Jesus Death Caused Quite A Stir

21 - We Had Hoped That He Was - Messiah

They were Blinded To Gods Plan --
By Their Own Agenda - Missionary - Bible School

22-25 Slow To Believe - Not The Women -
Not The Apostles - Nor The Angels

But The Prophets = Written Word!

3

26-27 - Beginning With Moses - What?

Today Bible Scholars Argue Over
Who Wrote Gen - Ex - Lev. - Num - Deut.

Jesus Had No Such Problem!
Things Concerning Himself - in Gen.?
What A Great Session! yes!

28-29 - If We Would Have Jesus Stay - -
Need To Ask

30 - In The Breaking of Bread - Ministry
31 New Windsor - Work Camps - Louise & Phylis
Our Eyes Will Also Be Opened

32 - When is The Last Time Your Heart
Burned Within You - As You Have
Recieved Insight & Teaching From Jesus?
Scripture is Alive!
33 - When We See The Risen Christ - We Will
Not Be Able To Keep it To Ourselves

36 - Jesus Made Many Appearances After Ressurection

Paul Says To More Than 500 People
At The Same Time

4

37-42 Again A Unique Body

44- Reaffirms - Moses - Prophets - Psalms

45- We Cannot Fully Comprehend The Scriptures - Without Divine Help!

Minds Get Polluted By World - Need Opened!

47- Repentence & Forgiveness - Preached

I Hope You're All Going To Take A Walk This Week --
And I **Know** That Jesus Will Walk Along With You

When We Walk With The Lord - in The Light of His Word - What A Glory He Sheds on our way - While We Do His Good Will - He Abides With Us Still - And With All Who Will Trust & Obey

Stand & Sing Hymn # 485

(Amazing Grace)

Amazing Grace

Best Loved Hymn of All Time
Christian - Secular
TV Show - Rock Concert-London

People Identify with This Hymn
As With Many Hymns - A Fascinating Story Behind

Written By John Newton 1779
Born in England
Son of A Sea Captain

Soon Learned The Vile Debauchery of A Sailors Life

In His Own Words - Proud - Blasphemous

2Pet 2:14 - Eyes Full of Adultery, insatiable For Sin

If All That Wasn't Bad Enough -
He Sank To The Lowest Depths -
Trading in Human Cargo
Captain of A Slave Ship

It was From Such A Life -

God Brought Forth This Testimony of Grace

— God is in The Business of Changing Lives !

Eph. 2:10 - We Are Gods - Poem

John NewTon - Rebel - ATheist
Violent Blasphemer - Slave Trader

Saved By The Grace of God

Now A Minister of The Gospel

Is Moved To PuT Words To Feelings

Open your Hymnals # ~~143~~ 433

Amazing - To John NewTon - ThaT God --
Holy - RighTeous - Ruler of Unieverse
Would offer His Grace

Ps 8:3-4

Grace - UnmeriTed Favor of God
Eph. 2:8-9

How SweeT The Sound - To Those Who Are
Being Saved - Foolishness To World

Irving BaTdorf - An IrraTional STep - To Break
The Cycle of HaTred - Anger - Murder

"Ever been lost?" I've been lost in the dark in the mountains during a hunting trip.

That Saved A Wretch — Some People Don't Like That Term

New Hymnal Sets it Right
Old Hymnal — Wrong!

Agree With God — All Have Sinned
Jer 17:9 — Heart is Deceitful — Desperately Wicked
Paul Before Saved — Religious Pharisee "Good"

After — Wretched Man — Who Will Save Me?
(Like Laodiceans)
Do Not Know You Are Wretched?
Rev 3:17

Lost – Found –
Ever Been Lost? (Hunting)

Eph. 2:3 – All Lost

4 – But God Found Us!

Blind – Spiritually — Cannot See The Things of God – Untill – Spirit of God Controlls

See – Powerful Emotions

Sing Together – Verse 1

I

Verse 2

'Twas Grace That Taught My Heart
To Fear

Grace Teaches Us About God!

Prov. 1:7 - The Fear of The Lord -
Beginning of Wisdom

Fear = Reverence - Awe

Same Grace - Shows God Loves Us
Has Provided A Way Into His Presence

How Precious Did That Grace Appear
The Hour I 1st Believed - Think Back To That Time + Place you Trusted Christ

John Newton Never Forgot The
Joy of Salvation - Don't Allow Satan
To Steal your Joy!

Sing Verse 2

2

Verse 3

Through Many Dangers - Toils - Snares

John NewTon - STorms AT Sea
MuniTiny

Toils - Hum Drum of Every day Living

Snares - Traps!

Grace - Will Lead Me Home

Paul PuTs IT This Way Rom 8:37

Grace Will Lead Us Home

Sing Verse 3

6

Verse 6 - When We've Been There 10,000 Years
When Time is No More

We Will Shine Like Angels

Rev 21:23

We've No Less Days -

Rev 5:11 → To Sing His Praise

For John NewTon His Words
Are Now ReaLiTy As He Joins
That Heavenly Throng

Sing Verse 6

John NewTon PasTored Churches AT OLney
& London From 1779 - 1807 WriTing
Numerous Hymns & Books

He Joined Together With {John WesLey & William WiLberForce}
in 1785 To PuT An End To EngLands SLave Trade

AT Age 82 John NewTon Died in 1807

He was hardly able to speak. William Jay leaned over the bed to catch his last words.

Newton whispered: 'My memory is nearly gone. But I remember two things: That I am a great sinner . . .'

He paused for breath. '. . . And that Christ – *is a great Saviour*!'

"Tribalism" Your tribe came before anything else, even before Christians and churches.

!!

What, in A Name?

Introduce Myself -

"Tell Them Who you Are" - Joe

Today is The Day of Looking After #1 - I - Me - Mine

Everybodys Trying To Make A Name For Themselves

Same As Gen. 11:4 -

God Had Just Destroyed The Earth Because of Sin -- yet There is No Mention of God

Today Very Few People Give God His Rightful Place In our Lives - We can Take Care of Ourselves!

In Africa This Manifests Itself As - Tribalism

Well - As A Builder - I had To Make A Name For Myself

Prov 22:1 - A Good Name is To Be Chosen Rather Than Great Riches

Darvin: "Preached at Sherk's Church, 1985-86."

2

There's Nothing Wrong With Establishing
A Good Name = Honesty – Integrity --

But As A Christian – I Found Increasing
Conflict – Whose Name was I going To
Promote ?

Mine --- Jesus

His Name Chosen By God – Angel Declared AT
Birth – you shall Call His Name Jesus =
Imanuel – God With Us
Saviour – Redeemer – Lord

When I Made Him Lord = He Began
To Teach His Ways --

If you want To Be Great – (A Name) --
Humble yourself And Be A Servant !

If you want Money – give iT Away !

Gods Ways – Are NoT our Ways

God Says – IT you want your Name in My
Book – you Must Exchange iT For Jesus

AcTs 4:12 – There is No OTher Name given
under Heaven Whereby We Must Be Saved

Jim ElliOT – He is No Fool who gives what He CannoT
Keep (His Life) – To gain what He cannoT Lose
(eternal Life)

2

IT wasn'T Long Before We Began Sensing Gods Call To Missions

STop-Making A Name For Yourself -

STarT-Making A Name For Jesus

As We Travel in Kenya - Whats your Name? What Tribe Are you From? = ChrisT-Tribe

This Morning - I Don'T Know your Name -- Are you Busy Making A Name For Yourself?

When I Leave Here - You Can ForgeT My Name

BuT Don'T ForgeT The Name of Jesus

God Says in Phil 2:10 -- There Will Come A Day - When Everyone In The World will Know The Name of Jesus

Every Knee Shall Bow - Tongue Confess

BeTTer To Humble Yourself Now --- And Know Him As Lord ---

than To Know Him As Judge

Life Stress – ...

Jesus – Man of Compassion

Funerals – Rank Among Top 3 Events in Life
Birth – Marriage – Death
Emotional – Stressful – Thought Provoking

This Funeral was Different – The only Son – of Widow
No Hope! Jews & Heathen
Jesus had Compassion = Quot. Pg. 39

Compassion = Allowing God To Break your Heart – with The Things That Break His Heart
Compassion – Comes From God
Several Facts, – 1. No one Asked Jesus To Intercede
2. No one Excercised Their "Faith"
3. The Act itself was Simple – young Man Arise
4. The main Benificiary was The Mother – The man would merely Die Again

The Response – 1. Fear – Awe
2. Glorified God
When God Acts in Power – Super natural Events
it is To Draw People To Himself
TesTimonies ImporTant
Whats Happening in your Life? Now! Today!

What is God Doing?

Testing = For Benifit of Student - Not Teacher
↑God is Teacher

Testing - Sun on film -
God is looking for the Gold - not the junk

Abraham - was Tested By God - because he was obedient

Lot - was Tested By the World - - because he was disobedient - compromised

Who is Testing You ?

We Don't Like Testing → Pain - Fire [I Pet 1:6-7]

Expositor Pg. 44 = The Last Supper is Over

Lessons in Humility - Calm Before Storm

Pg. 45 = The Importance of Prayer

Jesus needed This Time -
The Disciples needed it   Peter V:-31
We need it Also -
Example - Break in [July 8 - 9]

V-44 - Sleeping For Sorrow ??

MT. 26 - 12 Legions of Angels = 70,000   [Eph 6:11-12]

Jn. 18 - Peter Was Ready For Wrong Battle !
Not Enough Prayer !
II Cor. 10:4

Like There [illegible] Good Kings,
Power Corrupts

Ch 18 - Hezekiah son of Ahaz

V2 - His Mother Abijah 2 Chro 29:1
Isa. 36:
A Godly Influence

5 - None Like Him Since Solomon!

He Restored The Levites & Priests
Passover - 2 Ch. 30:26

13 - Trouble - Why?

2 Cor 1 ← Why Do Bad Things Happen To Good People?

Disciples - Why Was This Man Born Blind?

God Will Use This Situation
To Demonstrate His Power

Hezekiah Trusted in God - But
Did His Part - Prepared For War
Used His Head - Tried To Apease With Gold

17 13 years Between Verse 13 & 17

TarTan = Field Marshal

Rabsaris = Head of Palace Guard

Rabshakeh = Chief Cup Bearer

18 Called For The King -
He Sent 3 of Equal Rank - Smart!

19-25 - Ridicule & Intimidation

26 - Speak in Aramaic

28 - Called To The People

36-37

Ch 19

Now We See What This Man
is Made of.!

1 Humbles Himself
Came Before The Lord - Prayed

2 Ch. 7:14 If My People...

—

2- Sent For Isaiah

Isaiah Sends A Word of Hope

7 God Will Deliver You

Rumor = King of Ethiopia is Coming

9 Sends A Letter

14 - Hezekiah Rightly Determined That This Was An Attack on God

When We Are Attacked Because We're Christian - Turn it over To The Lord

Blessed Are You - When Men Revile You Great is Your Reward in Heaven

15-19 Prayer Short & To The Point

A Prayer of Faith

Save Us - For Thy Glory

4

20 Quick Answer

22 Mocked

25 God Was In Charge All Along

27-28 - They Are Finnished

32 -
34 - God is Able To Defend Himself!

35

Foot Note - A Time To Die

Hezekiah Had No Son
Wept Bitterly - Begged God

Manasseh - Undid Every Thing Hezekiah Had Done

Put Isaiah To Death!
Friends & Co Workers - Amp. Pg. 802

SomeTimes God Gives Us What We Want -
Rom. 1 Sends Leanness To our Soul Ps 106:15

Plagues - Over 9 Months

Magicians - Highly Educated - Priestly
Leaders
A Great Civilization - Advanced
in Human Reasoning

Ch. 8:25 Egyptians = Civilized

Jews - A "Bloody" Religion

Redemption - Wholly of God
Egypt - A Type of The World
Pharaoh - A Type of Satan - Prince of World
Moses - A Type of Christ
Blood - The purchase Price

How Do Intelligent People Come To
worship Frogs?

World - Worships The Creation Rather
Than The Creator Rom 1:18

"Hardened"

The Usual Translations obscure The Fact That It is Always Clearly STated when, IT was God who Did The Hardening, And when IT was Pharaoh who Hardened His own Heart. God Hardens Only Those Who Begin Hardening Themselves.

Rom Ch 1

Who is The Lord?

Egyptians Had Many Gods

Each Plague Had A Relationship To one of Egypts Gods

1. Nile - Was Worshiped
Turned Rotten

2. Frog - God of Fertility

3. Seth - God of Earth - Lice - gnats

4. Gods of Fire + Water Unable To Protect From Hail or Locusts

5. Ra - Sun God - Could Not overcome The Blanket of Darkness

(Jesus – fully God)

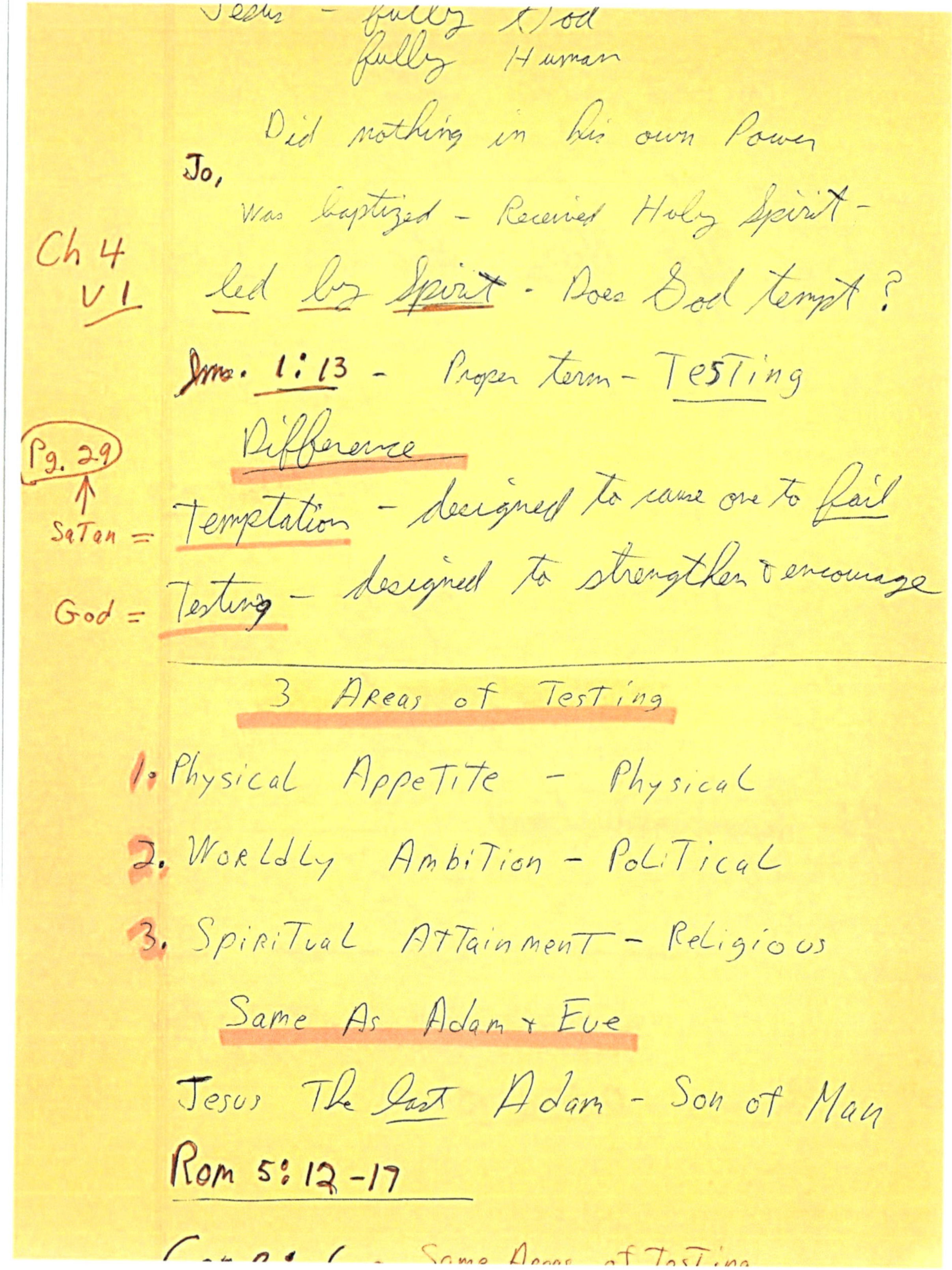

Jesus - fully God
fully Human

Did nothing in his own Power

So,
Was baptized - Received Holy Spirit -

Ch 4
V 1
led by Spirit - Does God tempt?

Jms. 1:13 - Proper term - Testing

Pg. 29
Difference

Satan = Temptation - designed to cause one to fail

God = Testing - designed to strengthen & encourage

3 Areas of Testing

1. Physical Appetite - Physical
2. Worldly Ambition - Political
3. Spiritual Attainment - Religious

Same As Adam + Eve

Jesus The last Adam - Son of Man

Rom 5:12-17

(Gen. 3:6 Same areas of testing)

V3 If you Are The Son of God

The Greek condition implies that Satan knew who Jesus was – even assumed that he had the power to turn stones into bread

U.S. News – Who Was Jesus?

What is wrong with turning stones to bread?

Did not Jesus later turn Water into Wine?

The Answer from Jesus Reply – Deut 8:3

Jesus gives us an example –

Don't rely on own strength or Wisdom ––
SCRIPTURE!

V5 Political Power

This implies that Satan has control of all The Kingdoms – Political structures – Governments?

Government is ordained by God = Rom ?

Answer Deut 6:13

09 Quarterly Pg 30 - A Taunt

The Pinnacle of Temple

Ps. 91-11-12

Satan also quotes scripture -
but he twists it to his own advantage -

He left some out! Do We?

To Keep Thee In ALL Thy Ways

God does not promise to keep his servants in
an act of foolishness - But only when
we are walking in God's ways

Answer Deut 6:16

13 Does Satan ever quit? No!
A more opportune time

Many great Christian leaders have fallen in
recent years - Why?

14 - Succesful Testing Results in
POWER!

Pg 32 An Encouragement To Us As
We Experience Testing & Temptation

When we walk with the Lord, In the light of His word.
What a glory He sheds on our way.' While we do His good will,
He abides with us still, And with all who will trust and obey.
Trust and obey, for there's no other way
To be happy in Jesus, but to trust and obey.

One Sunday evening, not long ago, our song leader, Pat Haldeman, led us in this song, and she emphaized the fact that we sing these songs, YeT We Don'T really listen to the words,- so I looked closely at the words,- and suddenly it ~~hit me~~ START → - TRUST AND OBEY - there's no other way to be happy in Jesus,
THERE'S no other way to grow as a Christian,
THERE'S no other way to fullfill Gods purpose in our lives,
THERE IS NO OTHER WAY!
Yet it is evident to me that we as Christians, are determined to try any other way, than Trust and obedience.

What is it about those two words that we don't like?

Let's look first at this word trust. To trust someone or something means to have faith in, to have confidence, in.

I believe one of the reasons we have so much difficulty in learning to trust, is because we live in an age of skepticism. Most people are very reluctant to take anything at face value, and we have been progeamed to question everything.

The prevelant thinking today is-that there are no absolutes, nothing seems to be trustworthy or reliable.

And one of the reasons we think that way is,-because all around us, we're constantly being lied to, we're being put on,- by phony advertisers, telling us that their product is reliable, but we find out otherwise, by government officials, and others in authority.
We become skeptical, almost daily we read about some respected person, someone we thought could be trusted, exposed as just another hypocrite.

Then we have an encounter with God, and He says to us, "trust me,"
and right away, - we say, - well prove yourself to me first,
then I'll trust you!

And then he gives us a whole series of rediculous principles to follow,
that we just know are not going to work, and our minds rebell.

For instance, everyone knows that the way to increase your financial
assets, is to invest wisely in stocks and bonds and so forth,

- - but God says no - - -

- - - the way to increase your assets is to give it away!

We say that if you want to be a leader, - a great man, you must work
yourself into a position of authority, a president, or Chairman of the Board -

- - - but God Says No

- - - if you want to be great - - - - be the servant of all.

We say if you want to be happy - - - then discover the desires of
your heart and do them - - - eaT - DRINK & Be MeRRY

- - - but God says, - if you want to be happy - -

- - you must die to self - - if you would find your life, - you must
lose it.

And so we can see very clearly, that Gods thoughts are not our thoughts,
in fact, he tells us that in Is. 55:8 "For my thoughts are not your thoughts,
neither are your ways my ways, says the lord."

and that makes it difficult for us to trust Him,

because we'd like to understand these things before we do them,

But God says no, - - my requirement is that first you have faith, - -

and then I'll give understanding! Have you Experience That

for he tells us in Prov. 3:5 "Trust in the Lord with all thine heart
and lean not unto thine own understanding."

GOD Says --- without faith it is impossible to please him, Hebrews 11: 6
And that makes it very difficult for the intellecual mind.

For we find that God has made foolish the wisdom of this world. In I Cor 1: 21 we read this "Has not God made follish the wisdom of the world, for since in the wisdom of God, the world did not know God through wisdom, it pleased God through the folly of what we preach, to save those who believe."

YOU WILL NEVER COME TO KNOW GOD THROUGH YOUR INTELLECT! your Mind

GOD IS SPIRIT,- AND WE MUST COME TO KNOW HIM IN AND THROUGH OUR SPIRITS.

3 PARTS - Body - SOUL - SPIRIT ROM 8: 16 - God's SPIRIT - Bearing Wittness WITH OUR SPIRIT

And what is faith?

Is it blind obedience?

Do we just launch out into the dark? NO!

God does not want blind obedience.

For we find in Prov. 3: 6 "If we will acknowledge him in all our ways, HE will direct our path."

But first we must acknowledge him!

"For whoever would come to God must believe that he is, and that he is a rewarder of those who diligently seek him." Hebrews 11: 6

And so the first step is up to us,

By a definite exercise of faith, we acknowledge God as God.

What then is faith?- and how do we receive it?

Let's turn to Hebrews 11 and find out . . . . (verse 1) . . .

Now how do we get assurance? How do we get conviction of things not seen

The Bible tells us that the moment we place our complete trust in the Lord Jesus Christ, and accept his finished work at Calvary as full payment for our sins, - - - and we confess this with our mouth, - - and believe (TRUST In - Rely) it in our heart, -- God sends the Holy Spirit to take up residence in our hearts, and his Spirit, bearing witness with our spirit, gives us assurance and conviction of things not seen. How Does This Work?

Look at verse 3. . . . . . Can I prove to you that the world was created in 6 days? - - No, but I believe it by faith, - - and God gives me conviction of things not seen, - - and I know in my heart that it was so.

And then it goes on to list some of the men and women of faith down through history, - who have stepped out in faith, and the writer makes it clear that because of their faith they were acceptable to God.

Continuing with verse 4 . . To - 32 . . .

Long Pause

In all 3 gospels we find these words of Jesus - whoever does not have faith like a little child, - shall not enter the kingdom of heaven.

That's a very humiliating thought for such enlightened, intelligent people as 2oth century Americans.

Well, - you know how gulliable a little child is!

He believes anything you tell him !

Did Jesus really mean that? ? ? I'm afraid so. .

Jesus says we must be like that little child.

And just as that little child takes his mothers hand, and takes those first faltering steps, - - so too we must place our hand in Gods hand - - and start out one step at a time, gaining confidence with each step until we grow to mature manhood, - - - to the measure of the stature of the fullness of Christ. Insert - Page 2

And as we walk with him daily, - we can say with assurance that neither death nor life - - nor angels - - nor principalities, - - nor powers, - - nor things present, - - nor things to come, - - nor height, nor depth, - - nor any other creation, shall be able to separate us from the love of God, which is in Christ Jesus.

And now let's look at this word obedience.

If you think its hard to trust God, you'll think its impossible to be obedient.

Obedience is one of those words we'd just as soon do without, it conjures up all sorts of things in our minds.

There's a part of us that just naturally rebells at the thought of obedience.

I remember Carl Ziegler, putting it this way - -

If someone says I must - - - - - - something in me says I won't!
And I think that's how we respond sometimes to the commandants of God.

But as we grow in our trusting of God, we should also want to be more obedient to Him, knowing that he directs all things for our good.

Now there is some popular thinking today that obedience is an optional sort of thing. When we read the Bible we decide which things are more important than others, and then we decide what we will be obedient to and what we won't! Some Say Pauls Letters Are Not Inspired - They Say Gen. Is A Fairy Tale - Rev. Is A Riddle - & The Gospels Are - Historical - What's Left? II Tim. 3:16 - All Scripture

I believe that God would say to us this ~~morning~~ Evening - - that obedience is not optional!

God has given us complete instructions for every area of life, and I believe that without a willful obedience to Him, we are in danger of falling out of fellowship with God .

Jesus said, If you say you love me - - - - keep my commandments.
Prove it, by being obedient.

Jesus, of course, was the greatest example of obedience,

never doing his will,

but always the will of his Father,

being obedient even unto a cross.

Now Just what is obedience?

Obedience is - - - - 1. doing exactly what you're told to do

2. imediately

3. with the right heart attitude.

Let me illustrate - - - if you are given instructions to do 4 specific things and you do 3 of them - - that is not obedience! You must do exactly what you're told.

Now suppose you do all 4, but it takes you 4 weeks to do them - - - no that's not obedience either - - - - you must do it immediately.

Now if you do all 4, and you do it right away - - - - but you grumble and complain all the while you're doing it - - - - that's not obedience either but do exactly what your told - right away - with a right heart attitude. That's obedience!

Obedience is very important to God, and always has been, and we can see very clearly as we follow the tragic account of Saul's life in I Sam. that continued disobedience to God, brings spiritual shipwreck.

Lets turn in our Bibles to I Sam. 10, and begin with verse 6 (To Verse 12)

There are 2 things I want to point out here

#1. God is definetely with Saul - - verse 9 says that God gave him a new heart - - - and verse 10 says the spirit of God came mightely upon him - - and he prophesied.

#2 Saul is given specific instructions - verse 8 - until I come

Now in the next 2 chapters we are given the account of the establishment of Saul, as Israels first king. Samuel writes up his duties and responsibilities, and also tells the people what is expected of them.

And then in Ch 13 Saul gets his army together, and goes down to Gilgal - to wait for Samuel.

Let's pick up at verse 5 Ch 13 .... (to verse 15)

Saul, because he did not trust God, did that which he knew was wrong, and then displays that age old malady that we excell in - -

r a t i o n a l i z a t i o n!

Well Lord, I had to do something!

the people were scattering - - - what difference does it make who offers the burnt offering anyway?

But Samuel says you fool, - - -

God would have established your kingdom forever- - - - -

but now, one of the consequences of your disobedience is - - - -

your kingdom shall not continue.

And everytime we disobey God - - we will suffer some consequence to our own ministry. Disobedience Is Sin - & Sin Must Be Dealt With

Now the Lord stepped in, and delivered the Israelites that day - - by causing confusion and panic in The Philistines Camp Ch.-14.

And now God gives Saul another chance. Lets read starting at ch 15 .1-9.

Again, Saul does 90% of what he was instructed, but does not seem to understand that complete obedience is necessary. (read verses 10-13)

Saul still rationalizing - lying to himself and to God. - Do We Do That?

But look at Samuels reply ,(verse 14) (read verse 15)

Then Saul begins to make excuses - the people did it - - -

so they could sacrifice to the Lord - - - your God

how often we do this same thing, we say we would have been obedient, but someone else did this or that, and we place the blame on them.

And again verse 18, Samuel says to Saul why did you not obey? and again Saul begins to make excuses - - - -

- - and then Samuel says, (verse 22-23)

Now you say how is rebellion like the sin of whichcraft?
you Say I'd Never Get Involved In The Occult - But God Says - Willful Disobed
Well, what really is whichcraft or divination - - - - Is The Same Thing!

- - according to the dictionary, - whichcraft,

- - is the practice of sorcery,

- that is using supernatural powers to work evil,

- by association with evil spirits or the devil

and I might add that is the Bible definition also,

thats why we're told not to get involved in it.

So whichcraft, is really exposing oneself to the realm and power of Satan.

And every time we are disobedient, - - rebellious - - we are in effect

saying, God, I don't want to do it your way, - my way is better.

and we take ourself out from under his authority

- - - and we expose ourselves to the power of Satan. !

Thats exactly what Saul did. - - he could'nt see why he had to destroy

everything, - - and the people wanted to have some sport with old King Agag,

and just keep some of the best sheep and cattle,

And He thought his way was better than Gods way.

today we call that "doing your own thing"

God calls it sin.

And Saul, even though he was chosen by God,

and was annointed and filled with His spirit,

because he was disobedient, - - rebellious,

he placed himself outside the authority of God,

and exposed himself to the power of Satan,

and from that time on, his kingdom went downhill.

In later years he fell into all kinds of sins, and at times acted almost

as a man posessed, as he tried to kill David, because of his jealousy.

Saul actually fell so far out of fellowship with God, that he consulted with a practicer of whichcraft, to seek some direction. Ch 28: verse 8

Yes, disobedience brings separation from God. Pause

We're always looking for new insights, - truth, - doctrines, -

- - but God is looking for obedience!

We're looking for new applications, - illustrations, - methods, -

- - God is longing for obedience.

We're looking for new messages, - programs, - revival,-

- - God is waiting for obedience.

I believe, that if each of us was just obedient to the truth that we now know, - - - we would have a revival that would set this Country on fire!!

Truth Recieved, Brings More Truth - But Truth Rejected Brings Condemnation.

When God speaks to you, - do you instantly obey?

When God reveals an area of truth form his word,

do you just give intellectual assent or acceptance?

or do you also obey?

Perhaps God is asking you to get rid of something in your life, that is not pleasing to him, - -

- are you listening to him?

- or maybe you've felt God leading you to go to someone and ask forgiveness for some wrong?

Is God burdening your heart, to just speak a word to some unsaved neighbor or friend? You Know It's Easy To Say No To God - Because He's Not Pushy. We Can Easily Drown Out His Still, Small Voice

The reason many of us do not hear God, is because we have conditioned ourselves to intellectual agreement, - - we say amen to what God says, - - - but fail to obey him.

We think because we go to Sunday School and Church every Sunday, and serve on some committee, and go to lovefeast twice a year,

- - that somehow God is very pleased with us. - - -

God is not impressed with our sacrifices,

- - he doesn't want our burnt offerings.

Listen to Him! "BEHOLD TO OBEY IS BETTER THAN SACRIFICE!"

When we walk with the Lord, In the light of His word,
What a glory He sheds on our way!
While we do His good will, He abides with us still,
And with all who will trust and obey.
Trust andobey, for there's no other way
To be happy in Jesus, but to trust and obey.

This sermon is recorded on Darvin Byler Family Sermons, "Trust and Obey". (Spotify/YouTube)

File folder marked "New Testament". Sermons written and preached by Darvin Byler.

MT. Ch. 3

V-1 John The Baptist - Lu. = Zecharia & Elizabeth (Cousins)

Jesus Said John was Greatest - MT. 11:11

Josephus - Non Biblical Witness

V-2 His Purpose - Prepare The Way

V-11 - Not The Messiah

V-2 His Message = Repent - Kingdom of Heaven is Near

V-2 Different! Are We Too Soft?

V 11 Baptism of Holy Spirit

V-13 - Baptism of Jesus - Not For Repentance

1. Identifies With People
2. Sets Example

Dove -
1. Not An Eagle But Harmless "
2. Doves " Mourn
3. Offered As Sacrifice

15-17 - Trinity in Action

Dove - Sign For John - Jo 1:29-

Later - John Doubted - MT. 11:2-3
Circumstances of Life
Missionaries Killed!
Ch 14 Beheaded

2

Ch. 4

The Temptation

V1 Led By The Spirit? Emptied Himself
Submitted To Fatherrs Will Set Aside His Diety

2-3 - Hungry - Satan Comes At Our
Weakest Point - Greatest Need

4 Jesus Sets The Pattern - Use The Word
Example For Us All From Deut! Moses!

5-6 Satan Quotes Scripture - Ps. 91: 11-12

7
8 Satan Has Access To All The kingdoms of
This World! Lu 4:6

MT. 5:1-16

"The Sermon on The Mount"

Jesus had just begun his public ministry - 1st Sermon

1&2 He went up on A mountain — he opened his mouth

He Talked About Happiness - and He Gives

8 Essential Qualities - For Happiness

3 1. Blessed - How happy Are Those Who Are - Poor in Spirit
Those who Are humble minded - who have given God
His Rightful Place at The center of Their Lives
Pride - Refusing To Allow God To Control

4 2. Mourn - Those who Allow God To break Their heart with
The Things That break His heart and gain His Goals
For Their Lives. Lack of Purpose - Direction

5 3. Meek - Those who give All possessions and personal Rights
To God And There after Look upon What They have
As Loaned To Them By God for His Work & Glory
Anger - Greed

6 4. Hunger & Thirst For Righteousness — Those Who have A healthy
Spiritual Appetite For Gods Word and The principles
Received From IT. Lack of Spiritual Interest

7 5. Merciful — Those who fully forgive All who injure or
Offend Them and Return Love and understanding
Bitterness - Resentment

8 6. Pure in heart - Those whose motives And Desires Are Under
The Control of Christ Moral - Sexual Impurity

9 7. Peace makers - Those who make Things Right with everyone They have wronged and By Their example guide Others To do The Same. Condem Others

10 8. Persecuted For Righteousness Sake - Those who have Identified Themselves with Jesus Christ So That Those who Reject Christ And His Principles Also Reject Them. Fear of Witnessing - Compromise Standards

11-12 Rejoice - Great is Your Reward in Heaven

13 - Salt = gives Flavor - Preserves

14 - Light = Reveals Truth - helps Us See

If These 8 qualities For Happiness Are Yours You will not only Be Happy --
you will Be Salt & Light

16 Let your Light So Shine --

MT. 6: 19-34 Lu. 16: 19-31

Jesus Tells A Story

A Rich Man - - - A Poor Man

They both die

1 went To Heaven - - 1 went To Hell

Why? Because He was Rich? No!

MT. 6: 19 + 33 Riches O.K. - If God Wills!

Abraham - was A Rich man

David Where is your Treasure?

Solomon

He went To Hell Because He

Trusted In His Riches - His Heart was Cold

1. Seek 1st The Kingdom of God

2. Do Not Be Anxious About Things - You Can't

Serve Two Masters MT. 6: 24

Worry - Is A Sin against God!

Verse 26 - 30

3. Where Will You Spend Eternity? v.24

Pleasure Now -- But what Later? Hell is Real!

Lu. 16 v. 25 Heb. 9: 27 II Cor. 5: 10

I Jo. 5: 13 - Do you Know That you Have Eternal Life?

Jo. 3: 16 - God wants you To Know Jo. 5: 24

Rom 8: 1 - No Condemnation

1. Seek God Before Riches

2. Don't Worry About Things

3. Make Sure Where You Will Spend Eternity!

(Mt. 8:28-)

Mt. 8: 28-

START - V 23 - Jesus Power - Calm The Storm
Heal The Sick.
Today - Cast out Demons

MRK. 5:1
LK 8:26

28 Gadgrenes - - Mark + Luke = Gerasenes
From Villiage Gerasa
From City Gadara District Called Gadara

2 Demoniacs - Does Not Say Men

Mark + Luke - Only one - Why? Perhaps
Husband + Wife?

They Lived Among The Tombs - Suggesting
Satans Realm - Bible Says - Satan is Liar. Murderer
Hates Bodies

Kenya - Old Morgue - Tools

They Attacked People Indiscriminately
Today?

Fact

V 29 1. Demons Speak Through People
2. Demons Recognise Jesus - What A Testimony!
They Know + Confess Jesus As Son of God!

It Is Not Knowledge That Saves Us!

Today We Say People Are "Mentaly ILL"

Jesus Differenciated Between Demon Possession & Sickness MT. 10:1

Wycliffe Pg 934 - Minds given To Satan

How? - Occult - Physic - T.V. Adds
Drugs

V 29 B - What Have We To Do With Thee - KJV

Possible To Know & Believe That Jesus is Son of God
And Reject Everything Else

Jesus Has Plenty To Do With Them - And
They Know IT!

Before "The Time"

Satan is Loosed For A Time -
But Judgement Is Sure - And They Know IT Jms 2:19

Facts - 1. Demons Know Who Jesus Is
2. Are Aware of Their Ultimate Doom
3. Always Give Jesus Absolute Obedience

V30-31 If you Cast Us Out ------

Why A Herd of Pigs? - Unclean Animals
Jews Forbidden

Fact - Demons Can Also Live in Animals
(Most Farmers Already Know This)

V32 Jesus Said -- Go - one Word!

Fact - Demons Are Commanded By The Word
of God --
Not By our Many Words or Rituals
(Exorcism)

32-B What Happened To The Demons?

33-34 They Begged Jesus To Leave --

Matthew Henry - "There Are A Great Many Who
Prefer Their Swine Before Their Saviour

MT. 9:1-8

Mark 2:1
V1 His own City = Capernaum - Luke 5:17

Through The Roof --
V2 - Saw Their Faith - The Bearers Also

— 1 —

Is ALL Sickness A Result of Sin?
Example = Job

V3 - Only God Can Forgive Sin

Fact - Jesus Knows Our Thoughts --- !!!

4-5 Easier? - Both Require Divine Power

V6 So That You May Know -

Dramatize - Carried in on Bed -
Now - Pick up your Bed - And Walk!

V8 They Glorified God ---

Fact -- When Gods Work is Done in
Gods Power - People Glorify God -
Not Men!

11 Parable of Sower
MT. 13

Parable = Earthly Story - Heavenly Meaning
Why Parables? V 10
Everyone Loves A Story - Those Who
wanted To Learn - Would see God
Those Who Would NoT - Listened To A Good Story
V 13
Seeing - Hearing - Understanding
Sin Gospel Salvation
Essential For Salvation

V 1 - That Same Day - Ch 12 - Long Day

2 - Great Crowds - Boat

3-9 Review Quickly -
We Don't Need To Guess AT Heavenly Meaning
Jesus Will Interpret - Also Tares - 24-37

V 18 - Hear The Parable Again
Hear = Understand
Many People in Church - Hear - Again & Again
Never Understand -- you Haven't "Heard" until You Understand!

Seed = Word of God - Powerful
Incorruptible yet Appears Dead - Mystery

1st Priority - Good Seed

2

Ground = Peoples Hearts - v19 when Any one
Not All The Same - Hershey - Palmyra - Limestone
Shale - Conewago - Red Clay
It Can Be Improved - Manure - Fertilizer
Tilled

1. 19 Path way = Foot Paths Through The Fields - Kenya
A Hardened Heart - Prov. 29:1
Easy Prey For Satan Root of Bitterness

Remedy - Break up The Fallow Ground
Hosea 10:12 - Read

2. 20 Rocky Ground
Soil on Top - Layer of Rock Underneath
Not Like Ely Lex
Springs Up Quickly - yet No Depth

When - Trouble Comes 1 Pet. 4:12
Why Do Bad Things Happen To Good
People ? 2 Cor. 1 Kenya

"Footpaths Through Fields"

Footpaths in a field are created by people and animals walking on the same ground continuously.

The ground becomes so hard that no crops would grow there.

"Eli Lex"

Every year my brothers and I would follow our neighbor as he plowed the same field. Why?

Because every year more rocks would surface.

We removed the rocks from the field so that he could plant his crops.

We used to say that Mr. Lex is in the rock business.

"Kenya-Old Morgue-Tools"

I would keep my tools in the old morgue in the hospital because the Kenyans were afraid of demons and death. My tools never went missing.

I often had to fix the motors that cooled the morgue. This required me to carefully and quickly work around the 20-plus bodies in a room made for nine bodies.

3

3. Thorny Ground - Weeds

Plants Get Good Start - Roots - Growth

Everything Looks Fine -- But Leave it Awhile

Weeds!

1. Cares of World ? Name Them ?

In Themselves - Not Bad

Like Weeds - Multiply - Silently - Relentlessly

Distract - Divert

2. Deceitfulness of Riches

Again - in Itself - Not Bad

Deceit = To Trust in - Rely

4. Good Soil - Difference → Fruitfulness

Doesn't Matter How Beautiful Plant is ---

Jo 15:8 - Bear Much Fruit

He Doesn't Say No Stones - Thorns

Some 100 - 60 - 30 - Different Talents - Abilities

The Parable of The Sower
MT 13:1-17

Jesus Christ Was The Son of God
The King of Kings - Lord of Lords
Yet He did Not Come To The Rich & Powerful - He Identified With The Poor - Laborers & Farmers

Many of You Are Farmers and Will Understand This Story.

Jesus Loved To Tell Stories - He Called Them Parables

A Parable Is An Earthly Story - With A Heavenly Meaning

Jesus ~~He~~ Used Parables Because The Common people Could Understand Them - And We See In verse 13 He Used them So Those Who were Spiritually Minded Could Understand.

He Said Some People Refuse To hear - They Have the Ability To See & Hear - But They Don't Want To

They Are The People the Prophet Isaiah Spoke of When He Said - (verse 14)

But You People Are Not Like That - He Told Them - Because You See & Understand

I Think The Same Is True About You People

Now To The Story

verse 4 A Man Went Out To Sow some Seed -

1. Some Fell on The Path way
2. Some Fell on Rocky Ground
3. Some Fell on Thorns
4. Some Fell on Good Soil

4 Different Kinds of Soil - But The Same Seed

Now What Happened?

1. The 1st Seed Fell on The Hard ground & Laid on Top & The Birds Came & Ate It.

2. The 2nd Seed Fell on The Rocky ground where There Was not much Soil, The seed sprang Up quickly, But when the Sun Came Out, They Withered & Died Because They Had No Roots.

3. The 3rd Seed Fell among The Thorns And As they Grew The Thorns Chocked Them out.

4. The 4th Seed Fell on good Soil & Grew & Yielded grain - A Hundred Times - 60 Times - 30 Times

Now You People Have Sown Seed - And you Have All Probably Had this Same Experience - Some will Grow - & Some Will Not - But Where Is The Heavenly Meaning? Where Is The Spiritual Application?

The Disciples Asked Jesus The Same question & In verse 19 Jesus Interprets the Story For Them

The Seed Is the Word of God - the Gospel - The Good News - The Soil Is Our Hearts

1. The 1st Seed That Fell on The Path way Fell on A Hard Heart - One that Refused To See & Understand - & The Birds Came & Snacthed It Away - Satan Is Like the Birds - He Takes Away the Seed Before It Can Grow.

2. The 2nd Seed Fell on the Rocky Ground - This Is Like A Person That Accepts the Word with Joy - & Imediatly He wants To Preach -- yet He Has No Roots -- He Lasts A Little While - But When Trouble & Persecution Comes - He Withers & Falls Away

3

3. The 3rd Seed That Fell among The Thorns - This Is Like A Person That Hears The Word - & Understands & Believes - But The cares of This World - Pleasures Riches - Buisness Choke it Out & Suffocate the Word & IT Bears No Fruit!

MT 6:25

4. But The 4th Seed That Fell on good Soil - This Is The Person Who hears The Word - & Understands & The Word Grows & Takes Root & Bears Fruit Some A 100 Times - Some 60 - Some 30

We Are Not All The Same - Some Have greater Ability - But We Should All Bear Fruit For the Lord

Where Do You See Yourself this Morning?

What Kind of Soil Are You?
Is Your Heart Hard?
Is IT Rocky?
Are there thorns In Your Life? Choking Out The Word?
Or Is your Heart Fertile Soil - Where The Word of God Can grow - & Bear Much Fruit
I Pray that IT Is.

MT 13

53-58 Jesus Came From A Real Family

Brothers + Sisters

James + Judas = N.T. Writers

Tremendous Witness!

Ch 14 Johns Death

2. PostScripts

Josephus = 1. Herod's Army was Defeated By AreTas King of PeTrea (Father in Law)

Herod + Herodias Both Banished To France

2. Daughter Fell into Ice - Head + Neck Sliced

V 14 Jesus Had Compassion

He Ministered To Their Needs = Sick

Africa = Famine - Again!

ITs Their Own Fault!

Compassion

15 Send Them Away

16 - No! You Feed Them!

17 - God Wants To Use our "LiTTLe"

18 - First - We Must Give it To Jesus
Great Spiritual Truth
Unless A grain of Wheat Falls into The Ground
And Dies -
Multiplies!

20. Not Just Something For Everyone To Eat -

No! Gods Way is Full & Overflowing!

Open The Windows of Heaven - Overflowing Bless

Why 12 Baskets?
One For Each Doubting Disciple!

22 Jesus Constrained Them Why?

Jo 6:15 - They Would Make Him King

23 Jesus Withdrew Again - Alone

Hunting!

25 - Fourth Watch - 3 - 6 A.M.

1. Jesus Ordered Them out - still Storms!

2. They Did Not Turn Back

3. Joy Comes in The Morning!

Walking on Water - Why?
Just To Prove He is God!

26 It is A Spirit!

We Are Still Frightened By The Spirit World

27 Perfect Love Casts Out Fear

28 Peter - Not - Let Me Walk on Water Too -
Rather - Let Me Come To You
An Expression of His Love & Need

Jesus Answer - "Come"

To Any Who Would - "Come Unto Me"

29 Peter Walked

We Shall do The Works of Jesus -
And Greater Works Shall We do!

God Does Not Often Suspend The
Laws of Nature -
But He Can & Does!

30 Even Peter Doubted
Took His Eyes off Jesus

He Was Afraid - We All

Lord Save Me! Great Prayer

31 Immediately - Christ Responds

Then Rebukes - Why Did you Doubt?

What Reason? - Our Doubts?

32 Jesus Calms The Storms - our Lives

33 He Recieved Their Worship

MT. 17:14 -

Jesus Casts Out Demons
Epileptic = Lunatic
Mark 9:14 -

V17 - O Faithless + Perverse Generation ?
Hard Words!

V 19 Why Could We Not Cast Him out?

Because of Unbelief! - In Jesus? NO!

Failure To Appropriate The Power + Authority Already Granted To Them
Ch 10:8

V20 Amplified

Half Shekel Tax (Temple Tax)

V 24 Payment Usually Made in Spring - Months Overdue!

1. Its O.K. To Be Delinquent on Taxes!

V25 Peter Spoke - Without Thinking - Again!

He Was Defending Jesus! Certainly My Master Keeps The Law

2

25 Jesus Knows EveryThing

26 Jesus Was A Son - He was Exempt

27 However - Not To Cause Them To Stumble

1. Great Christian Principle Freedom = Choices

In Christ We Are Free - Exempt 1. Alcohol
But - We Willingly Submit. 2. Sunday
So As Not To Cause Them To Stumble 3. Dress - Kenya Sandy-Pants
Paul - Meat - Idols

Today
27 Do You WithoLd Money From The Church? - Corrupt? (Staff)
(Elevator)

Jesus Said They Had Made The Temple A Den of Thieves

27 The Payment = From The Purse? Judas?

Peter Says Yes - We'll Pay - But Had No Money!
Jesus - For our Sakes He Became Poor
He Did Not Have A Half Shekel - 50¢

Out of A Fishes Mouth!

Second Principle
2. God Chooses To Work Through Us

3

1. Peter Must Participate - Why Fish?

Peter Was A Fisherman!
God Uses Us Where We Are

Peter Learned A Great Lesson – God is Able!
Fisher of Men

2. Jesus Gave Peter Dignity - Go & Pay For
Me & Yourself
Famine - Somalia

Ch 18

I Am The Greatest!

V3 Unless You Repent - Your Problem Won't Be
Who's The Greatest – Rather Will You Even Be
In The Kingdom?

A Child = Trusting - Loving - Forgiving - Humble
Harmless - No Malice - Envy - Airs

MT. Ch 18

Who is The Greatest ?

V3. Unless you Change - your Problem Won't Be Who's The greatest - Rather Will you Even Be in The Kingdom?

Change Your Mindset

4. Humbles Himself - Like A Child

A Child - Humble - No Airs - Pretense
Envy - Malice

Gods Ways - Not our Ways → Christmas

5 Do it unto The Least of These

6 Child Pornography

7 Necessary ?

8-9 - Drastic Measures

10 Ministry of Angels ↗ Not Just At Christmas

12-14 The Ninety & Nine - Not Fair ! Prodigal Son
2nd Son

MT. Ch 18

Who is The Greatest?

V3. Unless you Change - your Problem Won't Be Who's The greatest - Rather Will you Even Be IN The Kingdom?

Change Your Mindset

4. Humbles Himself - Like A Child

A Child - Humble - No Airs - Pretense
Envy - Malice

Gods Ways - Not our Ways → Christmas

5. Do it unto The Least of These

6. Child Pornography

7. Necessary?

8-9. Drastic Measures

10. Ministry of Angels → Not Just At Christmas

12-14 The Ninety & Nine - Not Fair! Prodigal Son
2nd Son

2

15 This is "MT. 18"
Archaic - Not Used

Why? These Are Jesus Words!

21 Forgiveness

23 Parable
24 Talents - A Huge Debt - 15 years Wages

Denarii - 1 Days Wages

32
33 - We Also should Have Mercy

35 - My Father will Do -

Is Forgiveness A Command?
A Choice?
A Feeling?
An Emotion?
A Gift?

Is it Deliberate?

Give Forgiveness This Christmas!

The Lords Prayer - Forgive Us - As We Forgive

1

Forgiveness Is Not Optional

Background MT. 18:15-20

Verse 21 - Peter Demonstrates Our
Attitude When Offended --
How Long Untill I get Revenge?

Then Jesus Gives This Parable
To Illustrate One Reason For Forgiveness.

Verse 23-35 - Use Gothard Pg 3

I Called This Message "Forgiveness
Is Not Optional" -- Because We Really
Don't Have A Choice -- That's Provided
We Want To Have Fellowship With God -
Want More of His Grace -
Want Him To Hear Our Prayers -
Accept Our Worship

Turn To Ch. 6: 12-15
Lords' Prayer
Another Principle

Mark 11:24-26 Unforgiveness Affects Our
Prayers!

(3)

In The Greek This Word - Basanistai Is Used To Describe Sickness And Adverse Circumstances

So What Jesus Is Really Saying Here Is -- If You Do Not Forgive Others From Your Heart -- My Father Is Going To Make IT Very Rough On You

And There Are Some Good Reasons Why Jesus Could Say That With Confidence

No. 1 He Knew Very Well That The Human Body Was Never Designed To Handle Guilt - Bitterness - Hatred - Envy

When We Harbor These Kinds Of Feelings We Create A Chemical Imbalance That Can Cause All Kinds Of Physical Sickness

Another Thing Jesus Knew Is That Our Bones Help Produce Our Blood And Bitterness Has A Direct And Devestating Effect Upon Bone Health. Ps 32:3

MT. Ch 21 Pharisees / Sadducees } Like Us!

23-27 By What Authority?
Jesus Taught With Authority
Came From Father

By What Authority Do We (Church) speak?

Do We Have Authority? Yes!
MT 28:18
NoT in Politics
Economics

24 Jesus Answer - Clever

These People Were Smoothe-Politicians

Baptism of John? - What Does That Have To Do with Any Thing?

Why Then Did you NoT Believe John? --
John Proclaimed Jesus As Messiah!

28 Having A Form of "Religion" is Dangerous

31 Ouch!

32 Jesus STILL Answering Their Question
John Came in RighTeousness = Heaven

2

Even When you Saw - Too Proud

More Concerned With Appearance
Having A Form of Religion is Dangerous!

33 Hear Another Parable Ha!

Very Clear - Gods Dealing With Israel

37 Jesus Authority - Sent By The Father

41 - These People Just Don't Get IT!

42 - The Punch Line

43 Nation - 1 Pet 2:7-9 A "Holy Nation"
Same O.T. Scripture Ps. 118

Warning! if we Do Not Produce "Fruits"

God will Also Take Away From Us

Paul - If God Did Not Spare The Branches
Neither Us - Grafted In

45 They Get IT!

3

Ch 22

Hear Another Parable

3. Oriental Custom 1st Invitation - 2nd Exact Time

Brazenly Rude

7 Gods Anger is Real

9 Calling of Gentiles

Good + Bad = Open Sinners
Morally Upright (Religious)

11 No Garment = Robe of Imputed Righteousness

We Must Insist - No Other Way!

15-22 We Laugh - Argue With God?

Do You Even Argue with God?

Is 1:18 - Come Let us Reason Together

Reason = Convince - Correct

4

2 Great Principles

Rom 13

1. v21 Render unto Ceasar The Things That Are His

We Are Subject To Civil Authority

We Do Not Withold Taxes in Protest

Rome Was A Corrupt Government!

2. 23-33 God is God of The Living

We Shall Never Die!

Sadduces Did Not Believe God!

Quote From Torah

29 You Are Wrong - Authority

ITs NoT Smart To Argue with God

Do Not Know Scripture or Power of God

5

35 Which is The GreaTesT Commandment?

How Can Anyone Be Commanded To Love?

How Can We Love With ALL our HearT - Soul - Mind?

Gods STandard - PerfecTion

Our Response - Always Falls ShorT
Gods Grace = Answer

39 Your Neighbor As Yourself

42 - Whose Son is He?

Ch 23

RespecT For PosiTion

David - Saul - I will NoT ATTack Gods AnnoinTed

PasTors - GovernmenT officials

6

5 Phylacteries = Small Cases Containing
Parchment on which were written
Ex. 13: 2-10 Deut, ~~[illegible]~~ it.
Worn on Forehead

Tassels on Garments - Show

7 But You - Humble Yourself

13 Seven Woes
Legalism

A Deadly Disease - A Mindset

23 - Mint - Dill - Cumming Garden Plants used
For Seasoning
Justice - Mercy - Faith

Gnat = Levitically Unclean insect that
might Fall into A Cup

Camel = Largest Unclean Animal

25 Focus on Outward Appearances

But God Looks on Heart

2

What is Legalistic?

Homosexuals - Abortion - Non Sexist Language
- Divorce
Peace Position - Brethrenism

Legalism - Strict Conformity To Law
Stressing The Letter of The Law
Rather Than The Spirit of The Law

MT. 25:1-13 Ten Virgins

Last Week - Easy - Jesus Interpreted

Not This Time

Ch 24 - Olivet Discourse - End Times

Middle East - Sadaam ?

Next Great Event - 2nd Coming

Tribulation - 2nd - Millenium

Rapture - ~~Tribu Millenium~~ - 2nd Coming

Who Are Virgins ?

Who is Bridegroom ?

Who is Bride ?

1. Primary Application Pg. 90

2ndary Application

Apply To Us!

One Interpretation - Many Applications

1. Primary Application = Be Prepared!

2

V 1 History of Jewish Weddings

1. Engagement 2. Bridegroom Comes For Bride 3. Feast - 7 Days

2 - Wise - Foolish Difference = "Character"
Wise = Prudent - Sensible - Practicle
Foolish = Heedless - Stupid - Stubborn

3 - No Oil - Why ?
Unprepared

Oil = Holy Spirit
Wise = True Believers
Foolish = Proffessing Believers

4-5 - All Slept - No Rebuke

Parallels Long Absence of Christ
Even True Believers Sleep

Church Today = Sleeping !

No Sense of Urgency

A.I.M. Paper

3

6 - Midnight - Sound Asleep
Least Expecting
I Thes 5:2-3 - A Thief in The Night
Peace - Peace!

Whether Rapture - I Cor 15:51
Rule - MT. 24:37

Be Prepared!

7 All Trimmed Their Lamps
Incredible! Wheat & Tares

Foolish Knew They Had No Oil!

8 What?

9 - Each Must Prepare - God Has No Grandchildren

10 - Tragic - No 2nd Chance

11 - On What Basis?
12 - Who Are You?

13 - Be Prepared!

Parable Of The Talents
(Matthew 25)

Verse 15 – To each In Proportion To His Ability

1. God knows Our Abilities & Limitations
2. God Deals With Us Individually

Verse 16 – Went At Once No hesitation

1. He Who Hesitates Is Lost
Many Times We Allow Satan Time To Talk Us Out of Things.

Verse 18 – More Here Than Meets The Eye

1. Old Hebrew Law – Buried Treasure Belongs To Owner of Field. MT 13:44

2. This Servant Was Really Trying To Escape His Responsibility.

How Do We Do This?

1. Work – No Time
2. Family
3. Comparison To Others
4. Fear – Because of Ignorance
Servant Did Not Really Know His Master
(Do We?)

(2)

5. Fear of Failure!
Are you Free? -- If Christ Sets you Free you Shall Be Free Indeed!
Freedom To Fail?

God Can Teach Us Many Things In Failure That We Can Never Learn OtherWise
When We Fail We Are Humbled -- God Gives Grace To The Humble
His Forgiveness Is Always There
DeuT 32:11 - A BeauTiful ScripTure
Like An Eagle STirs Up IT's Nest, That Flutters Over IT's young, Spreading out IT's Wings, Catching Them

One of The GreaTesT Joys of The ChrisTian Life -- Is To STep OuT In FaiTh - Knowing ThaT In & of Yourself you Can'T Do SomeThing - And Then See God SuperNaTurally Work Through you!

Give God A Chance To Show Himself Mighty In Your Life!

3

Verse 21 - God Wants To Give Us More
Joy - Blessings - Delight
But We Must First Be Faithful
With What He Has Given Us.

1. Faith Demands Action
2. Obedience To The Light We Have --
Will Bring New Light.

Verse 28-29 - Jesus Is Stating A Principle
MT. 13:12 -- MK 4: 24-25
Lu 8:16-18 --- Jn 15: 2
We Better Take Heed -- Because We
Have Seen & Experienced Some Truth

1. There Is A Job To Be Done
What Is IT? MT 24:14
We Need To Keep Focus ON
The Big Picture
Today We Are Living In Exciting
Times -- God Is Opening Doors As Never
Before - India - Indonesia - Maylaysia - Africa
Red China
1. Through Radio - Back To The Bible
J Vernon Mc Gee
Pass Port To Russia

(4)

2. News Paper Evangelism - A.M.G.

3. Wycliffe Bible Translators
Started In 1936 - Over 100 Translations
They Expect To Complete Their Work
In This Century - The Bible In Every
Language
Carl Forney

God's Work Will Be Done!

If We Don't Do IT -- He'll Use Someone
Else --- But He Wants Us To Share
In The Joy - Blessings That Come
From Doing & Acting By Faith!

You've Heard IT Said That We
Have A Very Talented Church -- That's True

SomeTimes That Can Be A Hindrance
1. - Always Waiting For Someone Else To Do IT

2. Trying To Do Things On Our Own
Example = Me - First Speech

Lu 9:57

V-57 - Pg 57 in Quarterly

Jesus Call Verse 23

V-59 - He was Obligated To Care For His Father Untill He Died

Let the spiritually dead - bury the dead - spiritually alive - follow Jesus!

V-62 Pg 58

Ch 10

V-1 Jesus must have Had a large following to be able to send 70 men out

2 - There is Always A Shortage of Laborers - A.I.M. Report

3 - Lambs - Wolves - NoT Pleasant!

4 = Salute No One - Greetings Pg 59

No Extra Baggage

2

7 - Not To Go Looking For The most Comfortable Housing

9 - Special Annointing - Temporary Power

10 - Not only Reject You - But Kingdom of God

12 - More Tolerable on Judgement Day for Sodom? Why?

What About America?

Average Family - 6 Bibles -
Churches on Every Corner
Radio - TV

13-14 -

16 -
17 - The 70 Were More Succesful Than The 12 - they Could Not Cure The Demoniac Boy - - -
But Demons Fled AT The Name of Jesus! Why?

18 - Power of Satan is Broken - Fall From Heaven?

20 - Do Not Rejoice in Momentary Victory
But Eternal Triumph

3

21 - Jesus Rejoices in The Spirit

Great Spiritual Truths Are Seen & Understood By Those Who Are Humble Not The High & Mighty

God Resists The Proud - Jm. 4:6

23 We Also Are Blessed To Have Our Spiritual Eyes Opened -

Parable of The Banquet
Lu. 14:12-24

Parable = Earthly Story - Heavenly Meaning
This One Easy To Understand

V12 - What Man? Back Up - Verse 1

Jesus & Pharisees - Quart Pg. 23

V2 - Just Like Brothers - A Dirty Trick!

Dropsy = A swelling of Limbs - Collection of Water in Body Cavities

V3 - Jesus Did Not Avoid The Issue

4 - Jesus Questioned Them - Silence

7 - 1st Parable - A Gentle Reminder

11 - Last Week?

12 - Jesus = Bad Manners!

15 - Great SS Answer

16 - 2nd Parable

2

V16 A Man = God
Banquet = Kingdom
Those Invited = Religious Leaders – OT Promises
Seed of Abraham
1st Invitation – Many Days Before

Event Oriented People – Kenya
All prepared To Come
O.T. Prophets = Prepare For Kingdom

V17 – 2nd Invitation – All is Ready –

John The Baptist – Jesus – Kingdom is Here

18 – A Strange Thing Happens
Honored Guests Don't Want To Come
Excuses! Why?

They Had Their own Understanding of Kingdom
When Jesus Revealed True Nature ---
What is Heaven Like?
They were Wrong – Change = Thought / LifesTyle

Have You Even Been Wrong?

Story of Missionary Lady – Watch

"Event Oriented"

Kenyans did not plan events ahead of time. When someone showed up

Then it became an event of several hours.

They would kill a fatted goat, prepare a meal, and celebrate.

You were not allowed to leave until they released you.

They released you with a blessing.

3

21 God is Angry
Poor – Maimed – Blind
Jewish Masses

22 – Still Room

23 – Outside The City = Gentiles
Compel Them – Unworthy
Are you Sure For Me?

24 – Those invited 1st – Will Not Enter!
Their Choice

Today – of All Groups – We in Church
Bear A Striking Resemblance To Pharisees

Legalistic – Tradition Oriented
Upper Middle Class – Lip Service To Poor
Proud – Brethren!
A Form of Religion – No Power

Lu. 18:9-14

The Context

Introduction - Ps 17 How ought we Pray

verse 9- Focus = Works Righteousness
All other Religions = Mans Attempt To Reach God
Christianity = Gods Attempt To Reach Man

Muslim
J.W. } Wide Appeal

Amish - Many Within Church
Mennonite

Self-Righteous People Always Despise
Others - Seperate

10. Pharisee = Respected Leader } opposites
Publican = Hated + Despised
MT. was A Tax Collecter
Jesus Loved The Hated
Zacchaeus - Ch 19 - 7

Mary Magdelene - Prostitute MT. 21: 31

2

11 The Prayer - Standing - By Himself
Seperation - Mark of Self-Righteousness

Thank you God I Am Not - A Gentile
Servant
Woman
An American ?

12 All He Said Was True - I - I - I !

Paul Also - But Came To See - Worthless

MT. 23:23 - Tithe yes - But More!

13 - The Sinners Prayer - Not So Much What
He Said - But How

Beating The Breast - Sign of Sorrow & Guilt
Are Others Sinners ? No Matter
He Knew His Sin - All That Mattered

14 - The Result - Sinner was Justified Why?
He Was Needy - Asked

Pharises Had No Needs - Did Not Ask Anything
Rev 3:14 Laodicea

3

The Punch Line
Sound Bites
Gods Way – Mans Way
Every One That Exalts Himself

1. Blow your own Horn PROV. 27:2
2. You Deserve The Best
3. Nice Guys Finnish Last

Jm. 4:6
4:10
Humble yourself And God will Lift you Up
Phil. 2:5
Humble – If you Think you Are - you Are Probably Not!

Lu. 23:32-46

Pg 92 Top

Prophecy

V32 - Crucified With Sinners Is 53:12

33 - They Crucified Him - Josephus

34 - Prays For Enimies Ps. 109:4

35-38 Mocked & Insulted Ps 22: 6-8

39 - ~~[illegible]~~ You Are The Messiah - Right?
Sarcastic

40-41 Rebuke

42 - Amazing Confidence - He Watched Him Dying &
Yet Believed!

Heaven?
43 - Paradise - Where God IS - Persian

44 - Sixth hr - Began At Sun Up 6:00 A.M.

45 - Could Not Be A Lunar Eclipse -
Full Moon During Passover Week

2

45 - Curtain - Seperated the Holy Place - where Priests Ministered - from Holy of Holies - when God Dwelt

It Was A Thick Woven Material - No one Could Tear It

Significance - No More Seperation From God - Jesus Death opened The Way - Directly To God

46 Jesus Was in Control - His Death was Conscience - Voluntary
No one Takes My Life - I Lay it Down

47 Centurian - Roman Soldier - Praised God!

48 Beating Their Breasts MT 27:51

Ch 24:13-

Pg. 96

V 25 - All That the Prophets Have Spoken

27 - Beginning With Moses = Genisis!

44 - Moses - Prophets - Psalms
Pg. 94 - Questions

MT. 27:

52 - Made His Grave with Rich

Joseph & Nicodemas

Ch 28

Read 1-10

17 - But Some Doubted Jn 20:24

Jn 21:1-14

Paul - 1 Cor 15:1-9

James = Brother of Jesus!

12-20

Christ Has Been Raised!

Lord of Life Jo. 11

Mary Martha Lazarus

Provided Jesus With The Closest Thing
To A Family - A Sanctuary During His Years
of Ministry - Bethany - 2 miles From Jerusalem

Evedintly A Wealthy Family
1. House & Life Style 2. Expensive Perfume $50.00 3. Jewish Rulers Came To Home

Need To Begin AT Verse 1 - Ch 11

V.2 - Mary anointed feet Jo 12:3

V.4 - Sickness Not Unto Death
5-6 - Jesus Delayed For 2 Days - Because He
Discerned That God was going To Do A Miricle

Hand out Paper!

14 Lazarus is Dead

17 in The Tomb 4 Days - Important!
Rabbis Believed The Soul Left The Body After 3 Days
Lazarus was Officially Dead - 3 Days in Tomb - Same as
Jesus - only 1 month Away

18-19 - Many People = Wealthy Family = Large Funeral

20-21 - Marthas Response = Quarterly Pg. 45-46

WOW! Amen! Right on! who is Writer?

32. Marys Response = If you had Been Here ----
33. Jesus Shows Compassion

35 - Jesus Wept - Even Though He Knew what He was To DO
37 - Back biters - Misunderstanding

38 - Horray For King James ! "Groaning"
Greek - Embrimaomai = Deep Indignation - Anger
a harsh agitated feeling -
Deep displeasure - over Sin & Death

39 - Jesus Takes Command - Martha objects

41 - A Public Prayer - Not For God - For People!
What does this say about Public Prayers?

43 - Lazarus - Come Forth !

Unbind Him! Jesus Gives Us Freedom!

What is Binding You Today?
Jesus will set you Free!

45 - Many Believed - But Not All - V-46
Some People will Never Believe

Lazarus goes on into Obscurity -
Remember - This Sickness was To Glorify God

(John 13)

Familiar Text
Always Learn Something New

The Setting

1. Before The Passover ?
His Hour had Come

Jesus Wanted A Quiet evening Together
A Few Last Words

2. Satan Planted The Seed - Jesus Never
gave Up on Him Pg. 71

3. A Great Statement - He Was God!
Phil. 2:5 - The Ways of God
Humble Yourself - God will Lift You Up

4. The Quiet Evening is Falling Apart!
Feet Should Have Been Washed By Someone
when They Entered - But Disciples were
Arguing - Who Was Greatest

5-6 Peter is Shamed - The Rest Sat in Silence
Peter Speaks - Never!
Peter Was A Jew - God Needed To Shake Him
in Order To Use Him! We Too

2

7-8 Jesus Was Gentle - Yet Firm

9-10 Peters Outburst - Gives us more Explaination
This is Not A Physical Cleansing

11 - Judas was Also Washed - What Love!
Jesus Knew His Intentions - Yet Continued To Reach out
How About Us? In The Church -
Wheat & Tares - Leave Them Alone - Harvest

12 - Do you Know What I Have Done?
Turned our World Upside down!

Gods Ways Are Not Our Ways!
MT 20: 25-26

18 He who Ate My Bread - - - Ps 41:9

21 Judas Played His Part Well - No One
But Jesus Knew - -
May be Another Reason No one Suspected
Judas was - The Seating Arrangement
or Lying arrangement!

23 Lying Close To The Breast
Barclay Pg 168

3

26 - Judas Was Close By -
The Morsel Also Has Special Meaning

For The Host To Offer A Special Tid-Bit
A Sign of Friendship -
Kenya - Goat Neck!

Still - The Disciples Did Not Get It
Jesus Must Have Done That Many Times
Before - Special Love for Judas

27 - Jesus Tried To The Very End -
But -- Pr. 29:1 He who is oft Reproved -
yet Stiffines His Neck - Shall Suddenly
Be Broken --
Time Ran Out For Judas

28-29 - The Money Box - Was Judas Corrupted Because
He Kept The Money?
OR - Did He Keep The Money Because He was Corrupt?
Moral of Story - Don't Be The Treasurer!

31 Judas is Gone - Jesus Can Continue
with His Quiet Evening Together

4

34 - Last - Last Words - Disciples Leaned Forward
So Should We

I am Going Away - You Cannot Come - Yet

A New Commandment - Love one Another

35 This Shall Be The Sign . . .

Not Feet Washing -

Not Speaking in Tongues -

Jo. Ch 13 - 33

33 Jesus Says I Am Going Away

34 A New Commandment - Love one Another

35 - By This - A Profound Statement

36 But Peter Doesn't Hear IT!
Where Are you Going?

37 Big Talk - Doesn't Cut it

38 Peters Failure - Encouragement - Rock
In Our Weakness - God Strong

Ch 14 = Funeral Talk!

Disciples Are Troubled

Jesus is Leaving -
Judas is Deserting -
Even Peter Will Fail

They Need Reeassurance

vs 1 Do Not Be Troubled

You Believe - Trust in God = Also Me

2

2. Dwelling Places

3. Jesus Himself will Prepare A Place - & Come For Us! A Great Promise!

Heaven is --- Where Jesus is

4. Jesus Says You Know The Way & Where I Am Going

5. Thankful For Thomas -

6. I Am The Way

Christians were Know As followers of "The Way"

Jesus - Did Not Say - I will Show you The Way
All other Religions - "Show The Way"
"Works Righteousness"
You Have To Work Hard To Follow Directions -
Jesus Says - I will Take You There!

I Am Truth = God

Satan = Father of Lies

3

I Am Life - can Exist without Jesus
- cannot Live!

Jesus Said - I Came To Bring you Life

No One! - Comes - But Through Me

very Clear - No One

Midas = Nobody

Reason is Very Clear -

If there were some Other Way ----

1. Jesus Would NoT Have Had To Die - Blood!
2. Jesus Was NoT Gods Son = Holy
3. God is A Liar - Plan of Salvation

Rev. Ch. 5

7-8 Disciples Are Still Lost!

Lets NoT Be Critical - Human

9 - Jesus + Father are ONE - God!

0-12 - Greater Works = ?

13 - NoT A Blank Check

John 14

V. 15 Keep Commandments - Because of Love
Not Works Salvation

Daniel Stoltsfus

16 - Comforter - Counselor = Called Alongside
With you Forever

17 - God is Truth - Jesus is Truth
The World cannot Recieve - Foolishness
Lives Within - A New Concept
Jer 31 - A New Covenant - in Their Hearts
Him - Him - He - Holy Spirit A Person

18 - Reassurance - Not Alone - Orphans

19 - Because I Live - You will Live
(Bill Gaither Musical)

21 - Obedience - Lou Holtz -
Obedience more Important Than Football Games...
God says obedience is Better Than Sacrifice - Samuel - Saul

23 - If you Love Me - Obey Me!
Bible our Final Authority For Life

23 - We will Come? - Father?
Trinity - Stoltsfus

25-26 Father Sends H-S in Jesus Name
Ch 16:13 - Declare Jesus - Glorify

Our Teacher - Not Human Teachers!

Christians Are Always Learners
Not Negative -- Exciting!

Eye Hath Not Seen
Nor entered into The Heart -

Bring To Remembrance = Gospels - Acts

27 - Peace -
Gods Peace -- Worlds Peace

Absence of Conflict

In The Midst of Conflict!

2Tim 1:7 - God Did Not Give us A Spirit of Fear
Power - Self-Control

30 - Satan - Ruler of This Present World
He Has No Power Over Us

Acts = Action!

Paul = One of The Greats
Jesus Said John was Greatest

Systematic – Exspository Style
Verse By Verse

Ch 9:1 Saul = Sincere – Dedicated – Religious
2 Stephen WRONG!
Many Today – Be Alert

3 Conversion – Wouldn't It Be Great If Every Believer Had This Experience?

But Every Believer Must Be Born Again

4 "The Ways of God"

Why Do You Persecute Me?
1. Jesus Lives in Every Believer
2. Persecution is Borne By Jesus

5 Jesus is Alive & With Us Today!

6
7 A Large Party Traveled With Him

2

8 Blinded - Humbled

1. God Cannot Use A Proud Person
Spiritual Pride = Worst

9

10 Ananias - #2 A Layman - God uses Ordinary People
Does God Still Speak Directly?

11 Street Called Straight - Archeology

12 - When God Calls Us To Do Something -
He Always Prepares The Way - Kenya!

13 But - But Its Still Scary!
O.K. To Doubt - No Rebuke

14 God's Ways Are Not our Ways - Jer

15 Go -
A Chosen Vessel - Kings

16 Suffering - Paul Gloried in it

17 Brother Saul - Tremendous!

2

25-26 – Here We See The Real Character of Barnabas

He Could Have Just Gloried in The Huge Church He had Built

He Knew These New Converts Needed Teaching -
Not His Gift –
So - He Went for Help

No Jealousy – Able To See Spiritual Gifts in Another

Together – They Taught - God Blended their Gifts

Paul = Intellectual – Intense - Jewish

Barnabas = Gracious – Forgiving - Easy Going

The Church = A Body - When All the Parts Are Working in Harmony

27-30 - Revival - Spirituality – Close To Lord
Always Leads To Action =
God Has Blessed Us - What can We Do For Others

II

Rom 5:1-11

Justification

1 Quarterly - Pg 33

Justification = 1st Result or Fruit of Salvation

1. It is An Immediate Gift
The moment you Believe - Received By Faith
Obtained - - - Not Attained

2. It is A Perfect Gift - There are No
Degrees of Justification
Weak Faith vrs Strong Faith = No more Justified
a little faith will bring a soul into heaven -
a strong faith will bring heaven into a soul!

3. It is A Gift To Be enjoyed - Something
God Has Already Done For Us - We need To
Posess our Posessions = Assurance

1st Possession = Peace with God

We have Peace Because Not Guilty

Do You Have Peace? if Not - - -
Did You Forgive Yourself?

2 Jesus Provides Access To God - We Stand
only By Grace -

Rejoice in Hope Pg. 33

To Share in Glory of God!
Joint heirs with Jesus

2

3 Is That enough For You? Paul says
Theres More!

You're Saved - Justified = Heaven
But only The 1st Step

God wants To Change Us - To Prepare
us For His Glory

Paul experienced This - Acts 9

And His Primary Tool is - Suffering

How Are We To Respond? - Rejoice!

Why? = Because We Know God Has A
Purpose - Look Beyond The Now - Eternity

1st Purpose = Endurance - Patience
Most of Us Would Never Develope This on our own

God whispers in our Pleasures -- but Shouts in
our Pain

Be honest - When Did you Experience Most Spiritual Growth?

4 2nd Purpose = Character - Amplified = Integrity

3rd Purpose = Hope - Joyful Confident Assurance

5 This Kind of Hope - Not Pie in The Sky
Never Dissapoints Because --

Gods Love Poured in Through Holy Spirit
Pg. 34

Jn. 13:34 - By This shall All men know -

3

6 The Depth of Gods Love - while we were weak -
Pg. 34

7-8 Tell Story Told After Breakin

9 Now some Deep Theology ---

Verse 1 - said - We are Justified By Faith -
verse 9 - says - We are " By Blood ?

10 verse 10 says we are Saved By His Death -- saved By Life

Saved From Penalty of Sin

Being Saved From Power of Sin

Someday Saved From Presense of Sin

Justified	-	Sanctified	-	Glorified
Death - Blood		Holy Spirit - Life		Presense of God

Pg 34 - How much More

11 If We ever Fully Understand What God Has Done For Us -- We Also will not Be Able To Stop Talking About iT

11 Rom 9-11

Ch 10:12 - No Distinction - Jew - Greek - Black etc

God wants To Bless Us - with every Spiritual Blessing

13 - every one - will Be Saved Pg. 63

~~II Pet. 3:9~~

Saved From What ? - Hell!

Sin

Seperation From God

69% of Clergy Do NoT Believe in Hell!

Jesus Did!

ThaTs Why They Don'T support Missions

DonT Blame iT on God - He Does NoT Desire ThaT Any should Perish II PeT 3:9

14 - BuT How Can They Call on Him who - - -

3 Billion People - who have Never heard!

2 Billion will have To Be Reached Cross - CulTurely

No "Living WiTness"

Kenya - 22 Mil. Zaire - 26 mil - Sudan 20 mil Tanzania

Uganda - Somalia - Zambia - Mozambique

And Yes - Even in This CounTry - A New generaTion growing Up - who will noT hear The Gospel

A Churches SpiriTual VITALITY is NoT Measured By what iT ATTracTs To ITself - (Membership numbers)

Rather By WhaT IT Sends OuT!

2

14b - And How Can They hear WithouT A Preacher ?
Did you Ever Stop To Think About The Method God Has Chosen To spread The Gospel ?

12 Disciples - THey Formed The Church - They sent OUT Preachers -- ITS Ludicrous - Folly

Paul - with His great Education - I Cor 2:1-2
I Cor 1:21

BuT God - in His GreaT Wisdom - Has made The Gospel so Simple - even A Child

Rom 10:9-10 = The Gospel

I Never Thought That I Would Preach ---
Many of you Could -

If you Could Share The Joy That Comes with Bringing Good News!

Too often We Missionaries Share only our STruggles & Trials - NoT Joys

Share LeTTers

15 - The Church is The Sending Body --
you Send Me - A.I.M. = ExperTise
BuT -- We Need To Do MORE

a Church our Size Should ~~Have AT Least~~ Do More

3

Not Just **Foreign** Missionaries

But Here At Home Also - Many Needs

1. Social Ministries - Good Job -

But Maybe We Need To Call & Send Full Time!

2. Bob Jacoby - Evangelism

16 - God Has Made us With The Freedom To Chose

Our Job = Preach - Sow - Plant

Gods Job = Harvest

Example - Sudan - years of Labor - Gone
Today - 4 are held Hostage

17 - Many People Want To Believe - But have Never heard A Clear - Complete - Straight From Bible

We Make it So Complicated - God Says It Simply

Ch 11 - We Can only Understand This Passage By 1st Stopping - & Reminding ourselves That -

1. God is God - Soverign
2. His Ways Are Better - Higher
3. He Sees The Big Picture - We Are only A Speck

Pg 63-64 - Gods Way

33-36 - Pg 64

I Cor. 1 & 2

Ch 1:2 - Written To US!

V-7 - Body of Christ - Unique!
Each Body Equipped By God - Every Gift!
We Are Not Lacking Gifts --- Need To Identify - Encourage

10 - No Division - Ideal
Unity - Not Uniformity

11-13 → Causes of Division

1. Misconception of The Message

Baptism - Not Message - 14-16

Message = V-17- 23 - Ch 2: 1-2

Simple Message - Why? - 2:5

Healing
Spiritual Gifts } Result of Message
Peace Etc.

Ch2:V 11-13 - The Holy Spirit Gives The Message
From Gods Heart To Our Heart

3 Types of People

1. Natural Man

2. Carnal - Baby Christians - Kenya - Picture of Ryan

3. Mature - Eph. 4: 11-16

2

Misconception of The Ministry

Ch3: V3 - Jealousy - Strife = Focus on Leader
Apollos - Peter - Paul

V5 - Apollos - Paul = Servants

6 - One Planted - One Watered - God gave Growth

Why Do We Make Super Stars of our Ministers?

Follow The World - Sports - Movies + T.V.
Music
Bakker - Graham - Swindoll

7 - God Chooses To Use Us - Doesn't Have To
Could Use A Donkey!

8-9 - A Team Effort
10
Football = Always Quarterback!

12 - Very Important

Gold - Silver - Refined By Fire

Lanny Arensen - 1 Pet 1:6

We Each Must Go "Through The Fire" - Motives

18 - Don't Deceive Yourself

21 - Don't Boast of Men

I Cor. Ch. 6

This Lesson Need To Start at End!

V 19-20 - Christian goal - Glorify God
Body = Temple of God

Do you Not Know ? = Theme of Ch. 6
V-19-16-15-9-3-2 = 6 Times
Paul Taught Them - O.T. Scriptures Taught
Jer. 31: 31-33
Previously God Dwelt in Tabernackle-Temple

V 9-10 - Amplified

Review Definitions

Barclay Pg. -60

11 - Such Were some of You - Past Tense!

But you were Washed - Blood

Sanctified - Justified
Set Apart - Cleaved Declared Righteous

Fannie Grove - penalty - Power - Presence

2

12- All Things Are Lawful = Grace

Ch 8 = Meat offered To Idols

Kenya = Sandy - Slacks

13- Meat For Belly = (Nescessary For one another)
Corinthinians Said Same was True For Sex

Paul Says NO! Body made For Lord
Dwelling Place

15- Principle - Our Bodies Are One
with The Lord

16- Marriage - Two Shall Become One

17- Jesus - You = One Spirit

18- Flee Immororality - Sexual sins Different?

Other Sins By Fight - This By Flight!

Ex. Joseph

Amplified

"Sandy Slacks"

Even though Sandy wears slacks,

she deferred to the convictions of the Kenya church and culture.

She wore skirts/dresses to not offend or weaken the faith of Kenyan Christians.

"Kenyan Funerals"

When we first arrived in Kenya,

we did not know what the loud drums and cries were that we heard throughout the night.

Someone had died and according to their traditions,

they were keeping away evil spirits.

My workers called a pump pliers "the parrot" because to them it looked like a parrot's beak, an adjustable wrench they called "a spanner" because they could span things, and my work shed they called the "Go Down" because I would tell them to go down to the shed to get things.

The AIC Kijabe Hospital had hundreds of people coming through every day. The bathrooms often needed extra cleaning because many people never saw a toilet and did not know how to use a toilet. I found out that the hospital cleaners only cleaned clean bathrooms! One necessary job that no one wanted to do became a job I took care of. One week the toilet system backed up in a student nursing dorm. Several days passed before someone told me about the problem. I was shocked to find that I needed to wade through three feet of sewage to fix the problem. I fixed the problem and cleaned up the mess.

Review - Conversion of Saul

Begin
9:20 - Immediately - He Proclaimed Jesus
"He is The Son of God"
22 - Proving - from The O.T. - Jesus Was Messiah

23 - Many Days - Desert ? Gal. 1:15
2 Cor. 12:1-7

25 - Escape
26 - To Jerusalem — Acts 4:36
27 - Barnabas = "Son of Encouragement"
28 - Joined Peter & James - Lords Brother
29 - Hellenists - Same Group That Stoned Stephen
Paul - Un Afraid of Death
30 - Brethren - Same People Paul Tried To kill
Now Protect Him!
Transforming Power of Jesus - Kenya

Paul Returns To Tarsus - Home

11:19-21 - The Church At Antioch
Cyprus - Cyrene - Greeks

22 - Send Barnabas
23-24 - Discernment = Spiritual Gift

Barnabas = Full of Holy Spirit
A "Good" man - Gracious - Encourager
We Need More Barnabases!

Ch 13 1st Missionaries
Many People Ask Why Missions?

1. God Commands IT MT 28:19-20 Acts 1:8
2. We Want To Share Good News
Forgiveness - Peace - Power over Sin
3. Hell - Kenyan Funerals - No Hope
→ universealism - Way - Truth - Life

Share A.I.M.

Lesson Start - v 13

14 - Antioch of Pisidia = Galatia
15 - Jewish Service
16 - Always Be Ready To Respond = Evangelism

17 - History - O.T. - Nadine & Jolene P.C.B.

22 - David - A man After Gods Heart ??

23 - Prophesy - O.T. - Fulfillment N.T.

26-40 - The Message - Still The Same
Jesus - Son of God - Crucified - Raised
Forgiveness of Sin - Justified - Sanctified - Glorified

42-44 - When Gospel is Clear - Excitement!
Joy!

I COR 15: 1-27 I COR 15: 51-58

The Ressurection

The Single Most Important event in Christianity
ALL other Religions Worship Dead Prophets
Christians Serve A Risen Living Lord!

V 3 Paul says it is of 1st importance

1. Christ Died - He was Dead - Professional Killers
2. Was buried - Tomb was Sealed by Rome
3. was Raised on The 3rd Day

The Stone was Rolled Away - His body was gone!
Christianity stands or falls on the ressurection
Was Jesus just A great Teacher? - Prophet?
OR -- Son of God

12 some Corinth were saying that there was no ressurection
13-14 Paul says - If Christ is Not raised - our Faith is in Vain!
20 - But it is indeed A Fact
The ressurection is one of the best proved facts of history
many men have set out to disprove it - only to become believers
Look AT The Facts - Actual appearances of The Risen Lord

5 1. Peter - The 12
6 2. more than 500 people at one time! still living - Paul says if you don't believe me - go ask them
7 3. James - the brother of Jesus
4. Jo. 20: 24 Thomas

Acts 1: 3 - 40 Days

I COR V 51-58

Greatest Proof = Changed Lives

Heb 9:28 (8:1) - Jesus now AT Right hand of God - Awaiting The Time of Second Coming - Are You Ready?

EPh. Ch.1

Eph Ch 2:11-22

3 years Ago I Began Here -- Now This Is My Last Sun

v 15 - In America - I had heard of your Faith
Now - I have **Known** IT

16 Thanks For you - Remembering you in Prayer

17 wisdom.

18 Eyes of Your heart -- That you may Know

19 Power

20 in heavenly Places

Ch. 2:13 - This Jesus Unites Us - Brings us Together
Once you were Far Away - Now you Are Near

14 - He is our Peace - Breaking Down The Walls
of HostiLiTy

19 - No Longer STrangers - FeLLow CiTizens
Brothers & SisTers In ChrisT

20 - Jesus Is The Corner STone

22 - God Is Building His Church
you Are A ParT - I Am ParT

Even Though We WiLL Be SeperaTed
Geographically -- We CannoT Be SeperaTed
SpiriTually -- Together We Are The Body
of ChrisT!

Darvin: "Preached this farewell sermon at a Kenyan church."

Eph 3

1. For This Reason – What Reason?
Gentiles Are Joint Heirs - Same Body

A Prisioner of Whom? Ceasar
Good Lesson For Us - ATTITUDE

Our World is Changing – Who is in Control?
Paul – A Prisoner – Because God Willed IT

On Behalf of You Gentiles – Letters!
We Can See Gods Purposes = New Testament

2. Stewardship = Responsibility – We Too
Give IT OUT

3. The Great Mystery = Verse 6 – 1 Body
Paul Taught By The Ressurected Lord Galilia
Preached 14 years Before Talking With Apostles
Gal 2:6

4-6 Paul Stands in Awe – Mystery Made Known To Him

8 – Humility - Because He Saw Jesus
Turtle on Fence Post

7 – Not Pauls Idea – Gift of God!

Ministry = We Are Responsible For Depth
God is Responsible For Width!
Fruit

9-10 Hidden For Ages - Now Through Church
You & Me - Made Known
1 Pet 1:10-12
Going To Teach Angels ?

11 All Things on Schedual

12 Boldness - Confidence - Because of Christ

13 Great Concern - Will They Quit ?
These People Facing Persecution Daily -
Many Places Also Today - Glory in Suffering
Example

14 All This Puts Paul on His Knees Again
1st Prayer - For Wisdom & Understanding
2nd - Power

15-16 We Need Wisdom & Understanding - But - -
No Good Without Power To Implement
Indwelt By Holy Spirit

17 Christ Also Dwell - Make His Home in You

Rooted = Tree = Baobab

Grounded = Keep Feet on The Ground
in Love - Gods

"Baobab Tree"

The Baobab is a large tree in Kenya that puts down deep roots

and stores water in its trunk to live through droughts.

Likewise, we need to put down deep roots in the love of God.

Store the Word of God in our hearts.

"Goat Head & Neck"

If the Kenyans wanted to honor me, they would serve me the head or neck of the goat.

One time Sandy put a goat ear in her pocket because she could not eat it.

The Bible School students would try to sit next to me because

They knew I would give them their favorite parts of the meat.

18 Power To Comprehend = Holy Spirit
To Understand Fully - To Embrace
The Love of God -
Always Growing
19 Amplified
Church & Sunday School = Knowledge
Experiences of Life Make us Act on our Faith
Once You See God Work in Your Life --
Trust Him - Filled Through All Your Being!

20 Paul - Filled & Flooded with God
Breaks Forth in Praise!

1

Rooted & Grounded

(Ephesians)
Ch 3:14 - I Bow My Knee

16 - According To His Riches
Key Word NoT A PorTion - Rather An ProporTion

STrengTh for The Inner Man

STrengTh The OuTer Man Is Perishing - BuT The
Inner Man Is Renewed Day By Day

By The Holy SpiriT Himself -
Indwelling our InnermosT Being

17 May ChrisT Dwell - SeTTLe Down
Abide - Make His PermanenT Home

Key Words

DepTh They Already Had ChrisT - Paul Calls
Them "SainTs" - Paul Asks For A Deeper
RelaTionship

Rooted & Grounded
2 DifferenT Dimensions

RooTed = PlanT World
Grounded = ArchiTecTural Term

2

Rooted - We Think of Trees
When We Saw The Redwoods
Tremendous Root System - Many Years Old

We Are Like Trees - Ps. 1

If There Is To Be Power In Our Lives -- Then There Must Be Roots!

Grounded - The Most Important Part Of Any Building - Foundation
Jesus Told About The Man Who Built His House On The Sand

EveryThing Looks Fine Untill The Wind Blows
The Wind Reveals The Foundation - The Roots
Many Christians Are Like That

You Can Be Sure Of One Thing -- The Wind Will Come

So What Are We To Be Rooted & Grounded In? LOVE

Not Mushy Love -- Rather Agape Love

3

And Who Was The Personification Of
That Love? - Jesus

That's Why Paul Says In I Cor 3 -
No Other Foundation Can Any Man Lay
Than Christ Jesus

18 - King James - RSV Say Comprehend - Wrong!
Comprehend Speaks of Mentally Understanding

Key Word → Apprehend = Greek = To Seize - To Posess
Amplified → To Take Eagerly

The Breadth - Length - Heigth - Depth
What Paul Means Here Is That It's
Beyond Measure

19 What Is The Result Of All This?
The Fullness of God

To Know The Love - Experience It

Amplified → To Be Wholly Filled With God!

Not Just Once - But Again & Again
Eph 5:18 = Keep on Being Filled

4

20 Now Paul Burst Forth In Praise!

By The Power = Dunamis - At Work In you -
To Do Far Above All That We Could Ask or Think

If We Insist On Running Our Own Lives -- The Best We Can Hope For Is What We Can Think of ---
But -- If We Let God Run Our Lives - He Can Do Things For Us That We Can't Even Think Of!

Eye Hath Not Seen - Nor Ear Has Heard
Nor Has It Entered Into The Heart of Man
The Things That God Has In Store For Us!
Halleluia!

21 But Why Does God Share His Power With Us?
So We Can Build Great Churches?

To Go off on Some Glorified Ego Trip?
NO! - NO!

5

To Him Be The Glory

And The Wonderful Thing Is -

The Things We Do In His Power - Will
Glorify Christ Throughout All Ages -
Forever & Ever!

The Best Is Yet To Come!

We're In Kind of A Dress Rehearsal --
getting Ready For That Day When We
Shall Continually Be In His Presence

Praising & Glorifing Him!

Closing = Sing Doxology - Slowly

Phil. 1: 1-11 + 27-30 3: 1-16

3/ I Thank God For You All
5/ Your Partnership in The Gospel

8-10 My Prayer For You

27/ In A Short Time I must Leave You - -
Whether I come - or Am Absent
"Let your Life Be worthy of Christ"

Today in The Church There Are Many Who
Boast In Themselves Ch. 3: 4-7 If Any man - -

3: 8/ For Christ Sake - - Paul Lost Everything!
But Counts It As Dung!
9/ No Righteousness of His Own
10/ That I may Know Him! - Power of Ressurection

Today The Church Has Lost Its Power - -
Because It Is Not in Him! It Looks To The
World - It Looks To The Shilling For Power

The Power of The Church is The very
Blood of Jesus Christ - Ressurection

Ch. 2: 1-11 → (Slowly)

Phil Ch 2:12 – 18

12 – Work out Salvation Eph 2:8-9

Not A Works Righteousness – Not Paul!

Salvation = Corporate – Church To Spiritual Maturity

2 Things Left of World – People – Word

Work out Salvation By – InterAction Within The Body = Sanctified

I Could Be A Great Christian – If IT Weren't For Other Christians!

Too Much Individualism Today –

Epistles Now!

Problems? Change Churches

God Uses Conflicts To Shape Us

Pastor Hepner – Church Hoppers

Do This in A Right ATTiTude – Reverence – Awe

Remember Who you Are – Who God IS Ps. 8

13 Not in Own STrengTh – IT is God Who gives us The Desire & Power To Will & To Work His Pleasure!

Gods Will – Gods Way – Gods Power =

Lasting Fruit –

A Paradox – Positive Thinking

2

14 ATTITude! - ATTITude! - ATTITude!

Negative Thinking is A Deadly Cancer

I'm Working in The "Real World" = Dauphin Home

Grumbling - Complaining - Fault Finding

Disaster For Church - Hospital - Kijabe

15 Without Spot or Wrinkle - Blameless Before Others

Not without Sin - before God

In The World - which is Spiritually Bankrupt

[Pigion Shoot Abortion] → Perverse

We Should Be A Contrast - Light in Darkness

Not Stars - But Moons - Reflecting Light

16 Offering The Word of Life

I Pet 3:15 Be Ready

[GoThard - Fear]

Day of Christ Return - Keep our Eyes Focused on Goal -

So That I May Have Something To Rejoice -

Casting our Crowns At His Feet!

[Epistles Now!]

That I might Know Him - and The
Phil 3:10 Power of His Ressurection
How Well Do you Know Him?
Dictionary
1. To Be aquainted with - Familiar with (Many Christians)
2. To Be sure about The Identity of - To Recognize (Emaus Road)
3. To have A Practical and operative grasp of
It's easy To Praise The Lord in U.S.
Great Music - Dynamic Preachers - Wonderful Fellowship
4. To have Learned By Rote - To have memorized
5. To have experienced - To have come To grips with
6. To have understanding - a Certainty
Do you Know Him?
Once we Really Know Him - everything else
Fades in Importance - Paul - had it made
Was Perfect - under The Law V-6
But v 7&8 - Counted it All Loss - Unimportant

The Power of His Ressurection
Are you Living in The Power of The Ressurection?
Jesus said That same Ressurection Power is
Availiable Jo. 14:12
But - we're Like Peter - He heard Jesus say
on The 3rd Day - I will Rise
We hear Jesus say - He who Believes in Me
Will Also Do The Works That I Do -
And Greater Works Than These - Do we Believe?

And May Share His Suffering
The Clinker!
Allow me To Give Some background on Me –
So – you'll know where I'm coming From
Attended 1st H. S. Conference
Attended Numerous B.R.F. "
Kenya = Suffering
Phil 3:1 1 Pet. 4:1 -- 4:12 (If)
Verse 10 → Amplified Bible – To so Share His Sufferings
as To be Transformed into His Likeness – even
To Death Dan Yutzy – I am Crucified with
Christ Gal. 2:20 – Col 3:1
If ye Then Be Risen With Christ – seek Those Things

Verse 11 – Paul not only Speaking of Physical Death
He knew and Believed in Resurrection – 1 Cor 15 – I Thes. 4
Amplified –
You see -- There are some People who Think They're
Really Living – but They're Already Dead! Jn 3:18
And Then – There are Some who have Already
Died – Crucified with Christ – who Are Really Living!

Verse 13 – Press on Towards The Goal = Christian Maturity
(So easy in This Country To Remain Babes – spoon fed)
20 – Our Citizenship is in Heaven! And We
Await our Saviour!

Colossians

4. "We Have heard of your Faith" - And your Love

6. They heard The gospel = Truth - grace - Jesus
And Believed!

9-20 Pauls Prayer

1. Spiritual Wisdom
2. Walk Worthy
3. Bear Fruit = Patience - Long Suffering - Joy

Joy - Not The Same As Happiness

Joy - Comes From God - Makes Us Thankful

Verse 13-20 Heavy Doctrine!

1. He Delivered Us - From Darkness
2. He Redeemed Us
3. He Forgave Us

15 The Exact Likeness - The Firstborn
Jo. 14:9 He That hath Seen Me Hath Seen The Father

16 He Created ALL Things = ALL Things Exist For Him
In Him & Through Him

18 ① He Is The Head Of His Body - The Church

② He Is The Begining - Originator

ALL Christians Are Baptized Into This Body By The Holy Spirit. 1 Cor. 12:12-13

③ He Is Pre-Eminent - No 1

Many Religions Revere Christ - As One of The great

19 Teachers -- But Paul Says He Is God!

21 We Were Seperated - From God

Jesus Has Reconciled Us

22 In Orde To Present Us Holy - Blameless

Irreproachable

COLOSSIANS Ch 1

City of Colosae - 100 miles East of Ephesus

Quarterly Pg. 38

Paul Never There - Church Begun By Epaphras

Gnosticism - Ancient History ?

or Present Day ?

1. Redemption Through Knowledge v14
Today = Humanism

2. Special Revelations of Wisdom - v9
Today = New Age Chanelling

3. Not The Only Way To God v25
All Religions seek To Bring People To God
Today = Universalism

David Frost - Billy Graham
God of Love - Required To Save ALL ?

2

Quarterly Pg 38 - In Addition --

4. Christ One of Many Prophets V15-16
Muslims

Material World = Evil Spiritual World = Good

Body is Evil = Sexual Immorality
Excuse Behavior - Same Time Be "Spiritual"

See Any of That Today?

Nothing New - Colossians Tried To Fit
Christ into Their Existing Beliefs &
Lifestyle
Don't We Do The Same Today?

If Any one Be in Christ - A New Creature
Different
Maybe Stopped Smoking - Speeding

We Say The Church is The Living Body of Christ =

Then proceed To Organize it The Same
As Our Buisiness - Same As World

Roberts Rules of Order? - Democrocy?

3

Bibles!

U1&2 Greetings

3 The Father - Not Mother God

Brethren Used To Be People of The Book - No More

4-8 Epaphras - A Faithful Minister

Billy Graham - Same Words

9 Prayer - Filled with Knowledge = Gnosis

10 Walk A Good Walk
A Good Lifes Verse

11 Endurance - Patience with Joy

Joy - Not Rooted in The Soil of Suffering is Shallow

Rom
12-13-14 - in Whom We Have Redemption

4

Who is Jesus? Best Answer

15-19 Who is He on Yonder Tree
Dies in Grief And Agony
Tis The Lord O Wondros Story
Tis The Lord The King of Glory
At His Feet We Humbly Fall
Crown Him! Crown Him!
Lord of ALL!

22-23 If you Continue --

Assurance is Present Tense - God Never Changes

24 Pauls Sufferings - For Them
Corporate Body

Jesus Said = Why Persecute Thou Me?

25-27 Great Mystery - 1 Pet 1-10 12

Now Revealed - No Secrets (Waco) Koresh

Christ in You - Hope of Glory

Col. 3

Raised With Christ

1. Before you Can Be Raised --
   you Must Have Died! vs 20

Aim at - Seek Eternal Treasures

Christ - seated At The Right Hand

2. Set = To Exercise The Mind
   Direct your Affections

3. Hid = To Conceal By Covering
   Blood Is Covering

5. Mortify = Kill - Deaden - Deprive of Power!

How? II Cor 10:34-5 Gothard

Covetousness = Idolatry? Yes!

Worship of Things

8. Verse 5 Didn't Hit you? - How About
   This One?
   Anger -- Bad Feelings Towards Others

2

But Maybe Someone Says I Remember Paul Says It's Alright To Be Angry Eph 4:26

anger is a signal - that we have not yielded one "right"

Not Be Angry K.J. - Rather When you Are Angry - give No opportunity To Satan - (Back To Gothand)

Ex. Cain Gen. 4

10 Ever In The Process of Being Renewed

11 The Ground Is Level At The Foot of The Cross

12 Clothe yourselves - Bowels of Mercy

Bowel = Splen = "spleen"

Intestine - Inward Affection

Kindness - gentleness - Patience - Humility - Longsuffering

Fruit of The Spirit!

13 Forgive One Another

3

14. Above All This - Love

15. Peace - Soul Harmony

Rule = To Act As An Umpire!

Have A Spirit of Thankfullness

16. Let The Word Have IT's Home In You

Sing Songs - Psalms - Hymns -
Making Melody To God!

Highest Form of Worship -
Singing Scripture Back To God

17. Whatever You Do - Do IT In The
Name of - In Dependence on Jesus

I Tim Ch. 1

1 Christ in you The Hope of Glory!

3 Remain AT Ephesephus

No OTher DocTrine - Gal 1:8

Biblical Absolutes

Only Major DocTrines - Major in Minors!

4 Genealogies - Blue Bloods

GnosTicism - Above The Law

Ground is Level AT FooT of Cross

5 K.J. = The End of The Law is - Love

Agape = Pure HearT = Clean Conscience

Jesus MT 22 - All of Law = Love God with

All HearT - Soul - Mind -

your Neighbor As yourself

6-7 Do NoT Desire To Be Teachers Jm. 3

Teach Gods Word - NoT Opinion

8 The Law is Good

Jesus = I Did NoT Come To Abolish

Law Leads To SalvaTion

9

9/ Laws Fo Un Godly

"Can't Legislate Morality"

Abortion - Murder ? Euthanasia ?
10 Homosexuality ?

Gods Law - Designed To Provide An Orderly Enviroment So That The Gospel Might Be Presented

Example - Kenya - Missionaries Son Killed
No Law & Order = No Witness
Sudan

12-17 - Pauls Testimony

18 - The Change - Keep The Faith

19 - Clear Conscience - How ?

Agree With God - Chief of Sinners

20. Hymenaeus - Infamous! Tragedy

2 Tim 2:17

I Tim. Ch. 6

6:5 - Error of Baalam 2 Pet 2:15 Nu. 18:7

TV Evangelists ?

I Tim 5:17

6:6 - Contentment - Grateful? & Thankful?

(Man Gives $100 Away)

6:7 - Hearse & U Haul

6:8 - Your Father Knows What you Need

6:9 - Who Crave To Be Rich - Obsessed

An End in Itself - Idolotry

10 Love of Money is A Root -

Leads To Temptations -

Examples of Jesus

1. Rich Young Ruler - 2. Zachaeus

3. Rich Man & Lazarus 4. Mary, Martha & Lazarus

11 Flee - There Are Times in Life - Flee!

Sexual Imorality - Joseph - Flee!

Aim AT Righteousness

Set your Mind on Things Above

5

12- Keep The Faith - A Battle

13

14 Keep your Eyes on Christ

17 - God Has Blessed Some Rom 12

18 - For The Purpose of Giving
(Paper)

19 - Lay Up Treasures In Heaven

20

II Tim, 3: 10-17

II Tim. 2:14-26

14 Paul Tells Timothy To Remind The people

15 We Are To Study The Bible - To Learn how To handle The Word of Truth Ch 3:16

16-17 Hymenae'us - Phile'Tus

19 "The Lord Knows Those Who Are His"

20 Vessels of Gold - Silver - Wood - Clay
We Are All Different - we have Different

21 Abilities - But Unless We purify Ourselves
We Are NoT Useful To God

22 Set A Goal - Aim AT Righteousness
He who Aims AT Nothing - will Always hit iT!

What Are your Goals?
For Christians = To be Like Jesus!
Study The Bible - Know The Truth
Grow in Grace - Love - peace

23-24 Correct with gentleness - They may yet escape The Devil
Lets NoT Be Ashamed when We Meet our Lord - Lets Study - Show ourselves Approved

Milk? - or Meat?

Heb 5:11 - 6:1-8

verse 8 - Obedience Learned Through Suffering

11 - Lost Spiritual Ears

12 - Easy To become Dependant on Milk
Spoon Fed

13 - Babes = Suckling growth Is Painful

14 Full Age = Teloi = Mature = Fully Trained Athlete
Able To discern Between good & Evil
Decieved - Jim Jones

6:1 - Doctrine of Christ?
1. Virgin Birth
2. Son of God
3. Messiah
4. Sinless Life
5. Death & Bodily Ressurection
6. Visible Return
7. Judgement

2 Baptisms - Laying on of Hands

3 Time to Move On!

Pg 2

4 - Heavy Scripture - Eternal Security?
If We Dwell on That - We Miss The Point

Paul is Issuing A Warning - If

And Because His Main Concern Is The
Lack of Spiritual Growth -
There Is Another Interpretation Possible
Wycliffe

We Can't Stand Still!
If We Don't Move Ahead -- We Will
go Backward!

6 - Look Again At Verse 6 -

How do We Crucify Jesus Afresh?

When We Name The Name of Jesus -
Make A Public Declaration - Then Refuse
To Allow Him To Transform Our Lives -
To Continue To Live As We Did Before
To Remain Spiritual Babies!

We Hold Jesus Up To Ridicule
By The World!

Pg 3

7:8 Now Paul Compares These People To A Field That Bears Only Weeds

The Final Test Is Always The End Product - Fruit

By Their Fruit Ye Shall Know Them

Jo 15:8

Not A Little Fruit - But Much Fruit

To Glorify God

Are We Producing Fruit?

Sometimes We Have A Hard Time Telling What Kind of Trees We See - Because Not Much Fruit -

When People Observe Your Life -- Can They Tell You're A Christian By Your Fruit?

Eph 4:11

This is the story of the van we borrowed from our neighbors to deliver a motorcycle to one of our Bible School students who began pastoring several churches. The plan was to drive several hours, deliver the motorcycle, and drive home before dark. We took along with us a Bible School student named Mercy. When we arrived at the pastor's house with the motorcycle, everyone erupted in a great celebration. We had to stay and eat with them. The celebration lasted for hours, even though we kept telling them that we had to return home before dark. With only one hour before dark, they released us with a blessing. As we drove down the steep bank, across the dry stream bed, and up another steep bank the van's engine stopped. Sandy found a flashlight in the glove box and I began to look at the engine. I discovered that the points had jumped off the post in the distributor cap. I did not have the special tool to make this repair. Mercy was standing outside the van talking with the crowd that suddenly appeared out of nowhere. Mercy came over to me and said, "Mr. Byler, are you going to fix this tonight? The men are talking about robbing you." I told her that I was working on fixing it. I asked God for help as I set the points on the post, put the cap back on the engine, and turned the key. The engine started and we quickly drove away from the crowd and made it safely home several hours after dark. Praise Jesus!

Hebrews 12

How Is IT with you Tonight?
Are you Down? Discoraged?
Feel Like quitting?

We All get weary In our Well Doing From Time To Time -- And This Ch. In Pauls Letter To The Hebrews Is A great Place To Go For Help.

As He Begins In verse 1 -- Paul PorTrays Here One of The Best IncenTives To Keep Us Going That you'll find In The Bible

VR 1 In Ch 11 He Just Finished Telling About Abraham - Issac - Jacob - Moses - ETc. All The Great Men & Women of Faith -- I'm Sure We Can Think of Some of our Own -- D L Moody - I.N.H. Beahm - Rufus Bucher J. Herbert - Perhaps your Father or Mother S.S. Teacher - Grove - Eby

Elisha

2 Kings 6:15 → All Gathered Around As A Great Cloud -- Watching - Urging Us On Can you See Them?

And Paul Is Saying - Look -- Don't quit Now - All These People Are Pulling For You!

I must Confess
How Are you? Spiritual Depression
Really?

Too Much Work - Too Little Fishing
2 Cars Broke Down - Can't Fix
Furnace on Last Leg
Mid Life Crisis?
Male Menopause?

Then I got My AARP Card in Mail!!

We All Get Weary From Time To Time
Heb. Ch 12
Pep Rally! → Antidote To Wearies

V1 - A Great Cloud of Witnesses - Ch. 11
Also - Mothers - Fathers - Husbands - Wives
Herb Miller - Fannie Grove - Harry Eby

All Gathered Around - Urging Us On

Can you See Them?

Need Spiritual Eyes

Elishas Servant - 2 Kings 6:15-16

Today? = Jesse Rank Funeral

2

Get Rid of Those Things That Are
Dragging You Down - Tripping You --
And Run With Perserverance The Race [Marathon]
That Is Set Before You

2 Looking To Jesus [Goal] The Pioneer [First] & Finisher [Last]

Who For The Joy --- What? The Cross
Yes -- Because He Knew The Ending!

So Can We -- Read The End of The
Book -- We Win!

3-4 Then He Says Think about This --
Have You Suffered As Much As Jesus?

You Think You Have IT Rough?
You Haven't Even Shed 1 Drop of Blood Yet!

We Always Like To Compare Ourselves
With Someone Who Hasn't Suffered As
Much As We -- OR Maybe Doesn't DO
As Much As We DO
But Then God Says Whoa!
~~Compa~~ Here's The Standard -
Compare Yourself With Jesus!

3/

5 And Besides -- Have you Completly
Forgotten That We Are Son's of God?
And He quotes Prov 3:11

6 That Is Why Paul Tells Us In Eph.
7 To Praise God In All Things
8 And James Tells Us To Count IT
All Joy When Trials & Temptations Come

God Is Bigger Than Any Circumstance
And He Can Remove Any & ALL Sources
of Irritations From Our Lives Right Now

8 But-- Paul Says If We Are Left
Without Discipline -- Then We Are Not
True Son's

9-10 Rather God Chastens Us -- To Make Us
More Like Jesus
With Gentleness & Love As A Father

4/12 So Then - Lift your Drooping Hands! -
Strengthen Your Knees

Why Does He Say - Lift Your Hands?
So We Can Start Praising The Lord!

There Is Power In Praise!
But you May Say - I Can Praise God
With My Hands Down -- I'm Not Going To Be
Like All those Charismatics -- Can you?

Try IT!
But you Say Is IT Scriptural?
You Bet IT IS!
Ps 28:1-2 - 63:4 - ~~119:48~~ - 134:2 - 141:2
O.K. you Say So David Was A
Little Charismatic - What About the N.T.?
Look AT 1Tim 2:8
I'll Give You Two More Reasons
1. Universal Sign of Surrender
2. Acts As A Funnel
Try IT! IT Just Might Help
You To Praise God
When We Start Praising God -- Even When We Don't
Feel Like IT - Then God Is Free To Remove
The Source of Irritation
Heb 13:15 - A Sacrifice of Praise

5

13-14 Holiness To See The Lord
That Used To Bother Me - Because I
Realized I was Never going To Make IT!

Untill I Learned That IT's Not Going
To Be My Holiness -- But Rather The Holiness
of Jesus - Imputed To Me - Grace of God
v15

15 Here Paul Warns Us of the Danger of
Developing A Bitter Spirit
If We Don't Shake Ourselves Out of
Our Self Pity - And Start Praising God
In Spite of Our Circumstances

Then We Are Open To Satan To
Sow The Seeds of Bitterness --
God Is Cheating you
Other Christians Don't Have To go Through this
You Deserve Better!
And When The Seed Takes Root
We Have A Crop of Rebellion

A Bitter Spirit Is Like A Rotten
Apple -- IT Contaminates Everything
Around IT!

6

16 And He goes on To Point Out
What Bitterness Can Lead To –
Immorality – Sacrilegious – Profane
17 To The Point Where Repentance Is
Very Difficult Example = Esau

18 We Are Not Come To A Physical
Mountain – Like The Israelites – –
19 Rather We Come To The City of The
20 Living God

22 And Again Paul Portrays A Vast Host
of Angels And The Redeemed of The
23 Ages – – – Notice – Those Made Perfect

24 And Jesus – Our Mediator of The
New Covenant Through His Blood

25 How Shall We Escape If We Neglect
So Great A Salvation? Heb. 2:3

26 Now Paul Reminds Us That God Is
Going To Shake Not Only The Earth –
II Pet 3:10 But Also The Heavens – And The Purpose?
So That What Cannot Be Shaken May
Remain

7

I Believe This Also Applies To The Church - Because In Verse 28 He Refers To A Kingdom

Also We Know That Jesus Is Coming For A Pure & Holy Church A Bride Without Spot or Wrinkle

Now That Doesn't Describe The Present Day Church

Do You Have A Piece of The Rock?
Could you Be Shaken Loose?

28 Once We Are Anchored In Christ = Completely Yielded & Controlled By Him -- Then We Can Offer Acceptable And Pleasing Worship To God

Now Tomorrow When Those Mon Morn Blues Hit you -- Think of Heb 12 ---
And Lift Your Drooping Hands

Praise God! Whether You Feel Like It or Not -- And See If It Doesn't Help

(the following page is from another sermon on Hebrews 12, but it is the only page in the file)

(Heb 12) 6

18 - We Do Not Come To A Physical Mountain

22 Rather We Come To The City of Living God!

23 Again Paul Portrays A Vast Host of Angels
And The Redeemed of All The Ages
Rev.
Always Singing! Christians = Music!

Kenya - 1st Sign of Conversion - Joyous Singing!
whichcraft = Somber
Can You Imagine Worship Without Music?
Greatest Music - Christians - Dick Hiler

Bach - Handle - "Messiah"
"Halleluiah Chorus"

Music = Universal Language

Halleluiah = Universal Language of Praise!

Let Me Demonstrate - Revive Us Again
Halleluiah Thine The Glory
We Praise Thee O God - For The Son of Thy Love -
For Jesus Who Died And is Now Gone Above

Darvin: "I often sang Revive Us Again in Kenyan – Kikuya." A page from my copy of Kikuya hymns.

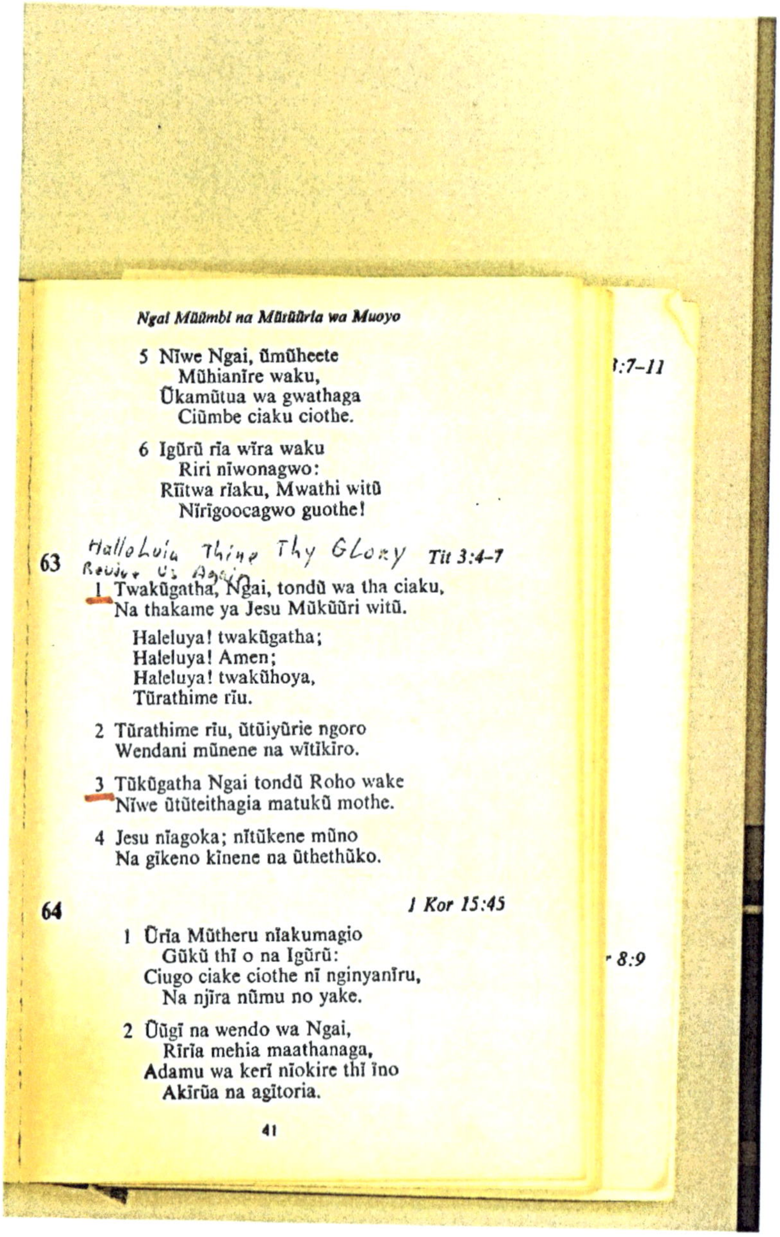

Ngai Mũũmbi na Mũrũũria wa Muoyo

5 Nĩwe Ngai, ũmũheete
Mũhianĩre waku,
Ũkamũtua wa gwathaga
Ciũmbe ciaku ciothe.

6 Igũrũ rĩa wĩra waku
Riri nĩwonagwo:
Rĩĩtwa rĩaku, Mwathi witũ
Nĩrĩgoocagwo guothe!

63 Halleluia Thine Thy Glory *Tit 3:4–7*
Revive Us Again
1 Twakũgatha, Ngai, tondũ wa tha ciaku,
Na thakame ya Jesu Mũkũũri witũ.

Haleluya! twakũgatha;
Haleluya! Amen;
Haleluya! twakũhoya,
Tũrathime rĩu.

2 Tũrathime rĩu, ũtũiyũrie ngoro
Wendani mũnene na wĩtĩkiro.

3 Tũkũgatha Ngai tondũ Roho wake
Nĩwe ũtũteithagia matukũ mothe.

4 Jesu nĩagoka; nĩtũkene mũno
Na gĩkeno kĩnene na ũthethũko.

64 *1 Kor 15:45*

1 Ũrĩa Mũtheru nĩakumagio
Gũkũ thĩ o na Igũrũ:
Ciugo ciake ciothe nĩ nginyanĩru,
Na njĩra nũmu no yake.

2 Ũũgĩ na wendo wa Ngai,
Rĩrĩa mehia maathanaga,
Adamu wa kerĩ nĩokire thĩ ĩno
Akĩrũa na agĩtoria.

41

A Somber Note – Heartbreak Hill!

25 Do Not Refuse Him!

26 God is Going To Shake The Church! II Pet 3:10

27 So That What Cannot Be Shaken Will Remain

Hows your Anchor?

28 Grateful – A Kingdom That Cannot Be Shaken!

29 Worship Acceptable To God
A Broken & Contrite Heart

A Consuming Fire

Pray!

(1)

I John - WRITING from The isLe of PaTmos
To CORRECT ERROR
Some were saying - possible to have no sin
Many Cults Today - Kenya!
What is Sin? = To miss The mark
 = ALL have Sinned 1:8

2:1 John says my wish is That you Do NoT Sin - - -
BUT - - we have an AdvocaTe PTL!
2/ And More Than An AdvocaTe - ExpiaTion
ChrisT is - Sacrifice - PaymenT PropiTiaTion
High Priest
3/ We may be sure we know Him - How?
Keep his Commandments
5&6 WaLk - The same way He walked
Can You see Jesus in Your own Life?
not Someone else - YOU!

TonighT - Love feasT = SeLf-ExaminaTion
Are You Looking Forward To meeTing Jesus TonighT?

2:28- NoT Shrink From Him in Shame
Why Don'T we hear more Today AbouT The
ReTurn of ChrisT? No one WanTs To See Him!

We need To See Sin For WhaT
iT Really is. (Page 9) 1. Agree with God

(2)

Unforgiven Sin- Seperates From God

When We See Our Sin- nailing Jesus
To The Cross -- Then God Can Use
Past Failures - To Remind Us That We
Belong To Him!

(sketch)

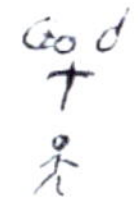

Now - Satan Would Use Past Failures To
Paralyize us with Guilt
He uses A Circle of Regret

if only ---
if only ----

Paul - our Example

Many Times Our Sin Involves Others
We need To Seek Forgiveness = Clear Conscience
There's A Reason why we have An Examination
service in The Morning -- And Love feast in The evening
Time To Seek Forgiveness
Why Don't we Do it? Because we believe
the other person was wrong!
The Splinter & Beam MT. 5:24 (Page 2)

R.E Freidly Seminar

Take Care of Your 10%!
Then See What happens
you Upset The Balance!
you Take Away The Blame!

(3)

Maybe you don't think you have
a problem - - - No Big Sins in
your Life
I have found We Bind one Another
BiTTerness - Unforgiving SpiriT - Gossip
PROV. 6:16 Some People Will Believe Anything
if - iTs Whispered!

Gods MosT HaTed LisT!
BackbiTing - God HaTes iT Because iT
DesTroys Fellowship

When we come together tonight - we should
be of one Spirit - we may not agree on
everything - - BuT - we All Agree
with What we Are Doing TonighT!

3:1 See WhaT Love - - By This Shall All men Know
ThaT you Are My Disciples - if you have
Love - one for another

I. B. Y. C.

(Revelation)

Encouragement - For Troubled Times

Universally Acknowledged The most Difficult book in The Bible

Calvin Refused To write A Commentary

Luther Avoided iT

G Cambell Morgan Said - There is No book in the Bible I have Read so Much, yet Understand so LiTTLe

Question → When is The Last Time you Read From Rev. ? | What is The 1sT Thing you Think of ?

Rev. is Noted for Gloom & Doom

a book For End Times About End Times

In our Day All news seems To Be Bad news iT Warps our Thinking - Causes Depression Despair

I Remember SiTTing in Sudan one Day - Thinking That The whole world could end in a Nuclear War - and I would Never Know !

BuT Now - To watch The evening News each night is Depressing !

That's A ShorTsighTed View of Rev -- AcTually --- Pg. 75 A Book of Worship

93 Hymns Inspired By Rev ! Pg. 79

Praise & Worship of Jesus !

He is The CenTral Figure Pg. 76

That's why it's so Important
we Be Bearers of Good News!

Who is in Charge? Pg. 76
Why Do Bad Things Happen To Good People?

What you Get – is what God Promised –
Already Secured – waiting For Us

STop! Questions Pg 79 b. – And c.

What is The Real Reason we Don't want
To Look Into Rev.?

Perhaps -- We Aren't Ready To Face Jesus

Perhaps -- We Are in Love With This World
Paul Compares Christians To Soldiers --
Don't get Bogged Down in Civilian Pursuits

"Eyes on The Prize" Ch. 33

We need To Keep A Proper Perspective --
Sandy & I Ask – Will iT Count 1 year From Now
10 " " "
Eternity

We Are Facing A Big Decision

Barber Shop – A man Works 45 Years AT
A job he Hates – Because of Job
Security And Retirement Benifits – Then
Dies – months After Retirement

He is No Fool who Gives What He Cannot
Keep -- To Gain what He Cannot Lose
Jim Elliot

SECTION FOUR: Old Testament Sermons Written & Preached by Darvin Byler. Kijabe Missionary Stories.

"Let not your heart be troubled. You believe in God. Believe also in Me. In My Father's house are many dwelling places. If it were not so, I would have told you. I am going to prepare a place for you. And if I go and prepare a place for you, I will come again and receive you to Myself, that where I am, you may be also. You know where I am going, and you know the way."

Thomas said to Him, "Lord, we do not know where You are going. How can we know the way?"

Jesus said to him, "I am the way, the truth, and the life. No one comes to the Father except through Me."

John 14:1-6 MEV

In 1987 we began our second missionary term. This time we knew what we were getting into and where we were going. It was a two-year term.

It was Nadine's first year in college. Sandy arranged with a local flower shop to send Nadine an arrangement of flowers every month. Nadine remembers the surprise and the thoughtful gifts of love being sent across the ocean.

Jolene graduated from RVA after our first year. She returned to Pennsylvania to join Nadine and begin her first year of college.

In 1982 we began with our whole family in Kenya and in 1988 we ended with half of our family in Kenya and half in Pennsylvania.

File folder marked "Old Testament". Sermons written and preached by Darvin Byler.

Explain Types - Scofield Pg 6

Cain & Abel - Gen 4

Cain = A Type of Natural Man
Abel = A Type of The Spiritual Man

Not Fair! ?

What made the difference?

4:7 Cain - did not do what God said
Man was sinful - needed a blood offering to make atonement - Heb 9:22
Cain Wanted To Come To God In His own Way - Without Confessing His Fallen Condition
He brought the fruits of the ground - which God had cursed! Vs. 17

Abel - Obeyed God (Had Faith!) - Acknowledged His Sin In Bringing A Blood Offering (Scofield Pg 9)
Heb 11:4

Cain is typical of the unspiritual man in 7 ways
1. He worships in selfwill
2. He is angry with God
3. refuses to bring a sin offering
4. Murders his brother
5. lies to God

6. become a wanderer
7. is nevertheless the object of divine grace
(verse 7)

In Cain we have the begining of all false religions - the essence of which is Man coming to God in his own way!

We have another type in verse 4
the lamb is a type of Christ
Jn 1:9 - The lamb of God who takes away the sin of the world

Why don't we study the Bible?

1. Dry history book
2. No real meaning for me today -
(Too Old)
3. Don't have time

Holy men of God - moved by the H.S. - Spoke 2 Pet 1:21

All scripture is inspired 2 Tim 3:16

More Than History

many applications - 1 interpretations

Because it's from God - perfect
gives principles to build our lives around

Everything in O.T. points towards Jesus

Many types of Christ are found in O.T.
Scofield - Pg 6

Example - Cain & Able Pg 8-9
Noah & The ARK

Moses & the Law = Exodus = all the things that happened to the Israelites = meant to show us that man is sinful - that the law cannot save us - that the mercy of God is great - etc. etc.

The Prophets - Issiah & Jerimiah
What meaning for us?

Do you know how you got to be a prophet -?

Not like today Jeane Dixon
50% correct?

They had to be 100% correct - or else they were stoned to death.

That's why they could stand up and say thus saith the Lord - they were sure

To give you a illustration - lets look at the story of Noah & the Ark -

very familiar - even to you!

The Ark - A Type of Christ

(Exodus 3)

Exodus 3

His - STORY !

Not Just HisTory - Rom 15:4

Jesus Called O.T. - Moses & The Prophets

Living Object Lessons - Types - Illustrations

Examp. Israelites - Slaves in Egypt
We - Slaves To Sin

Israelites - Are A Type of Unredeemed Man

Egypt - A Type of Sin

Moses - A Type of Christ - Deliverer

I Cor 10: 1-11
v11 - Example = Type - A Model - Pattern

Lessons From Moses

v10 1. Gods Call - Clear - Precise

2. Moses Response - Who Am I? - Send Someone Else!
Humility - Yes Worm? No!

3. When God Calls Us? - Faith
I can Do All Things Through Christ!

V12 - I Will Be With You

When you have Brought The People out

God Sees iT As Done

13 DoubTs SpeculaTion · WorsT Case Scenario

14 God's Name = Ungers

Cross Reference = Jn 8:58
Jesus Said "I Am"

15-22 - God Gives DeTails - Precise

Ch 4

1 - Moses NoT Convinced

2 - God's PaTience = Grace

Zeroes in on One Thing Moses Needed
To Give Up - LeT Go
WhaT is in Your Hand ?

A Rod ? - No ! - For Moses His Life

V 20 - The Rod of God

Evidence that God was with me in Kijabe and when I went on AIM Tech support trips to Ethiopia and Sudan. God provided a local pastor during the night watch at the border stop to take us one by one to his house to eat a meal prepared by his wife. Although we were held back for two days while the patrols searched our truck and hoped for a bribe, they neither found the Bibles we hid under the work supplies, nor did they receive a bribe.

In Sudan God was with us to release us from being detained at the airstrip on false charges, to protect me from the crocodiles in the Nile where I bathed, and to enable us to complete a water system using a large rock! We poured concrete channels on the rock to channel the bi-annual rainfall into two water tanks. Each rainfall provided the village and medical clinic with enough fresh water for six months. I was away long enough to grow my first and only beard!

v6 - A symbol of Defilement -
in need of Gods Cleansing

v9 - Nile To Blood

10 - Now its Not Humility - Fear -

Disobiedience - Refusal - Excuses

God Knows our Weaknesses - Availiable

11 - Gods Ways Are High Above our Ways

He Makes No Mistakes - Walk By Faith

12 God overcomes our Weakness
Paul Says I will Glory in My weakness
For When I Am Weak - God is Strong

13 Send Anyone But Me!

Joshua

Ch 1. Moses is Dead but God is Not

V1 God called Joshua - Joshua did not volunteer - Served Moses 40 years!

V2 - Go over this Jordan - Ha! How?
A Test already

V3-7 Be strong - Courageous Pep talk

8 - Study - Meditate - Do
Good leadership

9 - reminder

10 - A step of faith

16 - CommiTTment

Ch 2

Even Though God IS DirecTing -
1 We Must STill Think

Rahab the harlot

QuarTerly - -

Josephes Says She Was An Ex-Harlot
The Name Sticks

She Was A Zonah - A Working Girl
But She Now Made Cloth out of Flax

Rahab is Still Regarded As A Great
Hero of Israel - Listed Among The
Lineage of Christ - MT. - Heb. - Jms.

She Became The Wife of Salmon,
The Mother of Boaz - Husband of Ruth

v 3-7 Price of Sin = Her Name - Rahab The Harlot

v 8 - I know That The Lord Has Given The Land - -
How Did She know?

21 Covenent

Principle
God Works Through Some Unlikely People -
We Look on Out Side - He Looks on Heart

v 23-24
Spies Report - Said Nothing About Walls
Numbers of Soldiers etc.

(A Fore Shadow of Things to Come)

Types - A Fore Shadow of Things to Come

Joshua = Jehovah Saviour

A Type of Christ - Captain - Deliverior
Leads To Promised Land (Heaven)
Completes The Redemption of Israel

Crossing Jordan - Death To Past
A Type of our Dying To Sin & Self

Canaan - NoT A Type of Heaven "Conflict"
Rather A Type of our present position - in "Heavenly Places With Christ"

Joshua NoT A Law Giver -

The Law Could NoT Save & Deliver - Only Super Natural Power

Archaeological Notes

The Amarna LeTTers - Discovered in 1887
400 LeTTers writTen on Clay TableTs
Egyptian Gov. Officials & Various Groups in Syria & PalisTine
Dr. John GarsTang - Director British School
Extensive Work on All Cities - Confirmims DaTes & Comments in Bible Josephus

(Joshua Ch 24)

Joshua Ch 24

Just As Moses Had Done -

So Joshua Prepares To Die

Why is He So Worried?

Why Shechem? Not Shiloh

AT Shechem God 1st Promised Cannan To Abraham

Abraham Built An Alter Here -
Jacob Also Built An Alter

It Was A Holy Place

Is It Good To Have Special Places?

2ORS ARE Gathered

Holy Places? - Meca - Jeruselam

V14 The People were trying to serve many Gods - Kenya! Whichcraft

You Cannot Serve God & Mammon

No Retirement Plan?

Who is #1 in Your Life?

2

v16 For Be it From Us - That we Should Serve

19 These People Are Not Under The Blood

O.T. Law is Tough

Joshua Says "Count The Cost"

Christianity = Roses - Happy!

21 We Will Serve The Lord

23 What? Already Had Other Gods!

Did Not Obey God - Drive Out The People Utterly Destroy Them

Ch 13:13 Ch 16:63 Ch 16:10

Why Did God Command This?

#1. Halley - Pg. 113

#2. To Learn Obedience I Sam. 15:1-3 -7-

To Obey is Better Than Religion!

V. 26 - A Great Stone

V 29 Joshua Died

V32 Joseph - People Carried His Bones -
All Those Miles!

(Herb Miller was the pastor my mom sent to our cornfields to tell her boys to receive Jesus as their Savior & Lord.)

Last Lesson on Neh & Wall

Not Just A Wall - Not Just Any City

Jeruselam - Holy City of God

Rev 21:10-14

Destroyed By - Medes & Persians, Romans

Jeruselam - Always Rebuilt

Babylon - Never Rebuilt   Saddam Hussein

A Huge Task - A Diverse People   PR 29:18

God Sent A Leader - Gave A Vision - Help us Focus on Work

Nehemiah - How Did He get Them To Work?

He Set The Example - 6:14-16

Paul set Example - II Thes. 3:7

Byler Reunion - Christian Heritage = Work Ethic

My Father

Herb Miller - Came To Cornfield!

Ch 6-v1 Wall is Almost Finnished

Now Enimies Are Desperate - Get Nehemiah.

2 After Ridicule - Harrassement - Force

Peace Talks! A Neutral Site - You Pick it

2

A Good Leader = Godly Intuition

3 A Great Work - Because it was Gods Work

Are You Involved in A Great Work?

What Are You Doing That Will Count - 1 year From N
10 years
Eternity?

God is Building His Church
Letter From Margie Buhler - A good Work - A Great Work

Billy Graham - Offer To Be A Movie Super Star
"I Am Doing A Great Work"

4 Character Test - Four Times - Same Answer!

5 Intimidation

6-7-8 - Not True! Nehemiah Had Clear Conscience
Powerful - Could Not Intimidate!

9 Prayer - A Good Leader = Reliance on God

10 Now That Was A Clever Plot - Nice Try
But Watch This One!

Shemaiah - A Prophet } Traitors!
Noadiah - Prophetess } Sold Out!

10 The Sin of Baalaam 2 Pet 2:15

Using your Position - To get Gain
Today Pastors Selling Their Souls

11 But Nehemiah saw Through it - Because
He Knew His Bible!

Nu. 18:7

A Good Leader knows The Word!

We Also Need To Know What The Bible Says

12 Biblical Knowledge Brings -
Spiritual Discernment

A Good Leader Has Spiritual Discernment

15 The Wall is Finnished in 52 Days!

16 - A Great Work - 1. Done Gods Way
2. In Gods Power - Supernatural
3. Brings Glory To God - Humbles The Leader
And Fear To The Heathen

(Proverbs 1-3)

Proverbs - One of "Wisdom" Books
Job, Ecclesiasties
All Bible is Wisdom - Prov. is Special

Proverbs = Divine Wisdom - Applied To
Earthly Living
Wisdom - One of Attributes of God ÷ is Love / is Light

Proverbs - Fills The Gaps Between The other
Books of Bible

Verse 1 - Proverbs of God - Collected
By Solomon - And By Others
Ch 30 - Agur 31 - Lemuel

Solomon - Considered Wisest Man
Why? You Remember The Story
God Said - "Ask Anything You Will"
Asked For Wisdom - Received Everything Else
Same With Us Today! MT. 6: 25 - 33

Every Culture Has its own Proverbs
Wise Sayings Passed on Over The years

Kenya - Haraka - Haraka - When 2 Elephants Fight

Do You Remember Some?

"When 2 Elephants Fight"

The Kenyan's say that when 2 elephants fight the ground suffers.

This proverb means that when people with higher authority fight

only the people with lower authority suffer from their fighting.

The older ladies would bring bread and jam to church because they often waited a long time for a pastor to come and preach. I was surprised at how they were able to make a little bit of jam go a long way. They enthusiastically worshipped God with drums, singing, and dancing.

The hospital van was used as an ambulance and as Darvin's supply truck.

—

There is A Major Difference However Between These "Folk Proverbs" & The Book of Proverbs
1st is Just Common Sense

Proverbs is Wisdom From God

Verse 7 - Fear of The Lord
Fear = Awe - Reverence
Acknowledgement of Who God Is -
Who I Am = 3:7 - Ps 8:3

True Wisdom Comes From God - 2:6-3:19

Fool = One Who Rejects God
Ps. 14:1 - 53:1

Some Translations Use word Knowledge - Difference
Dictionary =
Knowledge = Result of, or Product of Knowing Information
Wisdom = The Power of True & Right Discernment

Education - Schools Teach Knowledge
Not Wisdom! Removed God!

There Are Those Who Say That Education Will Solve All of Mans Problems
No Way!

We Are Already Educated Beyond our Intelligence!

Examples of Kenyans

Fear of The Lord - His Wisdom - Only Way!

Verse 8-9 - Obey your Parents Eph. 6:1

10-19 - Warning Against Violence

20 - God Makes Himself Known Rom 1:20
They Are without Excuse!

22 - Three Groups of People

1. Simple - easily deceived - Peer Pressure

2. Scoffers - Those who Mock God & His People Gal 6:7 God is Not Mocked!
2 Pet: 3

3. Fools - Reject God
Hate Discipline - Work

23 - Gods Thoughts Are Not our Thoughts

4

24-33 - Gods grace Will NoT LasT Forever
Prov 29:1 - Rom. Ch 1 - God Gave Them UP!

Ch 2

Verse 1-6 - If you Seek Wisdom - Give God His RighTful Place in Your Life
God will Give iT 2 Chron 16:9
James Ch 1
Can Be very PracTical Wisdom -
Work AT Hospital - STory of Van

9-10 - You Will Find Wisdom

11-22 - Warnings AgainsT ImmoraliTy

Ch 3

5-8 - Wonderful Truths - God will Honor His Promises!
Our Ways Lead To DeaTh 14:12

9-10 - TiThing

11-12 - The Lord Disciplines The ones He Loves

Isaiah Ch. 7-9

History - Dull & Boring

Untill - You See How iT Applies
To Our Lives Today!

Ex, Sandy Civil War

Also - In History We Can see How
God Acted - His Character
Principles

Lets Look AT Isaiah - ~~His Call~~
~~Ch. 6~~ Scoffield Bible IntRo

His Call Ch. 6

His EnThusiasim - Send Me!

BuT The People Will NoT Hear!

Ch 7
Ephraim - LargesT Tribe of Israel
Joined with Syria

V 3 - God Sends Isaiah - & Son
Shearjashub = A RemnanT shall ReTurn

Ahaz was A Bad King
Openly Practiced Idolotry
Sacrificed His Sons To Baael

4-5 God Comes To Him in Grace

Doesn't Mention His Sin -
Be Calm - Don't Fear - I will Deliver You

6-9 This is The Way iT Will Be

Ahaz Can't Believe iT

God Wants Faith - BuT Understands our Limits

10 Ask For A Sign

Did You Ever Ask God For A Sign ?

Examples From Bible

Gideon

12 Now Ahaz Blows IT
He Refuses To Ask - No FaiTh

13-14 The Lord Himself Will Give You
A Sign
MT. 1:23

Prophesy - Now & FuTure
Scoffield Pg 142

Wycliffe Pg 618

Types - Scoffield Pg 144

15-16 - Immediate Fulfillment

18 - In That Day

Ch. 8 2nd Prophesy

God Names The Child Before
ITs BirTh

Maher-Shalal-Hash Baz = LongesT Name in
Bible

Means - Quick To The Plunder

4

V5 3rd Prophesy

The People Refuse God

8-10 Yet He is Still With Them

19 Mediums - Communicating With The Dead To Forsee The Future

Isaiah Says Consult The Living God

Ch 9

V 2-7 - Still Talking About This Child

Ch 11

Isaiah Ch 11

Courageous
↓
Great Men
Isaiah - Great Prophet - Jeremiah - Cistern!
Ch 6 - I saw The Lord!

Immanuel - Prince of Peace -
A Man of Sorrows
Wounded for our Transgressions Ch 53

Prophecy - This is What Sets The
Bible Apart From Other Books

Koran = No Prophecy Read AT Medical Center

Prophecy And Fulfillment

Higher Criticism = Undermine Bible Authority

Ch 45 Cyrus - Persian King 150 years Before!

Jo. 12: 37-41

Jesus - - Lu: 4: 16-21 - Is. 61: 1-2

Isaiah = Thus Says The Lord
Authority

Quoted in N.T. - 400 Times!

Ch 11: V1

A Shoot Shall Come Forth -
From The Stump --
Davids Kingdom Cut Down! Flat!

Ch 5 - Judgement & Exile

Ch 6 - 11-13 - Stump

V 4-6 Peace - Peace - Peace

Brethren Are Wrong!

Jesus Was The Branch - But They Crucified Him!

There Will Be No Peace Untill - He Comes Again!

MT 24 - 3-44 2 Tim 3 Paul

Ch 11 - 10 In That Day - What Day?

V-12 - Gathering of Jews - It's Starting Now!

Read Luke Ch. 2

Is. Ch 53

One of Greatest Portions of Prophecy

700 Years Before Christ

No Speculation = Interpreted By N.T. Writers
Quoted 24 Times in N.T.

Jn 12:38

Crucifixion = Roman Punishment
How Did They Know?
Ps. 22

V2 - No Majesty or Splendor - Worldly Standards

Remember The Root of Jesse?

V3 - People Still Turn From Jesus - Preferring An Historical Jesus - Instead of The Cross -
If Anyone Would Come After Me -- Take Up His Cross

V5 - Wounded - Hebrew - To Be Pierced

~~V7 - Opened Not His Mouth = Caiaphas - Herod - Pilate~~

~~V8 - From Prison - An Unjust Trial - Judicial Murder~~

~~V9 - Appointed His Grave~~

Day of Atonement
"Yom Kippor"

(2)

Cannot Fully Understand This Apart From Leviticus

God is Holy - No Sin in Presense

How Can The Gap Be Bridged?

Lev. 16: ALL This Was To Cover - Sin
Did NoT Remove! ThaTs Why They Had
To Repeat Every Year

Heb 9:1 - 10:1-2

V7 Opened NoT His Mouth - Caiaphas - Herod - Pilate

V8 - From Prison - An Unjust Trial - Judicial Murder!

V9 - Grave with Wicked - 2 Thiefs
Joseph of Arimathia - Rich Man

V10 - Gods Plan From The Beginning of Time

How Can A Dead Man See His Offspring?
Ressurection! - Spiritual Children = We

11-12 Philip. 2:5-11

Some of the unique emergency calls that I received were from the hospital when a piece of equipment stopped working mid-surgery. For instance, a lady was delivering a baby when the suction cap machine stopped working. I cleaned the motor amidst the nurses telling me to hurry because the baby was in danger. I got the machine working in time. Another time a man was under anesthesia for a heart procedure. The mat that he laid on would give an electric shock when the heart stopped beating. Well, the mat stopped working and the heart needed shocked. I followed the electric cord until I found a place that looked worn. I soldered and re-wrapped the cord, plugged it in and it worked. Another time the surgeon was using a laryngoscope when suddenly the light went out. I was called to fix the light before the patient came out of anesthesia. The bulb was tiny for me to work with, but I was able to reconnect the filament and get the light working in time. Praise Jesus!

When Sandy was scheduled for surgery, I went into the operating room to make sure everything worked correctly, and I cleaned the room. The surgeon had created an operating light by using ten car headlights. When I turned on the lights only four of them worked. I drove an hour into Nairobi to buy six headlights to replace the ones that did not work.

One day one of my workers brought me his transistor radio and asked me if I could fix it because it had stopped working. When I took off the back cover, cockroaches ran everywhere! Once I removed all the cockroaches, the radio worked.

The electricity for Kijabe came to a main panel on a pole and it was 220 volts. Kijabe was responsible for all the electricity at the mission station. There was a power break switch that we used to turn off the power when we needed to remove a fallen tree from the wires or work on connecting electricity to the new houses. Sandy remembers on one occasion that two men carried me into our house and put me in my bed. All they said to her was that I took an electrical shock and I needed to sleep it off. She recalls that they came back several times to check on me. Although I don't remember this electrocution, I thank God for saving my life.

Sandy's worst experience happened when we were asleep. A large rat ran across my head and woke her up. She saw it run up the wall and go behind the curtain. All night we searched for the rat. In the morning, we carried out the mattresses and continued searching until we found it drowned in the toilet in another room.

I took one trip with an AIM mission pilot to bring supplies and make repairs to one of AIM's most isolated mission station in a neighboring country. Two elderly women lived on this station. When I asked them why they lived so remotely, they responded that the people would kill anyone not from their tribe except elderly women.

Our grandchildren call Sandy "Sho Sho". This is the Kikuyu name for "grandma". One of Sandy's responsibilities was to be the Kijabe hostess. Many people came to Kijabe to tour the hospital and the nursing school. Sandy would serve chai and cookies, answer questions, and have local handcrafted items for sale.

Christmas and Easter sermons written and preached by Darvin Byler.

Matthew

A Publican - Tax Collector
Why would Jesus Choose Such
A Person?
Lu. 5:27 - Jesus Came For Sinners
What About Church?

Matthew - As Tax Collector
1. Good Record Keeper
2. Attention To Detail + Statistics
E. g. - Geneology Wow!

Bottom Line - God Looks on Heart
(Example David)

All Scripture Inspired - Instruction

v1. Book of Generation = Gr. Genesis = Origin

He Began His Earthly Life At Bethlehem -
But This Was Not His Origin

John = The Logos of God
Word Became Flesh

Christ - Christos - Annointed One
Messiah of God
Son of David - Son of Abraham
Luke = Son of Man - Joseph To Adam

2

Four Women - Unheard of!

Christianity Has Done More For Women
Elevated Them - in Christ - No Male-Female
Kenya - Feminist Convention

Two - Gentiles - Unheard of!

Three - Moral Blots = Grace!

1. Tamar - A Canaanite Woman
Judahs Daughter in Law

2. Rahab - The Harlot of Jericho

3. Ruth - A Moabitess Married To Naomis
Son, Later To Boaz

4. Baathsheba - Wife of Uriah

God Delights in Making Beauty
From Ashes!

v 11 Jechoniah - Jer. 22:24-30
Not Through Joseph - Mary!

Joseph & Mary - Both From David
All Scripture is Inspired - Profitiable

v 16 - Joseph - Husband(s) of Mary

v 17 Problem - Some Missing - Why ?

18 Birth of Messiah
Betrothed = Engaged = Same As Married

19 Mary Never Tried To Explain - Defend-Self

Joseph Showed Great Restraint

20 Ministry of Angels
Told From Josephs Perspective
Luke - From Marys "

God Explains - Defends Mary

21 Jesus = Jehova Saves - His Purpose

22 Prophecy - MT. Link To O.T.
(over 30 Prophecies)
23 Emmanuel For Birth

24 Jesse Jackson - Single Parent ?
Considered Abortion ?

25

4

MT Ch. 2

V1 - Born in Bethlehem - Not Nazareth
Only MT. Records "Wise Men"
(3 Wise Men ?)

2 Much Conjecture About Star
A Special Manifestation of God

3-4 Inquired ? Where ? - Old Testament !

Micah 5:2

9-10-11 - Over The House (Manger ?)

Traditions Abound - Facts Differ

Jesus - Several Months old - To 1 yr.

Christmas

Western = Deductive } 3 Parts
Analytic }

A Kenyan Sermon ? - Logic - Garden

Kenyan Christmas - Nothing! - 1st Christmas in Kenya

No Birthdays - Dishon - Roof

But They Love A Story - Parables

START ch1:1

Birth of Jesus = Great Story !

Most Important Aspect - Geneology - Tribes
who was Father

Tamar - Rahab - Rut,
Gentiles

Stop! What is God Doing?

A Woman? - Another Tribe?

God is God! His Ways Are Higher!

He's in The Salvage Buisness - David - Baathsheba

He Can Take A Gentile Prostitute - And Use Her in The Holy Lineage of The Messiah

Women Make Up 80% of Kenyan Church

They Need Encouragement - What About Us?

Bible is God Breathed - Every Thing There for Reason

Not Written For Western Mind - -

Written For All Peoples!

("Bible is God Breathed – Everything there for Reason")

2

Many Cults - Isms & Schisms in Kenya

Use Christmas Story To Teach Doctrine

1. Virgin Birth Vs. - 18 - 20 - 23 - 25

2. Ministry of Angels

Africans Live in Spirit World - Evil

They Know All About The New Age
Nothing New in New Age!

They Need To See Other Side of Spirit World
So Do We!

Christmas Story Full of Angels!

1. Instruct 2. Guide 3. Protect

1950's Story of Rift Valley Acca.

3. Satans Limitations - Respect Him - Yes

Put Him on A Level With God? - No!

Too Much of Darkness - We Are Children of Light

Ch 2 vs 13 U.S. Treasury
Working Through Herod - Tried To Destroy Jesus

Did Not Know Where He Was!

Satan is Defeated — Jesus is Lord!

("Story of Rift Valley Acca.", RVA, is recorded in Section One.)

3

4 Prophecy - God is in Control!

He Wants Us To Trust Him

Foretold The Events Hundreds of Years Before

Ch1:23 1. Virgin Birth Iss. 7:14 740 B.C.

Ch2:6 2. Bethlehem - Micah 5:2 720 B.C.

Not Nazareth - "O Little Town of Nazareth"

God Used - A Roman Emporer
Lu. 2:1 → Politics
Taxes

What About Even Today?
Russia - Iraq

Ch2:15 3. Flee To Egypt Hosea 11:1 730 B.C

Ch2:17 4. Weeping For Children Jeremiah 31:15 620 B.C

Many Prophecies in Bible - Most Fulfilled - 90%

Some Day - Another Christmas - Coming Again!

1st Christmas - Baby - Age of Grace
Our Choice - Take Him or Leave Him
Now is Day of Salvation
2nd Christmas - Judge

Recieve Him Now As Saviour - Later As Judge

Napoleon - Alexander - Ceasar - Myself Have Built Empires Based on Force - Jesus Alone Founded An Empire on Love - And To This Hour Millions of Men Would Die For Him!

|| The Good Shepherd

Lu. 2:1→ Read Slowly

Share About Christmas Tradition

Words Are So Familiar – We Miss Deeper Meanings

O.T. ⟶ Jesus ⟵ N.T.

Prophecy of Messiah

Gen 3:15 – Speaking To Serpent
22:18 –
49:10 Zech. 9:9
Ps. 132:11 Mal 3:1
Is. 7:14 Micah 5:2
9:6
61:1 – Jesus Quoted

God Worked Throughout History – To Fulfill Prophecy

Micah – Written 740 B.C.

Wise Men – Herod Asked – Where? MT 2:5

Joseph Lived in Nazareth – Caesar Augustus

Prov. 21:1 Is 45:1 – Sadam Husein?

2

verse 8 - Shepherds = Dirty - Smelly

God's Ways Are Not our Ways!

My Greatest Joy = Sharing Good News - God Loves You!

Fixing Cement Mixer - Self Image

verse 9-14 Angels Gabriel? Ch 1:26

Heb 1:14 Story of RVA

Billy Graham = Angels

John 10:11 - The Good Shepherd

Familiar Image - Sheep & Shepherd

Why Christmas? - Is 53:6 - All we Like Sheep

Sheep Are Stupid - Sin Flaws Our Thinking

v 11 - I Am Good Shepherd - Lay Down My Life!

3

Verse 9 - I Am Door - Jesus Didn't Come To Show us The Way - He IS The Way! He IS The Door!

V 10 Life = Gr Zöe = Spirit & Soul
Highest Blessedness

Opposite Bios = Physical Life

Abundantly = Very Emphatic = OverFlowing
Exceedingly Excellent - NOW!

14 - We Are Known By Him
Loved - Gives His Life

16 - Other Sheep ??

26-28 Eternal Life

Eternal Security

"The Kingdom of God"

IS

1. WiThin - must be born of the Spirit or we cannot see
Jn. 3:3 MosT have "SpiRiTual Eyes"

2. HumiLiTy - must be humble in Spirit
Lu. 18:9-14 must have a proper opinion of ourselves - Pg. 36
MT. 5:3 BeaTiTudes "WORM TheoLogy"

3. SeRvice - Then the King will say, come, inherit
MT. 25:34 the Kingdom

MT. 24:30 4. IneviTabLe - now it operates in the hearts of men
Dan. 2:44 Someday - it will come in Power Pg. 35

PeRsonaL ApplicaTion

Pg. 36 - Boxes Why do we live in boxes?
SecuRiTy - nothing can get in - - OR OUT!
A Box Has Walls - ITs Safe
BuT - To Be in Gods Kingdom means SeRvice
How can we serve others when we are in boxes?
We Can'T - ThaTs Why God "BReaks" our Boxes
Our WhoLe ExpeRience in AfRica Has Been
One of BRoken Boxes - PReconcieved Ideas - -
LimiTaTions of How God WoRks.

ExampLes - 1. BReak in & BuRgLaRy
2. DiffeRenT Ways of WoRship

2/

Once our Box is Broken - IT Frees Us
For Service But we need to be on
Guard - because the natural tendencies are
to build another box!

Pg 36 The Pharisees Lived in Boxes Too!
Their box was called LegaLism!
Legalism has always had great appeal and still
does today. IT is An Attempt To Write
Down A List of Do's & Don'Ts

So Jesus Said O.K. - you Want To
Reduce The Kingdom To A List of Do's
and Don'Ts - Here They Are!

MT.22 1. Give All of Yourself To God Pg 36
HearT - SouL - Mind
HearT = EmoTions SouL = our SpiriT
Mind = our InTeLLecT Sometimes we
forget to give God our intellect

2. Love Your Neighbor As Yourself
Goes back to "Worm TheoLogy"
1. A Proper Opinion of Ourselves
2. A Proper ReLaTion To God } = Love of Neighbor

3

Disqualifications For The Kingdom

We have looked at the meaning of the Kingdom - qualifications for the Kingdom

Jesus Spoke his Strongest Words against The Pharisees MT. 23:13-29

We Are Like The Pharisees ?? How?

1. Religious 2. Established Church
3. Accepted By Society

Pg 37 - They Thought Because They were A Part of Gods Program They were O.K.

But he Was A Sinner - And he Didn't Know it!

According To Jesus = 2 Things Disqualified Them

1. Self- Centered - Trusted Their own Judgement

2. Looked Down on Others - They thought more highly of themselves

Tax Collector = No Pretense - He was A Sinner & He Knew it!

The Passage Ends --- Exalted will Be Humbled
1st will be Last
Humble will Be Raised Up!

God is opposed to the proud - but give grace to the humble

Conclusion; Get Rid of our Boxes! How?
1. Recognize Them 2. Ask God To Break Them

Why Would God Allow you Into His Heaven?

Does Anybody Here Wana Die?

Does Anybody Here Wana Go To Heaven?

Universal Longing = But How?
Many Answers

Sermon Title Not Original with Me

Country Music Song! = Good Sermon!

Yes, Everybody Wants To Go To Heaven - But!!

Heb. 9:27 - It is Appointed Unto Man once To Die.

Enoch - Elijah Only Two

Every one Has A God Shaped Void At Center

Bible Says - We Are Made in Image of God - -
What Does That Mean?
Certainly Not Physical - Kenya

Kenyans Say Why We Have Long Noses

Our Spirit - Able To Commune - With Gods Spiri

Invite you To open Bibles

Lets Look At Text - - Rom. 10:3

Everybody Wants To Go To Heaven - Their Way

Its Gods Heaven! Prov. 14:12 - There is A Way Wh
seems Right To Man

Gods Way

Acts 4:12 - No Other Name Under Heaven Given Among Me
Jn 14:6 - I Am The Way - Truth - Light - No One.

"Kenyans say that we have long noses because we blow them all the time with a hanky!"

Rom 10:9-10 - Man Believes With Head

We Reason - Use Our Intellect

Paul means Much More Than Intellectual Belief

Greek Pisteuō = To Trust in - Rely Upon

Irving Battart - Put All your Eggs in Jesus Basket

10 - Believes with Heart = Justified - Made Right With God
Agrees With God -

Accepts Gods Way - Death - Burial - Ressurection

And - Confesses With Lips -- What ??

Jesus IS Lord !

Whatever Happened To Public Testamonies ??

Emory Hollinger

Important - 1. Verbal Expression = Confirms in our own Heart

2. Encourages Others

African Testamonies - Part of Worship
Peter - 60 years Old !

We Need To Share With Each Other - What God is Doing !

3

And So is Saved - From What?

Hell! Everybody Wants To Go To Heaven
Remember?

Hell - is one of Those Topics That Has Slipped
By The Wayside

A Recent Poll

The Reason is Simple - 70% of Clergy
Do Not Believe in A Literal Hel

What Did Jesus Say? - MT 10:28 = Read
Lu. 16. - Lazarus & Rich Man

Not Good Enough!

They Cite Modern Translations - Interpretations

Need To Be Very Careful -

Sandy ==== Sonday

Different Culture --- Laugh To Show Sympathy

A Question of Authority

Bible = Inerrant - Infalliable - God Breathed

Satans Method -- Question Authority of God
Eden - Did God Say?

Harold Lindsell - Battle For Bible

4

13. No Favorites With God - Everyone Who Calls

14 - Paul Asks 4 Pertinent Questions

Mission Leaders Estimate - Still 3 Billion People Never Heard!!

Most Need Cross Culture - No Living Witness

Even in This Country - Nadine At Camp Albany - Schenectedy

14 - How Can They Believe in Whom They Have Never Heard?

Without A Preacher -- Amazing! 20th Century

Computer Age - T.V. - Fax Machine

Still - God Blesses The Preaching of His Word

15. How Can Men Preach - Unless They Are Sent

Greatest Blessing of My Life - Preaching

Never Happen Unless You Sent Me!

Great! But We Need To Do More

A Churches Spiritual Vitality is Not Measured By What It Attracts To Itself (Members) Rather By What It Sends Out!

Not Just Foreign Missions - Here At Home - Opportunitie

5

1. Need To IdenTify Them -

2. Call People To Respond

3. Send Them OuT

15-B How BeauTiful is The Welcome --

African Churches - 300 - 400 People WaiTing
For A Preacher
Any Preacher !

16- No - They Will NoT ALL Believe - BuT Should Have Choic

17- FaiTh Comes From Hearing - AbouT Jesus

Our Job = Ambassadors → Jack & Dennis
(TesTamonies) → Preach - Sow - PlanT - WaTer

Gods Job = HarvesT He is Lord of HarvesT

Sandy & I - Thinking AbouT Kenya

God Used Ecclesiastes Ch11 - To Challange Us

Was IT The RighT Time ? Verse 4 & 5

We As A Church - Can Look AT The Clouds
Never Send ForTh - -

2 Tim. 4:6

MeanWhile 3 Billion People - A Godless ETernity
Everybody WanTs To Go To Heaven --- Don'T Know The Way

Begining of New Series To Lead us
To Easter

This Passage - Usually For Palm Sun.

Whole Procession Designed To Raise The Question -
was Jesus The Messiah ?

Much That was Done - To Fulfill O.T. Prophecy
Lu. 18:31 - ~~Zech. 9:9~~

1. The Occasion - Feast of The Passover Lu 22:1
Egypt - Sacrificial Lamb

2. The Donkey - Zech. 9:9

3. The Clothing - II Kings 9:13

4. The Entry itself - Blessed is He that Comes in The
Name of The Lord. Ps. 118:26

v 41 But Then Abruptly - The Party is Over

Jesus Weeps Over The City - Not 1st Time 13:34

43 He Phophycies Their Destruction Jer. 6:6 Dan. 9:26

44 Because - They Did Not Recognize Jesus

God Came To Jerusalem - He comes To Us
Why Don't We Recognize Him ?

When God Visits - we need To Make Decisions !
Jesus Made them Decide - was He The Messiah ?

2

If Jesus is Lord - We need To Make Decisions - About How we Shall Live

God Makes Claims on our Lives

God Demands Obedience

God Demands AccountabiLiTy - (Kenya)

In The Begining of Ch. 19 - Jesus Told This STory To IllusTrate AccountabiLiTy V. 11

Paul Reminds Us in II Cor 5:10 That We must All stand Before The Judgement Seat of ChrisT

NoT For SaLvaTion! BuT For Rewards

Every Word We Speak

Could iT Be - That we Don'T WanT To Recognize Jesus?

Pg. 7 We Also Can Ignore Him - ManipuLaTe Him

LimiT His Kingship BuT -- ULTimaTeLy - You will RejecT Him

Because - Jesus is EiTher Lord of All - or He is NoT Lord AT All

CLose - Pg. 9 - #8

Sequence of Events
Palm Sunday - Raising of Lazarus
6 Days Before Death
Greeks? Came To Phillip
Jesus Ignores Them - He Did Not
cater To Anyone
He Would Never Have Won An Election!

We Are Not in A Popularity Contest
Ex. - Kenya - Some People May Hate You
Paul Says We Are Soldiers - War!

23 - The Hour Has Come

24 - Jesus Will Be Glorified - But Not The
way we Would Expect
Is. 55:8 - Gods Ways Are not our Ways!
Hardest Lessons For Christians
Death is Key To Spiritual Fruitfullness
Example - Grain of Wheat
Unless it Dies - it Remains Alone
Die To Self - Be Reproduced in Others
Man Says - If you want To Be Great - Assert Yourself

God Says - Be The Servant of All

2

Man Says - Be First #1!
God Says - The First Shall Be Last

Man Says - If you Want To Be Rich - Hoard-Save
God Says - Give it Away!

Man Honors The Famous & Soon Forgets Them
God Honors The Unknown - & Never Forgets Them

Gods Ways Are Not our Ways

25 - If you Love Your Life - You will Lose it

Hate = To Love Less

27 - Humanness of Jesus - Save Me?
NO! - Glorify Thy Name!

28 - A Voice From Heaven Pg. 66

31 - Two Main Objectives

1. Defeat of Satan

2. Draw All Men To Himself

1

Condemned But Not Guilty

Who is on Trial ?

Many injustices - illegalities = night Trial

Last Week Before Sanhedrin = Pharisees & Saducees

Now Before Pilate - Why ? = Jews Had No Power

Sanhedrin = Religious Charges
Romans - Political charges

Pilate - Roman Governor Appointed By Tiberious
A Politician
Already in Trouble with Jews - near Riots

1. Pictures of Tiberious Near Temple
2. Took Temple Money To Build Aquedoct

Was Ordered To Keep Peace!

Scripture Lu. 23

1-2 The Charges
3 - King ?
4 - I Find No Fault

6-7 Herod = Family Name = Agrippa - Phillip
Antipas

8 - Happy To see Jesus - Because of Guilt

2

9 - Jesus Would Not Even Talk To Herod
Iss. 53: 7 = Prophecy

10-11 - Mocking
12 - Birds of A Feather

13-15 Pilate Finds Jesus Not Guilty
End of Trial!

16 - Compromise! = The Begining of Disaster

Romans Prided Themselves in Justice - An Elaborate System of Judicial Process To Protect The Rights of Citizens - U.S. System is Patterned After It

Pilate Sacrificed This Principle To Avoid Trouble

What Principles Are You Living By?

What Compromises Are You Making?

Examples - 1. Abortion - 2. Pre Marital Sex
3. Working on Sun. 4. Lottery

17 - R.S.V. Omits This Verse - Pilate Wanted To Release Jesus

18 - Barabbas - A man Who Was Guilty of The Very Crimes Jesus Was Accused of

Palm Sunday? - Bulletin

Jesus on The Cross

The Cross - Today Women Wear it around their Necks
In Jesus Time it was A symbol of Humiliation - Roman Method of Execution
A Public Spectacle

32 - Two Thieves - Hardened Criminals
Prophecy Fulfilled - Is. 53:12

33 It had To Be - if Jesus Died For The Worst Sinners
Luke Does Not Dwell on The Intense Suffering - They Crucified Him

34 - Jesus Prayer - While Jesus Prays - - They Divide His Few Possessions
Prophecy - Ps. 22:18

35 - Jesus Mocked By People & Soldiers
36-37
38 - Pilates Revenge - Pilate Pronounced Jesus Not Guilty - yet Gave in To The Crys of The People & Jewish Leaders

Now - He Posts The Exact Charge That was Brought Against Him!

Jewish Leaders Are Enraged! - Ask Pilate To Change it Jo. 19:21

2

39 – Thieves Castigate Jesus – If you're God
Save yourself & Us
Like Many Today – Christian Only
To See what God will Do For Them

40-41 – The other one – is Repentant

42 – What Faith!? When You Come Into your
Kingdom

43 – What A Promise! – He had Only Asked
Jesus For Future Remembrance – – –

But God Gave Him Salvation!

We Ask For Little Things – – –
But God Wants To Do Big Things!

Physical Signs Given By God

44 – No Ordinary Execution – Darkness 12 – 3

45 – the Veil was Torn – A Tightly Woven Veil
From Top To Bottom

No One – Could Go in To Holy of Holies
Now – Exsposed!

Symbolic Fulfillment of O.T. Sacrifices

Now No Longer Needed – The Way To
God Had Changed!

3

46 – A Loud Cry – "IT is Finished" – Jo 19
He gave up His SpiriT

Jesus Said – No one Takes My Life – I Lay
iT Down

47 – Roman Soldier is A Believer –

48 – Many People in Jerusalem For
" Passover
"Beating Their Breast" =
A Sign of Mourning & GuilT

Practical Points For Today

1. Since ChrisT Forgave even Those Who PuT
him To Death – We can know That His
Love & Forgiveness Has No Limits For Us

2. ChrisT Came NoT To Save Himself –
BuT Sinners – Us – OThers

3. Death is Gain To The Believer –
AbsenT From The Body – PresenT WiTh The Lord

4. Those Who Ridicule ChrisT Will ALso
Ridicule Those Who Follow Him

Lu. 24 : 13

Christianity Stands or Falls on The Ressurrection - Josh McDowell

Many Others Down Through History

The Empty Tomb is Not The most convincing Evidence - Peter - John saw
The Post Ressurrection Appearances Are

Kenya = Christmas - No - Easter Yes!

Acts 1:1-3 I Cor 15:1-8 - 55 A.D!

Todays Lesson Deals with only 1 Appearance

13-16 Their eyes were held ?

17 - What Are you Talking About ?

18 - Cleopas - Husband of one of Mary's

19 - A great Prophet - This is still The Worlds View - They Did not yet see Him as God!

20-24 - A Confused Tale of Disbelief

25 - O Foolish Men!

27 - Moses - O.T. - Tells of Jesus!
Daniel

2

28-29
30-31 - Jesus Took Charge - Host gave Thanks -
Eyes were oppened

Sometimes We Fail To See Jesus!

Just When They Recognize Him - He Vanishes!

We Cannot Manipulate Jesus

32 - Our Hearts Will Also Burn in The
Presence of Jesus!

33 - That Same Hour - Evening!
Good News Must Be Shared!
(Jacks Sermon Last Week)

34 - What An Excited Bunch!

35 -
36 - Jesus Ressurected Body - Not Confined
To Laws of Matter & Energy
37
38-39 - Not A Spirit

3

This Was No Coincidence!

In Gods Plan - Jesus - The Spotless Lamb
would Take our Place
Iss. 53 - Wounded For our Transgressions

20 - Pilate Tries once More - But - His
weakness is Evident - Once Compromise
is Begun - The end is Certain

21-22 - Pilate is Reduced To Pleading --
Now instead of Being The Judge - He
Himself is on Trial
Other Gospels Add Certain Events
MT, 27; 17-26 -
Pilates Wife

John 18-19 - Familiar - Read At Love feast

24-25
The Trial is Over -
Jesus is Condemned Not Fair!
Iss, 53; 12

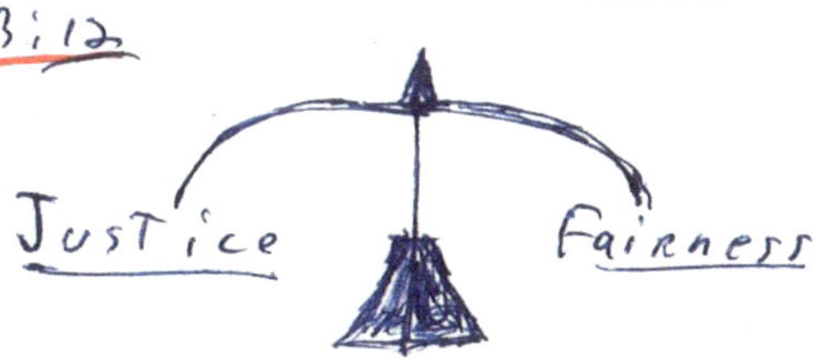

Pg, 6 Gothard

1. Father Forgive Them, For They know not what
Lu 23:34 They DO

Hard for us to control our anger -
But Jesus was absolutely without Resentment!

No Thought of Self - He Was More Concerned
About His Murderers!

2. Truly I Say To You, Today you Will Be
Lu. 23:43 With Me In Paradise

Again Jesus Has Time To Hear A Sinners Cry

And Look AT The Faith of That Thief!
He Had A Better Understanding OF The "Kingdom"
Than The Disciples Had.

He Was Mocked, Scorned, Jeered AT By
The Mob - On Top of That The Two Men
Crucified With Him Kept Up A Constant
MT27:44 "Railing" Against Him

Yet Something About Jesus Convicted
This One Thief - Perhaps Jesus praying for His
Enemys - His Total Display of Self-Denial

Convinced Him That Jesus Would
Triumph Over Death - And So Jesus --
Even While Suffering on The Cross --
Reached Out And Saved A Lost Sinner

Jn 19:26

3. Woman, Behold your Son - Behold your Mother

Still Thinking of Others

Amazing! Here He is, Fighting The Battle of the Ages -- The SALVATION of The Whole World Is AT Stake --

And Jesus Is Concerned About who will Care For His Mother!

Now Jesus was NoT Just Concerned About The Physical Needs of His Mother -- After All He Had Several BRothers who Could Take Care of ThaT -- BuT Jesus WanTed Her To Be with One Who Believed In Him

4. My God, My God, Why Have you Forsaken Me?

MT 27:46
MK 15

Jesus Had Been on The Cross For 3 Hrs.
Now Darkness Covered The Land

And Jesus Feels His Father Withdrawing from Him --- Turning From Him -- As He In That Awful Moment Became your Sin & Mine

II Cor 5:21 He Made Him To Be Sin - who knew No Sin That In Him we Might Become The Righteousness of God.

Think of IT! No Wonder John Newto WRote Amazing Grace How Sweet The Sound

Jn 19: 28

5 I ThirsT

Burning With Fever - Unable To BreaTh
Body Racked WiTh Pain - Tongue Swollen

This Tells Us Jesus Had A Body Like Ours
He Was Very Human - We Can Identify With Him

Jo 19:30

6 IT is Finished (completed)
What Is Finished?

The Wonderful Plan of SalvaTion

The Whole Purpose For Jesus Coming InTo This World - To Make ATonement - To Pay The price for our Sin -

VicTory over Sin & DeaTh
The DefeaT of SaTan

A TriumphanT Cry

How AbouT You TonighT?

Can You Cry WiTh Jesus, IT is Finished?

Are you Crucified wiTh ChrisT? - Are you Dead To Sin

We Are NoT our Own - We Were BoughT wiTh A Price

Generations worldwide are living by righteous and genuine faith in the Lord Jesus Christ.

"God, moreover, said to Moses, "Thus you will say to the children of Israel, 'The LORD, the God of your fathers, the God of Abraham, the God of Isaac, and the God of Jacob, has sent me to you. This is My name forever, and this is My memorial to all generations.'" Exodus 3:15 MEV

"Remembering the genuine faith that first lived in your grandmother Lois and your mother Eunice and that I am persuaded lives in you also." 2 Timothy 1:5 MEV

"Now also when I am old and gray, O God, do not forsake me, until I have proclaimed Your strength to this generation, and Your power to everyone who is to come." Psalm 71:18 MEV

"I will sing of the mercies of the LORD forever; with my mouth I will make known Your faithfulness to all generations." Psalm 89:1 MEV

NOTES

Section One

1. Mary Anderson Honer, *The Downing Legacy: Six Decades at Rift Valley Academy (New York: iUniverse, 2010), 104.*

Section Two

1. Links shared:

   kijabehospital.org/history.php

   rva.org/campus/ and https://rva.org/history/

   johnkamau.substack.com/p/kijabe-only-kenyan-town-with-no-bars

   moffatbiblecollege.org/about/history

Darvin Byler's sermons were written by him to communicate the Word of God, to share the love of Jesus, and to testify of his personal experiences as a Christian and a missionary. All references are only known as his notes show. The following resources were shared from his library.

1. The Holy Bible, New Scofield Reference Edition, Oxford, 1967. (Several pages are missing from the front. This information was found on the binding and introduction page.)
2. Strong's Exhaustive Concordance of the Bible with Greek and Hebrew Dictionary by James Strong. Published by Crusade Bible Publishers, Inc., Tennessee.
3. The Works of Josephus, translated by William Whinston, Hendrickson Publishers, Inc. 1987.
4. The Wycliffe Bible Commentary by Charles F. Pfeiffer and Everette F. Harrison, Published by The Moody Bible Institute, Chicago, 1962.

Scriptures in the narrative of the book are marked, AMP (Amplified), MEV (Modern English Version), RSV (Revised Standard Version), and TPT (The Passion Translation). We used Bible Gateway biblegateway.com/

TPT reference from my physical Bible, 2018 BroadStreet Publishing Group, LLC.

If you are interested in supporting Christian missions please consider:

Africa Inland Missions aimint.org

Victory Christian Fellowship (Palmyra, PA) Commission Club vcfpa.org

Thank you, Darvin, Nadine, and Shon

About the Authors

Contact us at darvinbylerfs@gmail.com

Listen to us at **Darvin Byler Family Sermons** on YouTube and Spotify.

Look for I Can Put In Windows and Doors Photo Album *"Darvin Byler Family Sermons",* by Darvin Byler, Shon Messick, and Nadine Rhoads.

Darvin Lloyd Byler graduated from Hershey High School and Moody Bible Institute Correspondence School. He married Sandy (Dechert) on March 3, 1962, in Palmyra, PA. Twenty years later they would serve together as missionaries to Kenya. Darvin and Sandy are blessed with four children, 22 grandchildren, and four great-grandchildren. Darvin continues to use his carpentry skills to bless his family and widows. Darvin and Sandy faithfully continue to support missionaries and their local church. Darvin enjoys traditional bluegrass and Southern gospel music. Doyle Lawson and Dailey & Vincent are a few of his favorite musicians. Darvin's favorite hymn, *I Stand Amazed In the Presence*, by Charles H. Gabriel, 1905. One of his favorite Scriptures is Ephesians 3:16-19.

Nadine Lynette Rhoads (Darvin & Sandy's oldest daughter) graduated from Lower Dauphin High School, Cairn University, Rhema Bible Correspondence School, and Western Governors University. She learned from her parents to seek first the kingdom of God and His righteousness, never quit, and always serve the Lord Jesus with gladness. She enjoyed working with her dad in his construction business building several houses together. Nadine continues the family ministry legacy as a youth pastor, together with her husband Nelson, at Victory Christian Fellowship in Palmyra, PA. Nadine and Nelson have authored several books (available on Amazon). Shon is the youngest of her four children. One of her favorite Scriptures is John 8:12, 32.

Instagram: @nadinelrhoads

Shon David Messick (Darvin & Sandy's grandson, Nadine's youngest son) graduated from Palmyra Area High School, Lebanon County Career and Technology Center, Rhema Bible Training Center, and Oklahoma Wesleyan University. God miraculously saved Shon and Nadine's lives when he was born ten weeks early by emergency C-section. He currently lives in Oklahoma fulfilling the plans God has for his life. Shon continues the family ministry legacy as a staff member serving in his local church and volunteering with a ministry with homeless people. Some of his favorite Scriptures are Philippians 4:4-7 and 1 John 3:18.

Instagram: @that_shon

Have you received salvation?
To know God and accept Him as your savior is the most important thing you can do in your life. If this book has touched your heart, stirred up your spirit or you just want to know God or renew your life to Him I invite you to join me in this prayer:

Dear Jesus,
I repent for my sins,
I ask for Your forgiveness.
I want to make You the Lord of my life.
I know that You sent Your son Jesus as a man to die on the cross for my sins.
And with this prayer, I ask You to come into my heart.
I do not want to live life the same.
I submit myself to You and Your will. I am no longer my own.
I confess this with my mouth and believe it in my heart.
I thank You for always loving me
In Jesus name, amen.

For those of you who would like to receive the Holy Spirit. He is the comforter that Jesus promised us in John 14:16,26. He is part of the Trinity and if you want to receive Him and speak in tongues, I ask you to say this prayer with me.

Holy Spirit,
I invite You into my spirit,
I want You to lead guide direct me,
I believe in the power of speaking in tongues.
I know that You are God
And I thank You for all that You are going to do and show me.
I want to be used by You,
Learn from You,
I speak it out and receive it by faith now,
In Jesus name, amen.

If you have said either of these prayers or want to reach out to us with a testimony or prayer request, please email us at **DarvinBylerFS@gmail.com**

"O my people, listen to my instructions.
Open your ears to what I am saying,
2 for I will speak to you in a parable.
I will teach you hidden lessons from our past—
3 stories we have heard and known,
stories our ancestors handed down to us.
4 We will not hide these truths from our children;
we will tell the next generation
about the glorious deeds of the LORD,
about his power and his mighty wonders.
5 For he issued his laws to Jacob;
he gave his instructions to Israel.
He commanded our ancestors
to teach them to their children,
6 so the next generation might know them—
even the children not yet born—
and they in turn will teach their own children.
7 So each generation should set its hope anew on God,
not forgetting his glorious miracles
and obeying his commands.
8 Then they will not be like their ancestors—
stubborn, rebellious, and unfaithful,
refusing to give their hearts to God."

Psalm 78:1-8 NLT

Made in the USA
Columbia, SC
15 December 2024

49433980R00280